Lecture Notes in Information Systems and Organisation

Volume 34

Series Editors

Paolo Spagnoletti, Rome, Italy
Marco De Marco, Rome, Italy
Nancy Pouloudi, Athens, Greece
Dov Te'eni, Tel Aviv, Israel
Jan vom Brocke, Vaduz, Liechtenstein
Robert Winter, St. Gallen, Switzerland
Richard Baskerville, Atlanta, USA

Lecture Notes in Information Systems and Organization—LNISO—is a series of scientific books that explore the current scenario of information systems, in particular IS and organization. The focus on the relationship between IT, IS and organization is the common thread of this collection, which aspires to provide scholars across the world with a point of reference and comparison in the study and research of information systems and organization. LNISO is the publication forum for the community of scholars investigating behavioral and design aspects of IS and organization. The series offers an integrated publication platform for high-quality conferences, symposia and workshops in this field. Materials are published upon a strictly controlled double blind peer review evaluation made by selected reviewers. LNISO is abstracted/indexed in Scopus

More information about this series at http://www.springer.com/series/11237

Bo Andersson · Björn Johansson ·
Chris Barry · Michael Lang ·
Henry Linger · Christoph Schneider
Editors

Advances in Information Systems Development

Designing Digitalization

Springer

Editors
Bo Andersson
School of Economics and Management
Lund University
Lund, Sweden

Björn Johansson
School of Economics and Management
Lund University
Lund, Sweden

Chris Barry
Cairnes School of Business and Economics
National University of Ireland Galway
Galway, Ireland

Michael Lang
Cairnes School of Business and Economics
National University of Ireland Galway
Galway, Ireland

Henry Linger
Faculty of Information Technology
Monash University
Melbourne, VIC, Australia

Christoph Schneider
IESE Business School
University of Navarra
Barcelona, Spain

ISSN 2195-4968   ISSN 2195-4976   (electronic)
Lecture Notes in Information Systems and Organisation
ISBN 978-3-030-22992-4   ISBN 978-3-030-22993-1   (eBook)
https://doi.org/10.1007/978-3-030-22993-1

This Springer imprint is published by the registered company Springer Nature Switzerland AG
The registered company address is: Gewerbestrasse 11, 6330 Cham, Switzerland

Conference Organization

Conference Chairs

Bo Andersson
Björn Johansson
Sven Carlsson

International Steering Committee

Chris Barry
Michael Lang
Henry Linger
Christoph Schneider

Track Chairs

Transforming Society with ISD

Ida Asadi Someh
Johan Sandberg
Trevor Clohessy

ISD Education

Arto Lanamäki
Lars Svensson
Peter Bellström

Human-Computer Interaction

Azadeh Savoli
John Sören Pettersson
Yukika Awazu

e-Health

Christina Keller
Joseph Wu
Sofie Wass

Information Systems Methodologies and Modelling

Birger Lantow
Darek Haftorn
Kurt Sandkuhl

Managing ISD

Emilio Insfran
Giuseppe Scanniello

Topics in ISD

Mostafa Mesgari
Michael Lang

Reviewers

Parisa Aasi
Silvia Abrahao
Jan Aidemark
Nam Aghaee
Asif Akram
Beatrice Alenljung
Henrik Andersson
Nour Ali
Vasco Amaral
Joao Araujo
Rogerio Atem De Carvalho
Eduard Babkin
Per Backlund
Rehema Baguma
Chris Barry
Dominique Blouin
Etienne Borde

Priscila Cedillo
Luca Cernuzzi
Michel Chaudron
Witold Chmielarz
Kieran Conboy
Alena Connolly
Björn Cronquist
Subhasish Dasgupta
Denis Dennehy
Lina Eklund
Fausto Fasano
Davide Fucci
Jesus Garcia-Molina
Martin Gellerstedt
Ahmad Ghazawneh
Guido Giunti
Abel Gomez

Janis Grabis
Carmine Gravino
Casandra Grundstrom
Bengt Göransson
Amir Haj-Bolouri
Darek Haftor
G. Harindranath
Hugo Hedlund
Hans Hedbom
Mairéad Hogan
Tomas Horvath
Miroslav Hudec
Amin Jalali
William Jobe
Katrin Jonsson
Gustaf Juell-Skielse
Bridget Kane
Dimitris Karagiannis
Mari Karjalainen
Pasi Karppinen
Grace Kenny
Andreas Koczkas
Erdelina Kurti
Michael Lang
Birger Lantow
Jouni Lappalainen
Ola J. Lindberg
Henry Linger
Michael Le Duc
Juhani Iivari
Ulrika Lundh Snis
Monika Magnusson
Osama Mansour
Jabier Martinez Tecnalia
Raimundas Matulevicius
Santiago Melia
Mostafa Mesgari
Amir Mohagheghzadeh
Tonja Molin-Juustila
Charles Møller
Makoto Nakayama
Peter Axel Nielsen
Ovidiu Noran
Jacob Nørbjerg
Stefan Nilsson

Jyrki Nimmenmaa
Daniel Nylén
Lena Pareto
Nearchos Paspallis
Raphael Pereira De Oliveira
Claudia Pons
Natallia Pshkevich
Thuy Duong Oesterreich
David Olson
Anders D. Olofsson
Christian Ostlund
Natallia Pshkevich
Iman Raeesi Vanani
Dorina Rajanen
Mikko Rajanen
Marios Raspopoulos
Vaclav Repa
Simone Romano
Sana Rouis
Boubker Sbihi
Betty Saenyi
Kurt Sandkuhl
Christoph Schneider
Di Shang
Ulf Seigerroth
Maria Spante
Janis Stirna
Karen Stendal
Frantisek Sudzina
Lars Svensson
Ann Svensson
Fredrik Söderström
Torben Tambo
Lars Taxén
Claes Thorén
Felix Timm
Justas Trinkunas
Tero Vartiainen
Benkt Wangler
William Wei Song
Juan-Manuel Vara
Christoper Vendome
Ulrika H. Westergren
Anna Wingkvist
Thomas Winman

Stanislaw Wrycza
Liisa Von Hellens
Dijana Vukovac
Alfred Zimmermann
Miguel Angel Zúñiga Prieto

Henrik Åhman
Lena-Maria Öberg

Preface

The **International Conference on Information Systems Development** (ISD) is an academic conference where researchers and practitioners share their knowledge and expertise in the field of information systems development. As an Affiliated Conference of the Association for Information Systems (AIS), the ISD conference complements the international network of general IS conferences (ICIS, ECIS, AMCIS, PACIS, HICSS). The ISD conference continues the tradition started with the first Polish-Scandinavian Seminar on Current Trends in Information Systems Development Methodologies, held in Gdansk, Poland, in 1988. This seminar has evolved into the International Conference on Information Systems Development.

Throughout its history, the conference has focused on different aspects, ranging from methodological, infrastructural, and educational challenges in the ISD field to bridging the gaps between industry, academia, and society. Advancements in information systems foster technological developments. The deployment of the resulting technologies in all areas of society, including public and private sector, the community, and in the home is greatly beneficial. ISD has always promoted a close interaction between theory and practice that has set a human-centered agenda focused on advancing the methods, tools, and management of IS.

This volume is a selection of papers from ISD2018, the 27th Information Systems Development conference hosted by the Department of Informatics, School of Economics and Management, Lund University, Sweden, and held in Lund, Sweden, on August 22–24, 2018. All presented papers have been published in the AIS eLibrary, which is accessible at http://aisel.aisnet.org/isd2014/proceedings2018. This volume contains extended versions of the best papers, as selected by the ISD2018 Proceedings Editors.

The theme of the conference was Designing Digitalization. It focused on mutual influences between information systems and organizational structures, processes, and people to promote research of methodological issues and ways in which IS designers and developers are transforming organizations and society through information systems. The conference provided a forum for discussing research and developments in this field. The ISD2018 conference attracted contributions in the general area of information systems development, as well as in more specialized topics including Transforming Society with ISD, ISD Education, Human-Computer Interaction, e-Health, Information Systems Methodology and Modelling, Managing ISD, and Topics in ISD. ISD2018 focused on these and associated topics in order to promote research into theoretical and methodological issues and ways in which these advances enable better synergies between theory and practice. We believe that the innovative papers assembled in these lecture notes will inform the reader of important contributions in this regard.

Lund, Sweden	Bo Andersson
Lund, Sweden	Björn Johansson
Melbourne, Australia	Henry Linger
Galway, Ireland	Chris Barry
Galway, Ireland	Michael Lang
Barcelona, Spain	Christoph Schneider

Contents

Advancing ISD Education Research with Bioecological Systems Theory

Niamh O. Riordan and Simon Warren

Abstract The Information Systems (IS) community designs and delivers IS curricula in higher education and faces pedagogical challenges in teaching some complex and technical material. Many of us are involved in the design, implementation, evaluation, adoption, and use of IS to support education and training in academia and in industry. Yet IS research on education is often based on technologically deterministic assumptions about the impact of technology on education outcomes and involves narrowly focused studies on the use and impact of technology in education. In this paper, we introduce IS to Bioecological Theory (BET), whose insights have had a transformative effect in the field of developmental psychology but not well known in IS. We use BET to map existing literature on IS and Higher Education and also outline how this theory can be used in IS to inform the design of technological artifacts to support students' learning processes.

Keywords ISD education · Bioecological theory · Systematic literature review

1 Introduction

The Information Systems (IS) community has had a sustained interest in education for many years. IS scholars have written about in the design and delivery of IS curricula (e.g. [11, 18, 63]). IS scholars have investigated some of the specific challenges in teaching some of the complex and technical material that comes under the umbrella of IS (e.g. [20, 43, 61]). IS scholars have engaged in quite a reflexive manner on the role

A prior version of this paper has been published in the ISD2018 Proceedings (http://aisel.aisnet.org/isd2014/proceedings2018).

N. O. Riordan (✉)
National University of Ireland Galway, Galway, Ireland
e-mail: n.oriordan@yahoo.com

S. Warren
Enheden for Akademisk Efteruddannelse, Roskilde Universitet, Roskilde, Denmark
e-mail: warren@ruc.dk

1

of Information and Communication Technologies (ICTs) in higher education (e.g. [7, 66]). Finally, IS scholars are involved in the design, implementation, evaluation, adoption, and use of IS to support education and training both in academia and in industry (e.g. [69, 72, 74]).

The IS community's research often borrows from established learning theories in education and related disciplines. These include the objectivist model, the constructivist model, the cooperative model, the cognitive information processing model, and the sociocultural model of learning (see [68]). For example, scholars often recognize that different learning models lead to different sorts of learning outcomes and account for some of the inconsistencies observed across IS education studies [37]. However, the IS community's main focus is usually on the technologies that can support different types of learning rather than on the pedagogical theories in themselves. For example, IS scholars have investigated the potential of the Internet and World Wide Web (WWW) to support asynchronous learning (e.g. [2]) via web-based virtual learning environments (e.g. [37]). Later, IS scholars investigated the usefulness of group support systems in collaborative learning (e.g. [15, 22, 23]) as well as virtual worlds for immersive education (e.g. [13]). More recently, IS scholars have studied the useful of gamification (e.g. [42]) and learning analytics (e.g. [3]) in technology-mediated training and education. As we illustrate in this paper, IS education research often overlooks many of the contextual factors that have been shown to influence academic performance.

Against this backdrop, we advocate for IS education research to be undertaken using Bioecological Theory (BET). BET explains how students develop their own abilities and skills via 'proximal processes' and has be used to explain why students' engagement in these proximal processes does not always directly correlate with students' ultimate achievements in education. Over the years, a large body of empirical research supported Bronfenbrenner's propositions about the kinds of ecological factors that affect students' academic performance. Its potential value in IS stems from the fact that it encourages scholars to take account of both the complex, reciprocal and subtle interactions among each individual's biological and personal characteristics and the significant social and ecological contexts that influence development [71]. We use BET to map existing IS education research and to confirm that IS education research has paid scant attention to many factors that are known to impact upon students' academic performance through BET. IS scholars can use BET to examine the impact of features of the broader ecological systems within which our students are embedded on their academic performance.

2 Introduction

2.1 Introducing Bioecological Theory

Urie Bronfenbrenner is regarded as a pioneer who has made outstanding contributions in the study of the ecology of human development [64]. Bronfenbrenner was among the first theoreticians to underscore the need to take into account both the complex, reciprocal and subtle interactions among each individual's biological and personal characteristics and the significant social and ecological contexts that influence development [71]. His Bioecological Theory (BET) altered the trajectory of research in field of developmental psychology; and it led to the conduct of ecological studies of human development in various disciplines including biology, psychology, anthropology, sociology, geography and education [73]. His works have been cited more than 75,000 times according to Google Scholar.

BET holds that individuals develop and actualise their potential by engaging in their environments in what are known as proximal processes (see [56, 57, 59]; see also [52]). Bronfenbrenner emphasizes the intentional and goal directed nature of an individual's interacting with and acting upon their environment as they move toward their currently adopted goal. He defines these processes as progressively more complex reciprocal interaction between an active, evolving biopsychological human organism and the persons, objects, and symbols in its immediate external environment. Bronfenbrenner explains that each individual proximal process requires "space and time and resources; it involves certain enabling structures and disabling structures; and it will require more or less effort depending on the process stage and the individual" [57].

Bronfenbrenner [53, 54] argues that a person's development is not solely a function of their own individual traits but is the product of a constellation of psychological, cultural, social, economic and political forces. His initial work concentrated on developing a better understanding of the environment itself and he later turned his attention to the role a person plays in his or her own development. He argued that to understand an individual's development, one must examine the entire ecological system within which growth occurs and one must do so using a systems perspective [53–55]. Using the analogy of the *matrioshka* (Russian doll), Bronfenbrenner argued that the environment consists of a set of nested structures, each inside the next: microsystem, mesosystem, exosystem, macrosystem and chronosystem. By examining this nested structure, researchers could better understand not only the proximal (direct) effects of the immediate social and physical environment but also the distal (indirect) processes that affect the individual's development [73].

According to Bronfenbrenner [54]:

- The *microsystem* is an immediate setting containing the learner (e.g., home, day care centre, classroom, etc.) A setting is defined as a place in which the occupants engage in particular activities and in particular roles (e.g., parent, teacher, pupil, etc.) for particular periods of time. The factors of place, time, activity, and role constitute the elements of a setting.

- The *mesosystem* comprises the interrelations among the major settings containing the learner at a point in his or her life. The mesosystem is the system of micro-systems.
- The *exosystem* is an extension of a mesosystem embracing the concrete social structures, both formal and informal, that impinge upon or encompass the immediate settings containing the learner and, thereby, influence and even determine or delimit what goes on there. These structures include the major institutions of the society, both deliberately structured and spontaneously evolving, as they operate at the local community level.
- The *macrosystem* is the overarching institution of the culture or subculture, such as the economic, social, educational, legal and political systems, of which local micro-, meso-, and exo-systems are the concrete manifestations. Such macrosystems are conceived and examined not only in structural terms but as carriers of information and ideology that, both explicitly and implicitly, endow meaning and motivation to particular agencies, social networks, roles, activities, and their interrelations.
- Finally, the *chronosystem* (see [56]) encompasses change or consistency over time not only in the characteristics of the person but also of the environment in which the person lives (e.g. changes over the life course in family structure, socioeconomic status, employment, place of residence, or the degree of hecticness and ability in everyday life). The nature of the dynamic relation between the organism and its environment is such that over time, the external becomes internal and becomes transformed in the process [59]. However, because from the very beginning the organism begins to change its environment, the internal becomes external and becomes transformed in the process. Thus, he believed that it is critical for research designs that permit analysis of the dynamic relation between the process of change over time within the person and the process of change in the environment [55].

The original contribution of BET was its conception of the developing person, of the environment, and especially of the dynamic interaction between the two [54, p. 3]. BET inherited from biology at a time when more mainstream theories of human development inherit the experimental and reductionist models of the physical sciences [73]. More specifically, it originated in Kurt Lewin's field theory, which asserts that an individual's behaviour is a function of the person and their environment; it is also influenced by Gestalt Psychology more generally [58, pp. 41–49]. In this view, the individual as a whole person is different from the sum of their parts, and these individual parts are interdependent and interact in a dynamic fashion; this means that looking at individual elements separately from each other and separate from the person's perceptual or psychological environment produces a misleading view of the causes of human behaviour and how it can be changed [60]. It also was, as its name implies, an ecological theory. This means that it explicitly recognized organism-environment interrelatedness and that human development occurs in the midst of a vibrant, complex environment [56]. This family of theories further recognized that our everyday experience involve, and are influenced by, constant, dynamic, mutually influential interactions between different conditions and between the person and the world [70].

2.2 The Potential Value of BET in IS

BET is potentially useful in IS. First, Bronfenbrenner's conceptualization of proximal processes offers some explanation of how individuals engage in particular tasks and can provide guidance as to how IS designers might design educational tasks for individual learners. Bronfenbrenner's work underscores the progressive nature of proximal processes, (i.e. that the complexity of proximal processes can increase over time), the fact that particular resources must be available to individuals to enter into these proximal processes, and that in order to understand an individual's development, one must examine the entire ecological system within which growth occurs.

Second, education scholars outside IS have long understood that students' academic performance is influenced by a range of contextual factors that are beyond their own immediate environment. Within IS, however, research on students' academic performance tends to overlook these factors. BET can be used in IS to address this gap. IS scholars can use BET to examine the impact of features of the broader ecological systems within which our students are embedded on their academic performance. BET is especially well suited to this task because it is based on a conception of not only the developing person or the environment (immediate and distal) within which they are based but also on the dynamic interaction between the two—this is its unique and compelling characteristic.

Finally, Bronfenbrenner's framework is comprehensive and well supported by multiple empirical studies carried out over decades. As we illustrate in this paper, it can effectively be used to map IS education research and to identify important gaps for future research.

3 Research Design

Our aim in this study was to evaluate existing IS education research using the lens of Bronfenbrenner's theoretical framework [54]. Our first step was to adapt Bronfenbrenner's framework to suit IS research (see Table 1). The framework posits that the ecological components of human development consist of five nested and interrelated structures; i.e. microsystem, mesosystem, exosystem, macrosystem and chronosystem. We developed a set of operational definitions of each ecological component of the framework that we could use to review the IS education literature.

We carried out a systematic literature review (SLR). An SLR is a distinct research method used to aggregate evidence (see [67]). It addresses a clearly formulated question and uses systematic and explicit methods to identify publications, select

Table 1 The bioecological model of human development in higher education, derived from [54]

System	Operational definition
Individual	The individual student who is at the centre of Bronfenbrenner's theoretical framework. Various characteristics of this individual are likely to be relevant to their academic development including their age, gender, ethnicity, social class, health and wellbeing
Microsystem	The institutions and groups that most immediately and directly impact the individual's development, e.g. college, college community, local community, family and friends
Mesosystem	Interconnections and interactions between the microsystems; i.e. interconnections and interactions between friends, college, college community, local community, family
Exosystem	Involves links between a social setting in which the individual does not have an active role and the individual's immediate context. For example, a student's experience at college may be influenced by their peers' experience at home or by their instructors' experience at work
Macrosystem	Describes the culture in which individuals live. Cultural contexts include developing and industrialized countries, socioeconomic status, poverty, and ethnicity. Members of a cultural group share a common identity, heritage, and values. For example, a student, his or her school, his or her peers, are all part of a large cultural context
Chronosystem	The patterning of environmental events and transitions over the life course, as well as sociohistorical circumstances. For example, leaving the family home is one transition; the increase in career prospects available to those who have graduated higher education is an example of a change in sociohistorical circumstances

publications relevant to the question critically appraise the publications analyse the data reported in the relevant publications report the combined results from relevant publications. As such, the method is designed to bring the same level of rigour to reviewing research evidence as should be used in producing that research evidence in the first place. The procedure we followed is based on recommendations set out in [65] and is as follows:

(1) Identify higher education (HE) journals listed in the ABS ranking with three or more stars in 2010 (i.e. Studies in Higher Education, the British Educational Research Journal and the Academy of Management Learning and Education) and identify the top "basket" of IS journals (i.e. Information Systems Research, MIS Quarterly, Journal of Association of Information Systems, Journal Management Information Systems, Journal Strategic Information Systems, European Journal of Information Systems and Information Systems Journal).

(2) Conduct a keyword search of all articles published in those three journals between 1996 and 2018 to identify those studies that reported on academic performance (various keywords were used; specifically, 'performance', 'outcomes', 'achievement', 'success').

(3) Review the titles and abstracts of these studies (n = 86) using pre-specified inclusion and exclusion criteria to eliminate those studies that either (a) did not concern higher education, (b) were concerned with retention and completion rather than achievement, (c) did not present findings regarding the factors affecting academic performance, or (d) did not provide an adequate account of the empirical methods used to generate findings.
(4) Analyse the remaining studies (n = 50) using an adaptation of Bronfenbrenner's initial research to both map and review the literature [54].

The strength of this systematic approach is that it can be replicated at any stage in the future to trace the evolution of research in this area over time. At the same time, whilst time constraints have necessarily limited the scope of this search, the same procedure can be replicated by future researchers with the capacity to conduct a broader search across a greater number of databases.

4 Results

Table 2 summarises research published in leading IS and HE journals between 1996 and 2018 regarding the factors known to impact academic performance (see also Appendix 1). The table summarizes (i) whether each study was carried out in a qualitative, quantitative or mixed methods mode, (ii) whether each study was student-centric or faculty-centric, (iii) the scope of the dataset used in the study, and (iv) which ecological components of achievement in higher education were assessed in the study.

Students' academic performance is a topic of enduring importance in both the IS and HE journals we examined between 1996 and 2018. There has been a steady stream of publications since 2013. Prior to that, a burst of publications in 2007 was preceded by an absence of publications in 2004, 2005, and 2006; and a burst of publications in 2002 was preceded by an absence of publications in 1998, 1999, and 2000. In total, we found thirty-two articles in the three HE journals (twenty-six of those had been published by Studies in Higher Education) and eighteen articles in the eight IS journals that met our search criteria. Space limits preclude an in-depth discussion of the fifty articles. Instead, the remainder of this section summarizes the results of our analysis of the dataset overall.

Overall, we found that the studies in the sample focus primarily on the individual and the institution within which that individual is embedded. Most studies focus specifically on individual student attributes (n = 14) or specifically on features of the microsystem (n = 10) or on a combination of individual and microsystem attributes (n = 17). These studies often investigate the impact of individual (i.e. student) factors on academic performance. These factors include student demographics, such as age (e.g. [5, 40]) and gender (e.g. [40]), prior academic achievement (e.g. [17, 21]), subjective experience of the learning environment (e.g. [25, 26, 33]) and supports (e.g. [35]), as well as behavioural approaches to higher education (e.g. [30, 32,

Table 2 Summary of academic performance research published in leading IS and HE journals between 1996 and 2018

Citation	Domain	Research mode	Orientation	Dataset	Individual	Micro	Meso-	Exo-	Macro-	Chrono-
[1] Bailey et al. (2014)	EDU	Quantitative	Student-centric	***		✓				
[2] Bargeron et al. (2002)	IS	Quantitative	Student-centric	*	✓					
[3] Bauman and Tuzhilin (2018)	IS	Quantitative	Student-centric	***	✓					
[4] Beenstock and Feldman (2016)	EDU	Quantitative	Student-centric	***		✓				
[5] Cassidy (2012)	EDU	Quantitative	Student-centric	***	✓					
[6] Clayton et al. (2012)	IS	Qualitative	Student-centric	****	✓	✓	✓		✓	
[7] Coppola et al. (2002)	IS	Qualitative	Faculty-centric	***		✓	✓			
[8] Crawford and Wang (2015)	EDU	Qualitative	Student-centric	***	✓	✓				
[9] Crawford and Wang (2016)	EDU	Quantitative	Student-centric	***		✓				✓
[10] Dancer et al. (2015)	EDU	Quantitative	Student-centric	*		✓				
[11] Dhar and Sundararajan (2007)	IS	Qualitative	Faculty-centric	****		✓				
[12] Diseth (2007)	EDU	Quantitative	Student-centric	**	✓					
[13] Franceschi et al. (2009)	IS	Quantitative	Student-centric	**	✓	✓				
[14] Galliers and Huang (2012)	IS	Qualitative	Faculty-centric	*****				✓		

(continued)

Table 2 (continued)

Citation	Domain	Research mode	Orientation	Dataset	Individual	Micro	Meso-	Exo-	Macro-	Chrono-
[15] Gasson and Waters (2013)	IS	Qualitative	Student-centric	****	✓					
[16] Grayson (2011)	EDU	Quantitative	Student-centric	****				✓		
[17] Gropper (2007)	EDU	Quantitative	Student-centric	**	✓					
[18] Hatzakis et al. (2007)	IS	Quantitative	Faculty-centric	**		✓				
[19] Heinze and Hu (2009)	IS	Quantitative	Student-centric	****	✓					
[20] Hustad and Olsen(2014)	IS	Qualitative	Faculty-centric	*		✓				
[21] Kuncel et al. (2007)	EDU	Quantitative	Faculty-centric	****	✓					
[22] Kwok et al. (2002)	IS	Quantitative	Student-centric	**	✓	✓				
[23] Kwok et al, (2002)	IS	Quantitative	Student-centric	**	✓	✓				
[24] Litmanen et al. (2010)	EDU	Quantitative	Student-centric	**	✓					
[25] Lizzio et al. (2002)	EDU	Quantitative	Student-centric	***	✓	✓				
[26] Loyens et al. (2007)	EDU	Quantitative	Student-centric	*	✓	✓				
[27] Malm et al.(2012)	EDU	Quantitative	Student-centric	**	✓	✓				

(continued)

Table 2 (continued)

Citation	Domain	Research mode	Orientation	Dataset	Individual	Micro	Meso-	Exo-	Macro-	Chrono-
[28] Mann and Robinson (2009)	EDU	Quantitative	Student-centric	***	✓	✓				
[29] Mansfield (2011)	EDU	Quantitative	Student-centric	**	✓	✓				✓
[30] Masui et al. (2014)	EDU	Quantitative	Student-centric	***		✓				
[31] Mathiassen and Purao (2002)	IS	Qualitative	Faculty-centric	*****	✓	✓				
[32] Newman-Ford et al (2008)	EDU	Quantitative	Student-centric	**	✓					
[33] Nguyen et al. (2016)	EDU	Quantitative	Student-centric	*	✓	✓				
[34] Nicholson et al. (2013)	EDU	Quantitative	Student-centric	**	✓					
[35] Ning and Downing (2010)	EDU	Quantitative	Student-centric	***	✓	✓				
[36] Ning and Downing (2012)	EDU	Quantitative	Student-centric	**	✓	✓				
[37] Piccoli et al. (2001)	IS	Quantitative	Faculty-centric	*	✓					
[38] Reinig et al. (1997)	IS	Quantitative	Student-centric	*		✓				
[39] Richardson (2008)	EDU	Quantitative	Student-centric	***	✓					
[40] Richardson and Woodley (2003)	EDU	Quantitative	Student-centric	****	✓					

(continued)

Table 2 (continued)

Citation	Domain	Research mode	Orientation	Dataset	Individual	Micro	Meso-	Exo-	Macro-	Chrono-
[41] Román et al.(2008)	EDU	Mixed	Student-centric	***	✓	✓				
[42] Santhanam et al. (2016)	IS	Quantitative	Faculty-centric	***		✓				
[43] Sheetz et al. (1997)	IS	Qualitative	Student-centric	*	✓	✓				
[44] Simonite (2003)	EDU	Quantitative	Student-centric	**	✓	✓				
[45] Smith and White (2015)	EDU	Quantitative	Student-centric	***	✓	✓				
[46] te Wierik et al. (2015)	EDU	Quantitative	Student-centric	***		✓				
[47] Thiele et al. (2016)	EDU	Quantitative	Student-centric	***				✓		
[48] Torenbeek et al. (2013)	EDU	Quantitative	Student-centric	***	✓	✓				
[49] Trigwell et al. (2012)	EDU	Quantitative	Student-centric	*	✓	✓				
[50] Wilkins et al. (2016)	EDU	Quantitative	Student-centric	***	✓	✓				

*Single module, single programme, single university
**Multiple modules, single programme, single university
***Multiple modules, multiple programmes, single university
****Multiple modules, multiple programmes, multiple universities
*****Multiple modules, multiple programmes, multiple universities, multiple countries

48])—especially surface versus deep learning (e.g. [12, 41, 50]). The mesosystem was examined in two studies [6, 7]. The exosystem was examined in two studies [14, 16]. The macrosystem was examined in one study [6]. This study was interesting as it investigated the impact of students' parents' education on their educational experiences and achievements. Finally, the chronosystem was examined in just two studies [9, 29]. These studies both investigated the impact of going on placement on students' subsequent academic achievements.

Methodologically, we found that most studies rely on quantitative techniques applied to large data sets, with very little variation across research methods used—very rarely to researchers investigate multiple variables and when they did, they generally failed to investigate any interplay that might take place between these variables over time. These studies therefore do no reveal any great insight into the dynamics of academic achievement over time and are not particularly helpful in seeking to understand the totality of an individual's situation and its impact on their development (see [61]).

There were several differences in the IS and HE articles in terms of the topics covered and also the methods and datasets used. First, the IS articles focused on two main topics: the design and delivery of the IS curriculum within the broader context of business education, and the development and use of new types of learning technologies. The HE articles, on the other hand, were far more specifically focused on predicting and explaining students' academic achievement and on issues related to grading practices within and across disciplines. Second, the IS articles featured a mix of qualitative and quantitative approaches as well as a mix of faculty-centric and student-centric studies. However, a significant proportion of the IS articles used module-specific data which can pose issues related to generalizability (i.e. the data was unique to individual modules within individual programmes within individual universities). Our first thought was that perhaps the qualitative IS articles were module specific but a closer inspection revealed that this was not the case. Instead, it was those articles that focused on specific learning technologies that tended to rely on module-specific data gathered during design science and action research studies and then analysed quantitatively. On the other hand, all of the HE articles in our sample used quantitative methods and were student-centric in nature. The majority of the HE articles we sampled used datasets that spanned modules and programmes and universities.

5   Discussion and Conclusion

Bronfenbrenner has made an enduring contribution to our understanding of the interplay between the biological and ecological factors that impact upon human development. Bronfenbrenner's BET provides a powerful lens through which a more holistic understanding of human development can be seen; an understanding of human development that takes the interrelatedness of individual, physical, sociohistorical and cultural aspects into account. Indeed, Bronfenbrenner is credited with bringing attention to contextual variation in human development and with increasing the ecological validity of studies of developing individuals in their natural environment [62].

Though he has had a substantial impact beyond IS, his work does not appear to be well known in IS or in HE research. In this short paper, we present the results of a systematic literature review of IS and HE research published in the past two decades carried out from a Bronfenbrennerian perspective. The analysis reveals that a great deal is known about the factors that affect academic achievement in IS and in HE, particularly regarding the role of the individual's own characteristics in shaping academic outcomes. However, when examined through the lens of Bronfenbrenner's work, it becomes clear that the literature has tended to focus primarily on the individual (or the microsystem) and to analyse one or possibly two factors at most, relying heavily on quantitative techniques applied to large data sets in doing so, and demonstrating very little variation across research methods. Many factors that have been shown to potentially influence academic achievement in other disciplines where Bronfenbrenner's work is more well-known have not yet been examined in IS or in business education, particularly those that exist beyond the confines of the microsystem.

Going forward, IS researchers can use Bronfenbrenner's work to better understand our students' engagement with the IS curriculum and with higher education more generally. In particular, Bronfenbrenner's conceptualization of proximal processes offers some explanation of how individuals engage in particular tasks and can provide guidance as to how IS designers might design educational tasks for individual learners. In addition, his work on the contextual factors that influence individuals' academic performance should inform the design of IT artifacts that support students' learning processes in higher education. Emerging learning technologies afford educators and researchers new opportunities to better understand and optimise the dynamics of academic achievement over time, perhaps to a point of being able to predict student success [51]. In particular, IS researchers are developing new learning technologies to enhance students' engagement with the IS curriculum and in higher education more generally (e.g. [13, 42]) and are using emerging learning analytics tools and techniques to monitor and respond to what Bronfenbrenner would call individual students' proximal processes (e.g. [3]). These tools and technologies can afford a fine-grained understanding of students' proximal processes and deliver fresh insights into the dynamics of academic achievement over time. But in the meantime, IS scholars should ask whether these tools are developmentally disruptive or developmentally generative. We also want to encourage more IS scholars to follow in the footsteps of scholars who are investigating the impact of meso-, exo-, macro- and chronosystems on students' experiences with IS and with higher education more generally.

Acknowledgements The authors wish to acknowledge that a portion of this research was carried out at the Centre of Excellence in Teaching and Learning (CELT), National University of Ireland, Galway.

Appendix 1: Results of Systematic Literature Review[1]

1. Bailey, M.A., Rosenthal, J.S., Yoon, A.H.: Grades and incentives: assessing competing grade point average measures and postgraduate outcomes. Stud. High. Educ. 1–15 (2014)
2. Bargeron, D., et al.: Asynchronous collaboration around multimedia applied to on-demand education. J. Manag. Inf. Syst. **18**(4), 117–145 (2002)
3. Bauman, K., Tuzhilin, A.: Recommending remedial learning materials to students by filling their knowledge gaps. Manag. Inf. Syst. Q. **42**(1), 313–332 (2018)
4. Beenstock, M., Feldman, D.: Decomposing university grades: a longitudinal study of students and their instructors. Stud. High. Educ. 1–20 (2016)
5. Cassidy, S.: Exploring individual differences as determining factors in student academic achievement in higher education. Stud. High. Educ. **37**(7), 793–810 (2012)
6. Clayton, K., Beekhuyzen, J., Nielsen, S.: Now I know what ICT can do for me! Inf. Syst. J. **22**(5), 375–390 (2012)
7. Coppola, N.W., Hiltz, S.R., Rotter, N.G.: Becoming a virtual professor: pedagogical roles and asynchronous learning networks. J. Manag. Inf. Syst. **18**(4), 169–189 (2002)
8. Crawford, I., Wang, Z.: The impact of individual factors on the academic attainment of Chinese and UK students in higher education. Stud. High. Educ. **40**(5), 902–920 (2015)
9. Crawford, I., Wang, Z.: The impact of placements on the academic performance of UK and international students in higher education. Stud. High. Educ. 1–22 (2016)
10. Dancer, D., Morrison, K., Tarr, G.: Measuring the effects of peer learning on students' academic achievement in first-year business statistics. Stud. High. Educ. **40**(10), 1808–1828 (2015)
11. Dhar, V., Sundararajan, A.: Information technologies in business: a blueprint for education and research. Inf. Syst. Res. **18**(2), 125–141 (2007)
12. Diseth, Å.: Approaches to learning, course experience and examination grade among undergraduate psychology students: testing of mediator effects and construct validity. Stud. High. Educ. **32**(3), 373–388 (2007)
13. Franceschi, K., et al.: Engaging group E-learning in virtual worlds. J. Manag. Inf. Syst. **26**(1), 73–100 (2009)
14. Galliers, R.D., Huang, J.C.: The teaching of qualitative research methods in information systems: an explorative study utilizing learning theory. Eur. J. Inf. Syst. **21**(2), 119–134 (2012)
15. Gasson, S., Waters, J.: Using a grounded theory approach to study online collaboration behaviors. Eur. J. Inf. Syst. **22**(1), 95–118 (2013)
16. Grayson, P.J.: Cultural capital and academic achievement of first generation domestic and international students in Canadian universities. Br. Edu. Res. J. **37**(4), 605–630 (2011)
17. Gropper, D.M.: Does the GMAT matter for executive MBA students? Some empirical evidence. Acad. Manag. Learn. Educ. **6**(2), 206–216 (2007)
18. Hatzakis, T., Lycett, M., Serrano, A.: A programme management approach for ensuring curriculum coherence in IS (higher) education. Eur. J. Inf. Syst. **16**(5), 643–657 (2007)
19. Heinze, N., Hu, Q.: Why college undergraduates choose IT: a multi-theoretical perspective. Eur. J. Inf. Syst. **18**(5), 462–475 (2009)
20. Hustad, E., Olsen, D.H.: Educating reflective Enterprise Systems practitioners: a design research study of the iterative building of a teaching framework. Inf. Syst. J. **24**(5), 445–473 (2014)
21. Kuncel, N.R., Credé, M., Thomas, L.L.: A meta-analysis of the predictive validity of the graduate management admission test (GMAT) and undergraduate grade point average (UGPA) for graduate student academic performance. Acad. Manag. Learn. Educ. **6**(1), 51–68 (2007)
22. Kwok, R.C., et al.: Role of GSS on collaborative problem-based learning: a study on knowledge externalisation. Eur. J. Inf. Syst. **11**(2), 98–107 (2002)
23. Kwok, R.C.-W., Ma, J., Vogel, D.R.: Effects of group support systems and content facilitation on knowledge acquisition. J. Manag. Inf. Syst. **19**(3), 185–229 (2002)

---

[1]The 50 papers that were analysed in this study are listed below.

24. Litmanen, T., Hirsto, L., Lonka, K.: Personal goals and academic achievement among theology students. Stud. High. Educ. **35**(2), 195–208 (2010)
25. Lizzio, A., Wilson, K., Simons, R.: University students' perceptions of the learning environment and academic outcomes: implications for theory and practice. Stud. High. Educ. **27**(1), 27–52 (2002)
26. Loyens, S.M.M., Rikers, R.M.J.P., Schmidt, H.G.: The impact of students' conceptions of constructivist assumptions on academic achievement and drop-out. Stud. High. Educ. **32**(5), 581–602 (2007)
27. Malm, J., et al.: Supplemental instruction for improving first year results in engineering studies. Stud. High. Educ. **37**(6), 655–666 (2012)
28. Mann, S., Robinson, A.: Boredom in the lecture theatre: an investigation into the contributors, moderators and outcomes of boredom amongst university students. Br. Edu. Res. J. **35**(2), 243–258 (2009)
29. Mansfield, R.: The effect of placement experience upon final-year results for surveying degree programmes. Stud. High. Educ. **36**(8), 939–952 (2011)
30. Masui, C., et al.: Do diligent students perform better? Complex relations between student and course characteristics, study time, and academic performance in higher education. Stud. High. Educ. **39**(4), 621–643 (2014)
31. Mathiassen, L., Purao, S.: Educating reflective systems developers. Inf. Syst. J. **12**(2), 81–102 (2002)
32. Newman-Ford, L., et al.: A large-scale investigation into the relationship between attendance and attainment: a study using an innovative, electronic attendance monitoring system. Stud. High. Educ. **33**(6), 699–717 (2008)
33. Nguyen, T.H., Charity, I., Robson, A.: Students' perceptions of computer-based learning environments, their attitude towards business statistics, and their academic achievement: implications from a UK university. Stud. High. Educ. **41**(4), 734–755 (2016)
34. Nicholson, L., et al.: The key to successful achievement as an undergraduate student: confidence and realistic expectations? Stud. High. Educ. **38**(2), 285–298 (2013)
35. Ning, H.K., Downing, K.: The impact of supplemental instruction on learning competence and academic performance. Stud. High. Educ. **35**(8), 921–939 (2010)
36. Ning, H.K., Downing, K.: Influence of student learning experience on academic performance: the mediator and moderator effects of self-regulation and motivation. Br. Edu. Res. J. **38**(2), 219–237 (2012)
37. Piccoli, G., Ahmad, R., Ives, B.: Web-based virtual learning environments: a research framework and a preliminary assessment of effectiveness in basic IT skills training. Manag. Inf. Syst. Q. **25**(4), 401–426 (2001)
38. Reinig, B.A., Briggs, R.O., Nunmaker Jr., J.F.: Flaming in the electronic classroom. J. Manag. Inf. Syst. **14**(3), 45–59 (1997)
39. Richardson, J.T.E.: The attainment of ethnic minority students in UK higher education. Stud. High. Educ. **33**(1), 33–48 (2008)
40. Richardson, J.T.E., Woodley, A.: Another look at the role of age, gender and subject as predictors of academic attainment in higher education. Stud. High. Educ. **28**(4), 475–493 (2003)
41. Román, S., Cuestas, P.J., Fenollar, P.: An examination of the interrelationships between self-esteem, others' expectations, family support, learning approaches and academic achievement. Stud. High. Educ. **33**(2), 127–138 (2008)
42. Santhanam, R., Liu, D., Shen, W.-C.M.: Research note-gamification of technology-mediated training: not all competitions are the same. Inf. Syst. Res. **27**(2), 453–465 (2016)
43. Sheetz, S.D., et al.: Exploring the difficulties of learning object-oriented techniques. J. Manag. Inf. Syst. **14**(2), 103–131 (1997)
44. Simonite, V.: A longitudinal study of achievement in a modular first degree course. Stud. High. Educ. **28**(3), 293–302 (2003)
45. Smith, E., White, P.: What makes a successful undergraduate? The relationship between student characteristics, degree subject and academic success at university. Br. Educ. Res. J. **41**(4), 686–708 (2015)

46. te Wierik, M.L.J., Beishuizen, J., van Os, W.: Career guidance and student success in Dutch higher vocational education. Stud. High. Educ. **40**(10), 1947–1961 (2015)
47. Thiele, T., et al.: Predicting students' academic performance based on school and socio-demographic characteristics. Stud. High. Educ. **41**(8), 1424–1446 (2016)
48. Torenbeek, M., Jansen, E., Suhre, C.: Predicting undergraduates' academic achievement: the role of the curriculum, time investment and self-regulated learning. Stud. High. Educ. **38**(9), 1393–1406 (2013)
49. Trigwell, K., Ellis, R.A., Han, F.: Relations between students' approaches to learning, experienced emotions and outcomes of learning. Stud. High. Educ. **37**(7), 811–824 (2012)
50. Wilkins, S., et al.: The effects of social identification and organizational identification on student commitment, achievement and satisfaction in higher education. Stud. High. Educ. **41**(12), 2232–2252 (2016)

References

51. Agudo-Peregrina, Á.F., et al.: Can we predict success from log data in VLEs? Classification of interactions for learning analytics and their relation with performance in VLE-supported F2F and online learning. Comput. Hum. Behav. **31**, 542–550 (2014)
52. Ashiabi, G.S., O'Neal, K.K.: Child social development in context. SAGE Open **5**(2), 1–14 (2015)
53. Bronfenbrenner, U.: Toward an experimental ecology of human development. Am. Psychol. **32**(7), 513 (1977)
54. Bronfenbrenner, U.: The Ecology of Human Development: Experiments by Design and Nature. Harvard University Press, Cambridge (1979)
55. Bronfenbrenner, U.: Ecology of the family as a context for human development: research perspectives. Dev. Psychol. **22**(6), 723 (1986)
56. Bronfenbrenner, U.: Ecological models of human development. In: International Encyclopaedia of Education, vol. 3, 2nd edn, pp. 1643–1647. Pergamon Press/Elsevier Science, Oxford (1994)
57. Bronfenbrenner, U.: Developmental ecology through space and time: a future perspective. Exam. Lives Context: Perspect. Ecol. Hum. Dev. **619**, 647 (1995)
58. Bronfenbrenner, U.: Making Human Beings Human: Bioecological Perspectives on Human Development. Sage (2005)
59. Bronfenbrenner, U., Ceci, S.J.: Nature-nurture reconceptualized in developmental perspective: a bioecological model. Psychol. Rev. **101**(4), 568 (1994)
60. Burnes, B., Cooke, B.: Kurt Lewin's field theory: a review and re-evaluation. Int. J. Manag. Rev. **15**(4), 408–425 (2013)
61. Cho, I., Kim, Y.-G.: Critical factors for assimilation of object-oriented programming languages. J. Manag. Inf. Syst. **18**(3), 125–156 (2002)
62. Darling, N.: Ecological systems theory: the person in the center of the circles. Res. Hum. Dev. **4**(3–4), 203–217 (2007)
63. Davidson, E.J.: 'Hey professor, why are you teaching this class?' Reflections on the relevance of IS research for undergraduate students. Eur. J. Inf. Syst. 133–138. Springer (2011)
64. Derksen, T.: The influence of ecological theory in child and youth care: a review of the literature. Int. J. Child Youth Fam. Stud. **1**(3/4), 326–339 (2010)
65. Dyba, T., Dingsoyr, T., Hanssen, G.K.: Applying systematic reviews to diverse study types: an experience report. In: First International Symposium on Empirical Software Engineering and Measurement, 2007, ESEM 2007. IEEE (2007)
66. Gupta, S., Bostrom, R.P.: Technology-mediated learning: a comprehensive theoretical model. J. Assoc. Inf. Syst. **10**(9), 686–714 (2009)
67. Kitchenham, B.A., Charters, S.: Guidelines for performing systematic literature reviews in software engineering (2007)

68. Leidner, D.E., Jarvenpaa, S.L.: The use of information technology to enhance management school education: a theoretical view. MIS Q. 265–291 (1995)

69. Liu, D., Santhanam, R., Webster, J.: Toward meaningful engagement: a framework for design and research of gamified information systems. MIS Q. **41**(4) (2017)

70. Papadopoulou, M.: The ecology of role play: intentionality and cultural evolution. Br. Edu. Res. J. **38**(4), 575–592 (2012)

71. Rosa, E.M., Tudge, J.: Urie Bronfenbrenner's theory of human development: Its evolution from ecology to bioecology. J. Fam. Theory Rev. **5**(4), 243–258 (2013)

72. Sharda, R., et al.: Foundation for the study of computer-supported collaborative learning requiring immersive presence. J. Manag. Inf. Syst. **20**(4), 31–63 (2004)

73. Tudge, J., Gray, J.T., Hogan, D.M.: Ecological perspectives in human development: a comparison of Gibson and Bronfenbrenner. In: Comparisons in Human Development: Understanding Time and Context, pp. 72–105 (1997)

74. Wan, Z., Compeau, D., Haggerty, N.: The effects of self-regulated learning processes on e-learning outcomes in organizational settings. J. Manag. Inf. Syst. **29**(1), 307–340 (2012)

Australian Undergraduate Information Systems Curricula: A Comparative Study

J. Richardson, F. Burstein, A. Hol, R. J. Clarke and J. McGovern

Abstract The paper describes the first comprehensive comparative study of Undergraduate (UG) Information Systems (IS) degree programs in Australia using the model curricula outlined in ACM/AIS IS2010 as a reference point. The study had three broad aims: (1) to compare the Australian IS curriculum with that of other major IS education systems internationally, (2) to identify what subject areas are considered mandatory and what are considered optional in Australian IS programs, and (3) to understand if the host academic division within different disciplines (e.g. Business or Science/Engineering/Information Technology) have an influence on the variations in the degrees. In a first phase, 2017 IS program data was obtained from university websites. In a second phase, this data was validated in consultation with academic staff from those universities offering the programs. The conclusion is that a high level of adherence to the IS2010 curricula was evident in core courses; considerable diversity was found in a long tail of non-core offerings; and the location of the host academic unit within Business or Science/Engineering/Technology influenced the subject areas offered.

A prior version of this paper has been published in the ISD2018 Proceedings (http://aisel.aisnet.org/isd2014/proceedings2018).

J. Richardson (✉) · J. McGovern
RMIT University, Melbourne, Australia
e-mail: joan.richardson@rmit.edu.au

J. McGovern
e-mail: jim.mcgovern@rmit.edu.au

F. Burstein
Monash University, Melbourne, Australia
e-mail: frada.burstein@monash.edu

A. Hol
Western Sydney University, Sydney, Australia
e-mail: a.hol@westernsydney.edu.au

R. J. Clarke
University of Wollongong, Wollongong, Australia
e-mail: rclarke@uow.edu.au

© Springer Nature Switzerland AG 2019
B. Andersson et al. (eds.), *Advances in Information Systems Development*,
Lecture Notes in Information Systems and Organisation 34,
https://doi.org/10.1007/978-3-030-22993-1_2

Keywords ACM/AIS 2010 model curriculum · Computing education · Bodies of knowledge · Core curriculum · Academic administrative units

1 Introduction

Information Systems (IS) academic programs first began to appear in the early 1970s, and the Association of Information Systems (AIS), the major US professional body, was only established in 1994 [2]. The IS academic discipline sits within the wider field of Information Technology (IT) along with disciplines, such as, computer science and computer systems engineering, and is broadly described as lying at the juncture of organisations (or business) and technology. Within Australian universities, the IS education function is primarily placed in Business, or in Science, Engineering & Technology (SET) academic divisions, though it is also taught in other domains, including the humanities. What is taught in IS academic programs, in part, defines the discipline [11] and distinguishes it from other areas of IT. It is important for the academic community and for the profession as a whole that IS curriculum is understood and examined in a global context.

This study examined the Undergraduate (UG) IS curriculum in Australia with three broad aims: 1/to compare the Australian IS curriculum with that of other major IS education systems 2/to identify what subject areas are considered mandatory (core) and what are considered optional in Australian IS programs, and 3/to understand what influence, if any, placement in Business or SET academic divisions have on this. Past research indicates that curriculum studies can take descriptive approaches, what is actually taught, or normative approaches, what should be taught [8]. This study will be primarily descriptive, though it also draws on normative approaches in comparing curricula to standard curriculum models.

2 Information Systems Body of Knowledge

Globally, a number of professional bodies define the required knowledge and skills of Information Technology (IT) practitioners and by implication what should be taught in the academic programs that prepare these professionals. In Australia, Information Systems (IS) curriculum is driven to a large degree by the Australian Computer Society (ACS). The ACS Core Body of Knowledge (ACSBoK) [1] guides professional certification for IT professionals as well as accreditation of academic programs. Almost all IS majors provided by publicly-owned universities are accredited at the professional level. ACSBoK references the international framework Skills for the Information Age (SFIA) [12]. In the UK, the British Computer Society [3] performs a similar role working with the UK QAA [16], which provides Subject Benchmarking Statements in the area of Computing [16]. In the US, the Association for Computing Machinery/Association for Information Systems (ACM/AIS) has developed a set of model curricula including IS2010 [14] that addresses undergraduate IS programs, and MSIS2016 [15] that addresses graduate programs, while the European Commission has established the European Foundational ICT Body of Knowledge [5, 6].

Of these, only the ACM/AIS IS2010 specifically targets IS undergraduate education, identifying and spelling out in detail seven (7) core IS courses (subject areas) in a model curriculum. Adding weight to the ACM/AIS IS2010 as a de facto global IS standard, the latest UK QAA Subject Benchmarking Statements for Computing [16] defers to the ACM IS2010 standard indicating that "... [ACM/AIS] documents are recommended to inform program design and curriculum content". IS2010 would appear to be the best candidate for a reference point. It is used in the US and UK, specifically addresses the undergraduate IS curriculum, and provides a model of core subjects, and examples of non-core subjects, with full topic lists and descriptions.

Particular IS programs are designed for different academic environments with their own imperatives, and views as to what knowledge and skills are important and required by graduates in 3–5 years. Different programs may uniquely package topics into units of delivery, and a variety of unit titles are used, even for similar or overlapping material. Two methods can be used to make comparisons, a topic-based approach in which units (of delivery) can be unpacked down to the topic (knowledge unit, skill or competency) level, or a subject-based approach where units can be broadly classified according to some common reference subject area, or typical grouping of topics. While the former method may be more accurate, it creates considerably greater effort in determining standard topics, and classifying, storing and processing them. This study employs a more pragmatic, subject-based approach, making use of the subject areas defined by IS2010 as a reference point.

3 ACM/AIS IS2010 Model Curriculum

IS2010 describes a model curriculum of 7 core IS courses (subjects/units) providing detailed syllabuses for each of the following semester-subjects:

- Foundations of IS (IS2010.1)
- Data & Information Management. (IS2010.2)
- Enterprise Architecture (IS2010.3)
- IS Project Management (IS2010.4)
- IT Infrastructure (IS2010.5)
- Systems Analysis & Design (IS2010.6)
- Strategy, Management, and Acquisition (IS2010.7).

The topic list for each subject facilitates classification of units of delivery. IS2010 provides for a capstone course and encourages consideration of electives and specialisation for career tracks. The reduction of the core from ten (10) to seven (7) core courses is a major change from IS2002, encouraging greater flexibility, particularly in enabling career tracks. The reduced number of core courses has impacted on program designs by flattening the pre-requisite structures [10]. IS2010 also provides a list of possible model electives [14]:

- Application Development
- Business Process Management
- Collaborative Computing (listed, but not specified in detail)
- Data Mining/Business Intelligence (listed, but not specified in detail)
- Enterprise Systems
- Information Search and Retrieval (listed, but not specified in detail)
- Introduction to HCI
- IT Audit and Controls
- IS Innovation and New Technologies
- IT Security and Risk Management
- Knowledge Management (listed, but not specified in detail)
- Social Informatics (listed, but not specified in detail).

4 IS Programs and Curriculum

In the UK, Stefanidis and Fitzgerald [13] studied IS curriculum, examining 806 modules (units) from 43 Undergraduate (UG) IS degree programs offered by 13 universities in the Greater City of London. They classified modules into the 16 UK QAA Subject Benchmarking Statement Computing Body of Knowledge descriptors in operation at the time.[1] The most common categorisation of core modules occurred in Data, Information & Knowledge Management (offered in 98% of programs) and Development, Implementation & Maintenance of IS (93% of programs). There were no modules offered in the categories of Compression Technologies, Content Management Systems, Personal Information Systems and Digital Libraries. 18% of core modules could not be placed in any of the 16 categories. Only four subject areas appeared in all studies: Programming, Database, Data Communications, and Systems Analysis & Design. IS Concepts was the next most commonly cited subject area.

Hwang et al. [8, 9] studied the alignment of IS programs with IS2010 in the US, examining 2229 courses (units) from 394 UG IS programs. Their sample included Advance Collegiate Schools of Business (AACSB) accredited programs, non-AACSB accredited programs, private and public providers, and Ph.D. granting and non-PhD granting institutions. They found that Data & Information Management (IS2010.2), along with Systems Analysis & Design (IS2010.6), were the most common units offered as core. Units with a development focus: Programming Language, Application Development and Web Development, were the most commonly offered subjects areas from outside the IS2010 model core. They also found that 27.4% of

---

[1]The UK QAA SBS was updated in 2016.

programs offered units in subject areas that were outside of the IS2010 model core and the top 9 non-IS2010 subject areas.

Also in the US, Bell et al. [4] examined the IS2010 Curriculum Guideline alignment of 127 UG IS programs from AACSB accredited Business schools. The results were of a similar order in both studies, though there were statistically significant differences (these results are shown later in Table 4). A simple z test ($P \leq 0.05$) on the two samples indicated no significant difference in the adoption of Systems Analysis & Design (84 and 80%), and Enterprise Architecture (17 and 14%), but indicated that the results of the Adoption of the IS2010 Curriculum Guidelines review of AACSB programs was significantly higher for Data & Information Management (97 vs. 87%), Foundations of IS (87 vs. 63%), IT Infrastructure (70 vs. 32%), and Strategy, Management, and Acquisition (29 vs. 16%). The larger more general IS2010 alignment study of Hwang et al. [8, 9] found a significantly higher take up for IS Project Management (29 vs. 16%). It would appear that AACSB programs (the Bell, Mills and Fadel study) had higher IS2010 adherence rates at least in some subject areas. However, Hwang et al. [8, 9] found no significant difference overall between adoption by AACSB and non-AACSB programs. The AACSB-only IS2010 alignment study [4] also examined the level of adherence to the full requirement of IS2010, finding that only 2 programs included all 8 courses (7 courses + capstone) with 77% having 3–5 courses. On average, the alignment of IS2010 core units by the programs surveyed was 3.4 from the 7 possible units of the IS2010 model core.

With respect to the core subjects offered by programs that were not specified as part of the IS2010 model, the findings of the two US studies were also similar. Application Development (Programming/Application Development) was the most common subject category, being present in at least 70% of programs. Web Development was the next most commonly occurring requirement in up to a third of programs. In both US studies, E-Commerce (E-Commerce/Mobile), Business Intelligence (Business Intelligence & Analytics), Cybersecurity (IS Security) were found to be core requirements in less than 1 in 6 programs [4, 8, 9].

The two US based curriculum IS2010 alignment projects reported studies that collected data in 2011, soon after the introduction of IS2010, and perhaps too early for the new model to influence programs. In both cases, data was collected from readily available web sites and online catalogues.

In addition, the AACSB focused study [4] followed up their data collection with interviews at a sub-set (a calculated sample size) of heads of programs to validate the collected data, but also to assess perceived adherence against their measured adherence. Interestingly, they found that perceived adherence was significantly higher than their observed adherence.

In the Australian context, a comprehensive analysis of the state of the IS discipline was conducted in 2006, identifying 46 areas of IS activity across 37 Australian universities[2] [7]. The influence of both business and technology is evident, with IS professional education being managed by Business (25 programs), Science, Engi-

---

[2]They included two private universities, Bond University and Notre Dame, but not Charles Darwin University.

neering and Technology (12 programs) and Information Technology (4 programs) academic divisions. In some cases, multiple IS programs existed in the one institution, with one or sometimes more in Business academic divisions and one or more administered by SET-based academic divisions. The study addressed distinctive features of the IS curriculum, but the focus was on breadth rather than depth, and the findings described a flavor rather than consistent curriculum design, detailed quantitative data [7].

5 Method

All 36 publicly owned Australian universities were included in the study. Only those undergraduate IS majors that had an intake in 2017, were analysed. The collection of data took place in two phases, an initial data collection phase and a subsequent data validation phase where appropriate academic staff from those universities that provided the IS programs were consulted.

In the first phase of the study, IS program data describing the location within the university structure was obtained from public information available on the web. In most cases, there appeared to be enough up-to-date information to provide a reasonable basis for analysis. Further searches were often able to reveal more detailed information, if needed. The identification of IS programs is not always straightforward. In many cases, titles were clear, but in some cases, particularly in major areas of study such as Software Development, judgment was required. In general, where program titles indicated IS or IS Development and associated professional roles, they have been included.

A reference list of subjects was used to classify units offered in the various IS programs. The reference list was initially constructed from the IS2010 model core and IS2010 example electives [14]. After a pass of units offered, the IS2010 example elective Data Mining/Business Intelligence was replaced on the reference list by two more commonly occurring topic groupings (at least in the Australian context): Data Analytics/Data Mining and Business Intelligence/Data Warehousing. When offered units were encountered, that did not match existing subject areas on the reference list, additional subject area descriptions based on these units were added to the reference list.

Only in a very few cases do unit descriptions exactly match subject descriptions on the reference list, and units were classified more in terms of capturing the "spirit" of the standard in its aims, the level of the offered unit, as well as the inclusion of important topics. In essence, the reference subjects are intentionally referred to as subject areas and treated more as categories. The absence of a match with a subject area in the reference list does not mean that topics are not covered, but rather that there is no single identifiable unit that can be argued to focus on the content of the reference subject area. Overall, 140 distinct subject areas were used to describe the offerings in this study. The first phase was conducted over several months in early

2017 producing mappings of units offered for each IS major to the reference list of subject areas.

In a second phase conducted in late 2017, all IS providing universities identified in the first phase were consulted to verify the selection of IS programs, and the classification of unit offerings. Heads of IS programs were contacted and generally access was given to an academic staff member with detailed knowledge of the program, typically a program coordinator or director. The preliminary analysis (mappings) of their programs and the list of reference subjects were distributed to these academic coordinators and feedback sought, in most cases through phone conversations. The final decision on whether or not a particular major was an IS major, and how units should be classified was left to the program coordinators. In the consultation phase, two programs were removed, one was added, and a number of revisions were made to the lists of core and non-core IS units offered.

The approach used in this study required interpretation of high level catalogue entries and the classification of units into subjects areas based on a 50%+ match reference subjects. This means some subject areas may be covered in total across the curriculum, but have not been included in any particular item. A focus on topics, without consideration of their packaging into delivery units, may provide a slightly different picture. While some classifications are clear and agreed, some required subjective judgment, and other assessors may have made different classifications. In the consultation phase, the final arbiters of unit classification were the program coordinators.

6 Data Analysis in the Australian Context

A subject-based approach based on IS2010 and the methods used by Hwang et al. [8, 9] and Bell et al. [4] provide a practical guide to assessing large numbers of programs. It also enabled the Australian IS academic community to compare their programs to those of the US. In addressing its overall aim, this study uses a similar subject-based approach to address the following specific questions in the Australian context:

– Where are IS academic programs placed in terms of academic divisions?
– What are the core IS units delivered in IS programs?
– How does the delivered core align with IS2010?
– What non-core IS units are offered in Australian IS programs?
– How does the level of alignment with the IS2010 core in Australia compare with that of US studies?

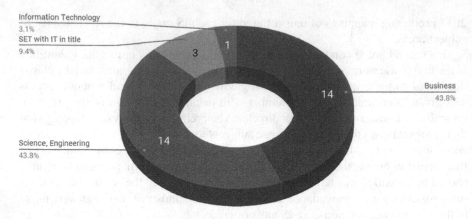

Information Technology
3.1%
SET with IT in title
9.4%

Business
43.8%

Science, Engineering
43.8%

Fig. 1 Administering academic divisions

6.1 Academic Programs Placement in Academic Divisions

Of the 36 universities in the study, 6 did not offer an undergraduate IS major. From the remaining 30 Universities deemed to have IS UG majors, 32 different academic organisational divisions administered the selected programs. Only in one case did different divisions from the same university provide IS UG majors relatively independently. Figure 1 illustrates the location of the vast majority of IS UG majors in SET or Business divisions. Twenty-eight (28) of the 32 academic divisions were split evenly between these divisions. Three additional SET focused divisions contained the term Information Technology, Information Science or Computing in their title. There was only 1 high level division (a faculty) dedicated to Information Technology. Twenty four (24) of these main academic units were further divided into Schools, Departments or Discipline groups.

IS continues to be offered across Business and SET focused academic divisions in Australia, though there has been some change since The Information Systems Discipline in Australia study reported in 2008 [7]. IS programs administered by Business academic divisions decreased from 25 to 14, while those administered by SET have increased from 8 to 17. The number of dedicated first level IT academic divisions has decreased from 4 to 1. The increased presence of IT in some division titles, primarily SET, may be a result of the merging of dedicated first level IT academic divisions into other SET-based academic divisions.

6.2 Core IS Subject Areas

From the 30 universities, 49 IS majors were identified. Of these 49 IS majors, 1 university had 4 majors, 3 universities had 3 majors each, 10 had 2 majors each and

Table 1 Units required as core in Australian IS UG programs

Subject category	Count	(n = 33) (%)
Systems Analysis & Design (IS2010.6)	32	96.97
Data & Information Management (IS2010.2)	31	93.94
Fundamentals of Programming	26	78.79
Foundations of IS (IS2010.1)	25	75.76
IS Project Management (IS2010.5)	23	69.70
Professional Skills (General, incl ethics)	15	45.45
IT Infrastructure (IS2010.4)	15	45.45
Data Communications & Networking	15	45.45
Web Applications/Technology	12	36.36
IS Project (Single Unit)	11	33.33
IS Project (Double Unit)	11	33.33
Strategy, Management, and Acquisition (IS2010.7)	10	30.30
HCI	9	27.27
Professional Skills (Communication)	8	24.24
Business Process Management	7	21.21
Enterprise Systems (ERP)	6	18.18
Business Analytics Foundations/Business Stat Methods	6	18.18
Application Development	6	18.18
IT Security & Risk Management	5	15.15
E-Commerce	5	15.15
Business Intelligence/Data Warehousing	5	15.15

16 had a single IS major. Of the 14 universities that had multiple majors, 8 of these had discernible "Y" structure, where a common core accommodated mostly 2 but also 3 streams. These 49 majors were further collapsed into 33 distinct programs. An IS program is defined as one or more majors designed and managed by the same group of academic staff. For example, a "Y" structure with the same stem and different branches would be classified as a single program, where units offered were counted once only. Table 1 shows the subjects required as core in 5 or more programs.

Units offered were divided between those that were core to a program and those that were not core (non-core). Core units are those units that must be completed by all students doing any of the IS majors in a particular program. In essence, core units are needed by all graduates, and are compulsory in all majors within a program. Non-core units are those units that are elective or not core to all majors. In total, 648 IS unit offerings were identified across the 33 programs, 365 core units and 283 non-core units. Each of these units was classified according to the best match (at least 50%) in the reference list of subject areas. The 365 core units were collapsed into 68 distinct subject areas, and the 283 non-core units into 113.

Placement within Business or SET appears to have an impact. SET-placed programs have a more extensive core. The 19 SET-placed programs required 233 core IS units over 63 distinct subject areas, with an average of 12.3 core units per program. The 14 business-placed programs required 126 core IS units over 38 distinct subjects area, an average of 9 core IS units per program. For non-core, the differences are not so marked. The SET-placed programs offered 162 IS units over 91 distinct subject areas, an average of 8.5 non-core IS units/program, and the business-placed programs offered 106 IS units over 61 distinct subjects areas, an average of 7.6 non-core IS units per program. The location of IS program within the university structure also appears to have an impact on the types of units offered. SET-placed programs have higher levels of technical content as core, while business-placed programs require more business focused subject areas.

Of the top 22 core subject areas, there is no significant difference (at $P \leq 0.05$ level) in adoption by Business and SET placed programs for 15 subjects areas. For the other 7 subject areas, Fundamentals of Programming, HCI, Data Communications & Networking, IS Project Management (IS2010.5) and IT Infrastructure (IS2010.4) were more often core in SET-managed programs, while Business Process Management and Business Intelligence/Data Warehousing were more often required as core in Business-managed programs.

6.3   Core Alignment with IS2010

Units that correspond to the IS2010 core model subject descriptions, Systems Analysis & Design (IS2010.6) and Data Information & Management (IS2010.2) are required in almost all of the 33 IS programs, 32 and 31 respectively. Foundations of IS (IS2010.1) and IS Project Management (IS2010.5) are required in a majority (25 and 23) of programs. IT Infrastructure (IS2010.4) is required in 15 programs, Strategy, Management, and Acquisition (IS2010.7) in 10 programs, and IS Architecture (IS2010.3) is a distinct unit in only 2 programs.

Of the non IS2010 subject areas commonly required as core, Fundamentals of Programming appears in a majority of programs, 26 of 33. Data Communications & Networking is required in 15 programs and Web Applications/Technology in 12 programs. Units identified as HCI, Enterprise Systems (ERP), Business Analytics Foundations/Business Statistical Methods, Application Development, Business Process Management, IT Security & Risk Management, E-Commerce, and Business Intelligence/Data Warehousing are required in between 5 and 10 of the 33 programs.

Figure 2 shows that most of the surveyed universities have core units of delivery that align with over half of the IS2010 model core subject areas, with a normal-type distribution of around 4 subjects areas in the core. No university adopted all IS2010 core subjects and only 3 programs required less than 3 subjects from the IS2010 core.

Overall, Australian IS programs have an average core adoption of 4.2 of the 7 core IS2010 subjects, compared to 3.4 from 7 found in the US [8, 9]. SET-placed programs (average of 4.6) have significantly higher alignment than Business-placed programs (3.8).

Fig. 2 Adoption of IS2010
by Australian IS programs

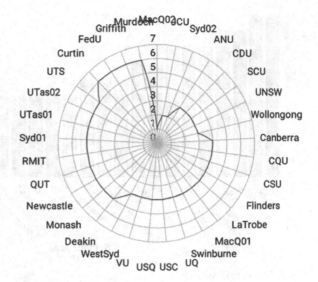

6.4 Non-core IS Subjects Offered in Australian IS Programs

Figure 3 shows the IS-related subjects classified as non-core. From the IS2010 model core, Strategy, Management, and Acquisition—IS2010.7 (10 of 33), IS Project Management—IS2010.5 (6), Enterprise Architecture—IS2010.3 (4), Data & Information Management—IS2010.2 (2), and Foundations of IS—IS2010.1 (1) are offered as non-core. Outside of the IS2010 core, Application Development (Mobile), Data Analytics/Mining, IT Security & Risk Management, Enterprise Systems (ERP), Application Development (Web), Business Intelligence/Data Warehousing and Business Analytics Foundations/Business Statistical Methods appeared in 6–10 of the 33 programs.

There is a long tail of 89 non-core subject areas offered in less than 4 programs. 53 subject areas are offered in only one program. Notable IS subject areas in this tail include: Web Applications/Technology, IS & Cloud Computing, Accounting Information Systems, Social Informatics, IT Management, IS Innovation, Global IS, and Health Informatics. A number of subjects areas cover more advanced topics in areas of specialisation, such as: Business Analysis, Application Development (Mobile), Application Development (Web), Data Analytics, Game Technology & Development, and Business Process Management. A small number of programs provide options in the area of professional skills (consulting, organisational behaviour, communication for English as a second language) and capstone activities (subjects and projects). The most common non-core capstone was actual industry experience, no doubt indicating the selective nature of industry placements. Desirability of the industry placement opportunity by students was typically driven by an understanding of the importance of the experience to graduate employability.

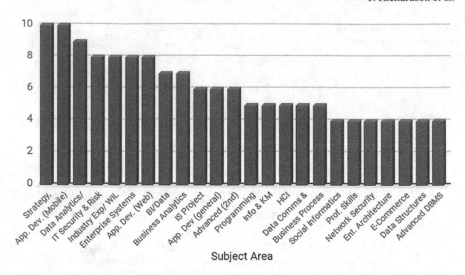

Fig. 3 Non-core IS subjects

There is significant difference in their level of adoption by Business-placed and SET-placed academic divisions in 5 of 24 non-core subject areas. Application Development (Web) and Social Informatics were more likely to be offered by SET-based programs as non-core, while IS Project Management (IS2010.5), Data Communications & Networking, and Business Process Management are more likely to be offered as non-core in Business-based programs.

Forty-seven (47) non-core subject areas are offered by less than 5 programs. Twenty- four (24) subject areas are offered by only 1 program. This long tail includes niche and emerging areas of IS, and different ways of offering professional skills learning and capstone experiences. Niche and emerging IS subjects areas include: Data Analytics/Data Mining (3 of 33), Social Informatics (2), IT Audit & Control (2), IS Innovations (2), Decision Support Systems (2), Service Management & Customer Support (2), Introduction to Games Technology & Development (1), and IS & Cloud Computing (1). Unique capstone activity included Industrial Placement Experience (4) and IS capstone activity delivered more in the form of a classroom experience (3). Relatively unique dedicated professional skills units included problem solving skills (3), working in industry (1) and collaboration and teamwork (1). Overall, these results indicate more diversity than that found in the US. In Australia, the proportion of units, 62% (227 of 365) classified into subject areas outside of the IS2010 model core is significantly higher than the 37% (820 of 2227) found by Hwang, Ma and Wang [8, 9].

6.5 Comparison of IS2010 Alignment in Australian and US Studies

Table 2 compares the IS2010 core subjects required in this study with those required as core in the US studies of Hwang et al. [8, 9], Bell et al. [4].

Overall, the results are of a similar order, though there are some significant statistical differences (at $P \leq 0.05$ level). There are no significant difference in the core requirement for Data & Information Management (IS2010.2) and Enterprise Architecture (IS2010.3). Adoption of Systems Analysis & Design (IS2010.6) in Australia was significantly higher than that found in both US studies, while IS Project Management (IS2010.5) and Strategy, Management, and Acquisition (IS2010.7) had higher adoption than that found in only one of the US studies. Foundations of IS (IS2010.1) and IT Infrastructure (IS2010.4) had significantly lower levels of adoption than that found in the US AACSB focused study [4]. The UK study reported in 2010 [13] does not use the IS2010 as a reference and a comparison of all subject areas cannot be made. However, in the subject areas of Data & Information Management, and IT Infrastructure, there are similar levels of adoption.

Programming and application development units, which are not part of the IS2010, are still widely required as core in Australia, the US and the UK. Units that build on a first programming unit for application development in general, mobile applications

Table 2 Comparison of core subject area: Australia, US and UK

Subject category	Count	% (n = 33) (%)	US AACSB [4] (%)	Hwang et al. US [9] (%)	Stefanidis & Fitz-gerald [13]	UK BoK (These do not align well with ACM/AIS Model Curriculum)
Systems Analysis & Design (IS2010.6)	32	97	84	80	60%	IS Design
Data & Information Management (IS2010.2)	31	94	97	87	98%	Data, Information & Knowledge Mgmt.
Foundations of IS (IS2010.1)	25	76	87	63	>50%	No single category
IS Project Management (IS2010.5)	23	70	38	66	93%	Dev. Implementation & Mtce (This category includes programming and project management.)
IT Infrastructure (IS2010.4)	15	45	70	32	58%	ICT
Strategy, Management, and Acquisition (IS2010.7)	10	30	29	16	53%	Mgmt. of IS & Services
Enterprise Architecture (IS2010.3)	2	6	17	14	Up to 50%	No single category

and web applications are also common in the curriculum. Gaming is beginning to appear as an option in IS programs, possibly as a vehicle for IS development skills, including analysis, design, HCI, and programming. In the UK and Australia, the professional bodies with their focus on the broader IT professional, may influence this, but the IS2010 core includes no recommendation around programming, suggesting that academic program designers still consider programming and development as central to the IS discipline.

Within the Australian context, the influence of the local professional body, the ACS, is clear, with the prevalence of professional skills units, and of specific capstone projects, equally divided between one and two semester units. Some programs offer actual industry placements, generally in a competitive selection process, but the majority aim to provide an authentic as possible industry experience without students being embedded in workplaces.

Within Australia, the ACS has a strong requirement of IT programs to include professional skills, such as ethical frameworks and the professional code of conduct, communication and teamwork skills. Almost a half of programs (15 of 33) required a general professional skills unit that included ethics. Fifteen (15) programs embed or integrate these topics into multiple subject areas across the curriculum, but others provide units that target particular professional skills such as communication (8), problem solving (3), collaboration and teamwork (1), and working in industry (1). Some programs had more than one professional skills unit.

Similar to professional skills, capstone activity is a clear requirement for ACS accreditation. Twenty-two (22) of the 33 programs include one or two semester-unit projects. Four (4) programs require industry experience, and 2 mandate a capstone subject, where integration of topics is covered in a more traditional classroom format. Five (5) embed or integrate capstone requirements into other subject areas.

7 Conclusion

This research has identified 648 distinct units that can be classified into 140 subject areas across the Australian IS curriculum, suggesting a considerable range in packaging of topics and potential attempts to address niche or emerging areas of the discipline. Overall, when viewed collectively, there would appear to be a high level of agreement between what should be included in an UG IS program in Australia. Alignment with IS2010 in Australia is on par, if not higher than that of the US. Systems Analysis and Design (IS2010.6), Data & Information Management (IS2010.2), Foundations of IS (IS2010.1), and IS Project Management (IS2010.5) have common and accepted units of delivery that are core to the vast majority of programs. Along with Fundamentals of Programming, these are the big 5 of the UG IS curriculum. Interestingly, Data Communication is required core in almost half of Australian programs (45%), compared to only 5% of US programs. The IS2010 IT Infrastructure (IS2010.4) subject area includes substantial data communications and networking components which are often seen as adequate for IS professionals.

This study raises questions about the packaging of topics or subject areas in the IS2010 model core. Clearly, Systems Analysis & Design (IS2010.6), Data & Information Management (IS2010.2), Fundamentals of IS (IS2010.1) and IS Project Management (IS2010.5) are widely accepted sets of topics. IT Infrastructure (IS2010.4) and Strategy, Management, and Acquisition (IS2010.7) are less commonly accepted as necessary IS subject areas, while Enterprise Architecture (IS2010.3) is rarely required as a distinct subject packaging, at least in undergraduate programs. Outside of the IS2010 model core, Fundamentals of Programming, and in Australia, Data Communications & Networks are deemed at least as important as IT Infrastructure (IS2010.4) and Strategy, Management, and Acquisition (IS2010.7). Further studies are required to investigate undergraduate versus post graduate degrees in Information Systems, in particular in regards to the topic packaging characteristics and the effects accrediting bodies may have on the core topic components.

Acknowledgements The authors gratefully acknowledge the financial assistance of the Australasian Council of Professors and Heads of Information Systems (ACPHIS) in conducting this project, and the help of all of those IS program coordinators who participated in the consultation process.

References

1. ACS: The ICT Professional Body of Knowledge Professional Standards Board, Australian Computer Society (2013)
2. Avison, D., Elliot, S.: Scoping the discipline of information systems. In: King, J.L., Lyytinen, K. (eds.) Information Systems: The State of the Field, pp. 3–18. Wiley, Hoboken (2006)
3. BCS: Guidelines on course accreditation: Information for universities and colleges, British Computer Society (2015)
4. Bell, C., Mills, R., Fadel, K.: An analysis of undergraduate information systems curricula: adoption of the IS2010 curriculum guidelines. In: Communications of the Association for Information Systems, vol. 32, Article 2 (2013)
5. EC: e-Skills for ICT Professionalism: Creating a European Foundational ICT Body of Knowledge. European Commission (2014)
6. EC: The European Foundational ICT Body of Knowledge, Version 1.0. European Commission (2015)
7. Gable, G., Gregor, S., Clarke, R. Ridley, G., Smyth, R.: The Information Systems Academic Discipline in Australia, ANU E Press (2008)
8. Hwang, D., Ma, Z., Wang, M.: The information systems core: a study from the perspective of IS core curricula in the US. In: Proceedings of the Information Systems Educators Conference, Baltimore, Maryland USA, vol 31, no 3049. ISSN 2167-1435 (2014)
9. Hwang, D., Ma, Z., Wang, M.: The information systems core: a study from the perspective of IS core curricula. US IS Educ. J. **13**(6), 27–34 (2015)
10. Reynolds, J., Ferguson, R.C., Leidig, P.M.: A tale of two curricula: the case for pre-requisites in the IS model curriculum. Inf. Syst. Educ. J. **14**(5), 17–24 (2016)
11. Ridley, G.: Characterising information systems in Australia: a theoretical framework. Australas. J. IS, **14**(1) (2006)
12. SFIA: SFIA6: The Complete Reference Guide. SFIA Foundation (2015)
13. Stefanidis, A., Fizgerald, G.: Information systems curricula in the UK: a survey of undergraduate courses (Research-in-progress). In: Innovation in Teaching and Learning in Information and Computer Sciences, pp. 87–99, Routledge (2010)

14. Topi, H., Valacich, J.S., Wright, R.T., Kaiser. K., Nunamaker Jr., J.F., Sipior, J.C., de Vreede, G-J.: IS2010: Curriculum guidelines for undergraduate degree programs in information systems. In: Communications of the Association for Information Systems, vol. 26, Article 18 (2010)
15. Topi, H., Karsten, H., Brown, S.A., Carvalho, J.A., Donnellan, B., Shen, J., Tan, B.C.Y., Thouin, M.F.: MSIS 2016 global competency model for graduate degree programs in information systems. In: Communications of the Association for Information Systems, vol. 40, Article 18 (2017)
16. UK QAA: Subject Benchmarking Statement, Computing. UK Quality Code for Higher Education (2016)

Cargo Cults in Information Systems Development: A Definition and an Analytical Framework

Tanja Elina Mäki-Runsas, Kai Wistrand and Fredrik Karlsson

Abstract Organizations today adopt agile information systems development methods (ISDM), but many do not succeed with the adoption process and in achieving desired results. Systems developers sometimes fail in efficient use of ISDM, often due to a lack of understanding the fundamental intentions of the chosen method. In many cases organizations simply imitate the behavior of others without really understanding why. This conceptual paper defines this phenomenon as an ISDM cargo cult behavior and proposes an analytical framework to identify such situations. The concept of cargo cults originally comes from the field of social anthropology and has been used to explain irrational, ritualistic imitation of certain behavior. By defining and introducing the concept in the field of information systems development we provide a potential diagnostic tool to improve the understanding of one of the reasons why ISDM adoption sometimes fail.

Keywords Agile development · Cargo cult · Method rationale ·
Self-determination theory · Social-action theory · Information systems
development · Information systems development methods · Software
development · Software development methods

A prior version of this paper has been published in the ISD2018 Proceedings (http://aisel.aisnet.org/isd2014/proceedings2018).

T. E. Mäki-Runsas (✉) · K. Wistrand · F. Karlsson
Department of Informatics, CERIS, Örebro University, Örebro, Sweden
e-mail: tanja.maki-runsas@oru.se

K. Wistrand
e-mail: kai.wistrand@oru.se

F. Karlsson
e-mail: fredrik.karlsson@oru.se

© Springer Nature Switzerland AG 2019
B. Andersson et al. (eds.), *Advances in Information Systems Development*,
Lecture Notes in Information Systems and Organisation 34,
https://doi.org/10.1007/978-3-030-22993-1_3

35

1   Introduction

Inefficient information systems development (ISD) is a prevailing challenge in many organizations. For example, over the years the Standish Group CHAOS reports [1–3] have showed that ISD projects have had difficulties in meeting their targets. In response to this challenge organizations adopt various kinds of information systems development methods (ISDM). The adoption and use of ISDMs is not a new phenomenon, since ISDMs first appeared during the 1960s as a response to what was once coined the "software crisis" [4]. Early approaches tried to handle problems identified in ISD without any plans, often by developers who did not know the business context the suggested systems were planned to support [5]. Today, a vast number of different ISDMs has been proposed. Jayaratna estimated already in 1994 that approximately 1,000 named ISDMs existed [6]. This number has most likely increased even more today. A problem related to many of these ISDMs is that they became more and more administratively heavy, and more difficult to follow and understand [7].

As a backlash against this development, agile ISDMs were proposed which aimed at flexibility and faster delivery [8–11]. These ideas were unified in 2001 when a group of experienced practitioners and researchers formulated what became known as the Agile Manifesto [12]. The manifesto stated that four main values are important in order to succeed with agile ISD; (1) individuals and interactions over processes and tools, (2) working software over comprehensive documentation, (3) customer collaboration over contract negotiation, and (4) responding to change over following a plan. These main values resulted in twelve principles that systems developers should adhere to while working. The point of this manifesto was to increase ISD efficiency. All agile ISDMs should implement these fundamental ideas, which for example means involving customers early and continuously, and responding to change through continuous software deliveries. Another fundamental point is to always welcome changing requirements and having an open working environment where business people and developers work together with an effective and short timescale, delivering software at a constant pace. The individuals involved should be kept motivated throughout the whole process in order to promote team spirit.

Nowadays many ISD organizations have adopted various kinds of agile ISDMs [13, 14] and thus making them common. An inherent characteristic of agile ISDMs—being lightweight methods—is their apparent lack of clear guidelines and direct instructions of how to conduct ISD. An obvious benefit of agile ISDMs is that they are presented as easier to follow, more flexible and easier to adopt than more traditional ISDMs [14]. Thus, many ISD organizations, which have adopted some kind of named ISDM, claim to be agile. However, it is unclear to which degree they are actually being agile, i.e. following the underlying values and principles of the agile manifesto. That said, some ISD organizations who claim to be using agile ISDMs are very successful, such as Spotify and King. At the same time, an extensive number of ISD organizations seem to fail in their efforts to adopt an agile ISDM [15, 16].

Both results are natural, considering that systems developers use their situational and local character of knowledge when adopting an ISDM, resulting in differences in method-in-action [17]. Although our discussion above uses the more recent developments on ISDMs and agile ISDMs in particular as an example, this challenge applies to the adoption of more traditional types of ISDMs as well. All ISDMs are normative artifacts, which means they are based on values that have guided the method design. Thus, irrespective of the chosen ISDM there is a need to be compliant with its values in order to be true to the method. Despite that this is known and that ISDMs have been on the research agenda for several decades, scholars have mostly focused on to what extent ISDMs are claimed to be used [cf. 18] and local adaption of methods [e.g. 17, 19, 20]. Less attention has been given to flawed or failed adoption and the reason behind these situations.

In order for practitioners and researchers to identify challenges related to ISDM adoption there is a need for useful analytical frameworks that direct attention. One way of pinpointing challenges in adopting ISDMs is to explore to what extent unsuccessful attempts are examples of "cargo cult" behavior. The concept of cargo cults originally comes from the field of social anthropology and is used to explain irrational imitation of rituals [21, 22]. This concept has been used among consultants as a metaphor when describing how an ISD organization fails to adopt an agile ISDM because they act upon and follow method descriptions, or imitate others, without understanding the underlying values and reasons behind the method. This results in misconceptions and ritualistic behavior, which does not contribute to reaching the actual ISD goals. Examples of how cargo cult has been used as a metaphor in the industry can be found in blogs by James Shore, Maxx Daymon, Jose Luis Soria and others [23–25]. Originally, the concept was used to describe ritualistic, uncontested imitation by different cultures in the Melanesian islands. These futile attempts to replicate the western visitors' behavior were carried out with the purpose to be rewarded with gifts from the gods. These gifts, or "cargo", were regarded by these cults as something magical, which would appear when they performed certain rituals [21].

Against this backdrop, the aim of this conceptual paper is twofold: (a) to define the concept of information systems development method cargo cult, and (b) to suggest an analytical framework that could be used to identify information systems development method cargo cult situations in ISD organizations. To this end we employ the original definition of cargo cult by Worsley [21], Weber's [26] typology of social action as interpreted by Kalberg [27], and Self-Determination Theory [28]. The typology of social actions is used to distinguish between rational, irrational and non-rational social actions with regards to the goals and values of the chosen ISDM. Self-Determination Theory is used to describe the orientation of the motivation behind social actions. Subsequently, this paper provides information system (IS) researchers with an alternative theoretical perspective and an analytical framework to identify flawed adoption of ISDMs. It provides managers and systems developers in ISD organizations with a potential diagnostic tool making it possible to identify cargo cult situations in organizations, which opens opportunities for future process improvements and organizational development.

The paper is organized as follows. The next section presents an overview of research related to cargo cults and to what extent cargo cults have been addressed in IS and ISD. This is followed by a theoretical section on ISDM, which provides a background to understanding the complexity of this type of artifact and why misconceptions and ritualistic method behavior can occur. The next section contains our conceptual development, resulting in our definition of ISDM cargo cult and the suggested analytical framework. Finally, we end this paper with a short conclusion and discussion of directions for future research.

2 Research Related to Cargo Cults

As discussed in the Introduction, the concept of cargo cults was identified among the natives in Melanesia and defined by Worsley [21] from a socio anthropological perspective. Many examples of cargo cults have been reported, typically describing the phenomenon in different cultures less technologically advanced in comparison to western society [21, 29–31]. These studies described the seemingly futile attempts to imitate western visitors in the hope that the gods will reward them with gifts. An example could be to construct an airfield in the dirt and an airplane out of palm leaves to lure the gods to the island. The interpretation is that the natives of Melanesia did this because they did not understand why the airplanes came in the first place. Nor did they understand the purpose of an airfield and how a construction must be coordinated with other efforts in order to make sure airplanes will actually come.

The purpose of an airplane is to go from A to B. Usually in order to deliver something, persons or cargo. If you choose to build an airfield, you have to make sure that this airfield is known to others, typically people interested in directing airplanes from A:s to B:s. You must also understand the basic requirements for an airfield. These could be aspects concerning length and material of the runway to accommodate airplanes up to a specific size. You must also understand regulations regarding air traffic control systems, possibly radar, air routes, fuel, security, customs, logistics and so on. This requires coordination and communication with others and most importantly an understanding of how and why the airfield is supposed to operate with other actors. The natives of Melanesia simply replicated what they observed without understanding the underlying reasons and requirements for an airfield; they were exerting a cargo cult behavior. The problem was not really the location of the airfield itself. Many islands in Melanesia have since then gotten airfields of their own. However, these airfields have been designed with a different kind of understanding. Just building an airfield through imitation does not result in airplanes landing. Other things do.

Typically, a cargo cult is understood as a temporal situation, which means that it is possible to overcome this state. That said, there are examples of cargo cults that persist in some form over decades. One such cargo cult is the "John Frum" cult of Tanna [32], which still exists today. Moreover, it is important to acknowledge that cargo cults are not only found in cultures considered less technologically advanced in comparison with western society. One example of a cargo cult in a western society can be found in the case of the UFO-sect Heaven's Gate. In 1997, 39 members of this sect committed suicide in the hope that their souls would be picked up by a UFO accompanying the Hale-Bopp comet. They were found at their compound in San Diego, CA, dead by poisoning and each one covered by a purple cloth. The inspiration for this came from science fiction and their leader Marshall Applewhite convinced the members that this was the rational thing to do [33]. The behavior is in line with what is typical for a cargo cult.

The concept of cargo cult has been sparsely used in the IS field. However, when it has been used, one can see it has been used disparately with many different meanings. McConnell [16] tried, in an editorial, to introduce the concept by explaining this behavior in ISD organizations. He wrote about impostors and misuse of processes, however he did not present any research to validate his opinions. We can also see the metaphor being used to describe robot research [34] and interaction design prototypes [35]. Cerf [36] used the concept in information technology environment development and explained how industrial parks are created through imitation with the blind belief that they would generate the same success as others. These examples all describe a certain behavior, which involves imitating others without understanding why.

Imitating behavior implies trying to act like someone else. Uncontested imita-tion without regards to, or comprehension of, the underlying reasons could lead to meaningless rituals. Feynman [22] introduced the concept of cargo cult science as a metaphor for describing scientific research of low validity and referring to the uncon-tested imitation of research methods without regard to whether they were actually appropriate in the intended studies. As methods are common in ISD, one can question if not the same situations might occur in different ISD organizations, leading to the following of meaningless rituals. Obviously, this might inhibit an ISD organization in reaching the desired success.

The notion of cargo cults in ISD can also be related to attempts to understand how ISD organizations deviate from standard ISDM application principles. For example, one way to describe such deviations in the agile context is to refer to them as Scrum-buts. This indicates that an ISD organization is using Scrum, "but" still chooses to not implement Scrum in full, omitting possible important aspects. Such deviations have been described using the term Anti-patterns as a way of describing agile malpractices [37–39]. So far, the research on Anti-patterns have not been aimed at finding a theoretical framework that could explain the problems concerning agile malpractices, but rather to collect instances of malpractices, suggest remedies, and record them as different types of Anti-patterns.

3   Information Systems Development Methods

Earlier we concluded that ISDMs have been around for a long time. This means that scholars have invested a lot of effort into understanding and explaining what an ISDM is. Hence, there exist a number of definitions [40–47]. However, Karlsson and

Ågerfalk concluded [40] that although these definitions are slightly different, there seems to be a shared understanding that an ISDM has three main parts; concepts, activities and notations.

Let us take two of the practices of an agile ISDM, Daily Scrum and Product Backlog, as illustrative examples of these three parts. Daily Scrum contains a description of what is meant by this practice; it should be carried out as time-boxed daily meeting, to synchronize the ISD team's efforts and plan the work for the next 24-hours [48]. In other words, concepts relevant in a Daily Scrum are; time-boxed, daily meeting, synchronizing efforts and short-term planning. Concepts in this sense emphasize what is considered important in the ISDM. Concepts must be operationalized and have certain activities making sure that the ISD team focuses on the concepts in a fruitful way, typically by asking questions. If the Daily Scrum is meant for the ISD team to synchronize development issues, questions need to be asked during the meeting to create a shared understanding for everyone involved in the project. These questions should help the team members to understand the current state of the system, the progress of the ISD activities, and current tasks and challenges. Since this meeting is being carried out every day, shared understanding is therefore created on a daily basis. Typically, the results of ISDM activities are recorded in some way, constituting the method's notation. However, since no shared records are produced during a Daily Scrum, the notation is an individual choice of the ISD team members—sometimes being nothing more than mental notes.

Our second example, a Product backlog consists of a list of things that need to be completed. The list is organized as prioritized and estimated work items that an ISD team picks in order to know what should be done during the next iteration [48]. Some of the concepts relevant for a Product backlog are; work item, priority, and estimation. Activities that relate to these concepts are, for example, to divide the work that needs to be done into specific work items, prioritize these work items, and thereafter to estimate how long time it will take to develop each work item. The result is documented using a table structure containing a list of prioritized and estimated requirements for the system. This constitutes the notation of a Product backlog.

An ISDM's content, such as Daily Scrum and Product backlog, are the result of the method designer's decisions concerning the method. Therefore, an ISDM's activities, notations, and concepts exist as a result of what the method designer has regarded as important. For example, Jayaratna et al. [49] have argued that "if [...] the rationale for the action is implicit then by definition the activity set cannot be considered a methodology". So, these reasons are an important part of an ISDM and they are according to Goldkuhl [50] expressed as part of an ISDM's perspective. Similar ideas are also found in Brinkkemper [43]. Hence, all of them acknowledged method rationale as an important part of an ISDM. Rossi et al. [51] have defined method rationale with the meaning of all choices made when designing the ISDM and the reasons for these choices; Ågerfalk and Wistrand [41] have made a less inclusive operationalization, with the meaning of explicating goals and values behind the ISDM. In this paper, we use the latter, less inclusive, notion of method rationale. Regardless of the chosen operationalization of the method rationale concept, it can be used to analyze the kind of rationale that is expressed in a method artifact. For example, Ågerfalk [52] used the less inclusive notation to analyze the rationale in the agile manifesto. He identified 12 different goals anchored in 5 different values. Method rationale has also been used as a starting point for situational construction or tailoring of ISDMs. For example, Rolland and Prakash [53] and Ralyte' et al. [54] used the concept of intention, while Brinkkemper [43], Harmsen [55], Gonzalez-Perez et al. [56], and Karlsson and Ågerfalk [40, 57] used the goal concept. Thus, this research has mostly focused on the method artifact itself and has paid less attention to how systems developers perceive information systems development methods and the rationale behind them.

However, it is important that the systems developers are aware of the goals and values of the adopted ISDM. Otherwise they run the risk of using the ISDM's activities, notations, and concepts based on wrongful assumptions and/or with wrong interpretations [58]. This might in turn result in not reaching the ISDM's goals, and possibly a cargo cult to occur. If we return to the Daily Scrum example, the goal is to create a shared understanding of the project status, create short term planning and achieve better interaction within the ISD team. If the team does not understand this, they might not understand the basic concepts and how to carry out the activities. They might thus end up having a meeting where they have focused on the wrong things. The right questions, as suggested by the activities, have not been asked and the wrong (or no) shared understanding is the result. The reason for this is that the ISD team has missed the fundamental goals and values of this type of interaction and, as consequence, they are not adhering to the method's rationale. They think they are agile, but in reality, they are just having a coffee break standing up.

In the example of the product backlog, the goal is to have a dynamic, living overview of the requirements of the system, in line with the vision. The ISD team could miss out on the goal of creating a product backlog if they do not focus on describing the work items in a distinct way, do not prioritize them, or make wrongful (or no) estimation of the work items. The value of a product backlog is to generate a higher degree of customer collaboration and to focus on working software. If the ISD team does not succeed in generating this type of product backlog, they risk ending up with a non-functional product backlog and they could be focusing on the wrong work items. In the end it could mean working on items that provide limited or no value to the customer.

However, the account of ISDM research given above does not mean that researchers have not addressed problems in this area, such as systems developers' awareness of the goals and values of the adopted ISDMs. Stolterman [59] discussed the importance of systems developers having an understanding of the perspective behind a method. Stolterman and Russo [60] used the terms public and private rationality, which can be thought of as partially intersecting sets. Public rationality is an inter-subjective understanding about why an ISDM prescribes activities, notations, and concepts and what kinds of results that can be reached by using them. Thus, it is similar to the concept of method rationale used by Ågerfalk and Wistrand [41]. Private rationality is, according to Stolterman and Russo [60], "in the skills and in the professional ethical and aesthetic judgments" of a person. It means that if an ISDM is to be used at its fullest potential there needs to be a harmonizing overlap, or rationality resonance, between the systems developer and the method. Hence, this concept focuses on aspects similar to cargo cult. However, with a few exceptions it has been applied with a focus on explaining individual systems developers' use of ISDMs. Wistrand [61] as well as Karlsson [62] have made fruitful attempts to study rationality resonance at group level. That said, rationality resonance focuses mainly on the existence of an overlap between the rationality sets and from the systems developers' perspective, i.e. rationality resonance as an expression of perceived usefulness of the ISDM or some of its parts. Hence, the potentially non-rational or an irrational use of an ISDM is less present, and to what extent such use is based on imitation.

Karlsson and Ågerfalk [63] and Karlsson [62] have used rationality resonance when analyzing to what extent systems developers stay true to the original method's intentions when tailoring a specific ISDM. Thus, these studies try to incorporate both perceived usefulness and the key ideas of the chosen method in the analysis. That said, both studies investigate this as part of structured tailoring of ISDMs, which to a large extent assumes that these actions are intentional and based on proper understanding of the method and its rationale, i.e. goals and values. Hence, they do not explicitly pay attention to possible irrational and non-rational tailoring or use of the ISDM.

Fitzgerald et al. [17] discussed the notion of goal displacement, which is connected to rigid or slavish adherence to methods [64]. It refers to situations where following the prescribed ISDM becomes a goal in itself and the systems developers lose sight of the real goal, i.e. to develop an information system. However, this kind of phenomenon is not necessarily equal to a cargo cult as long as the systems developers are aware of the rationale behind the method. The reason is that such actions can still align with the method rationale. That said, goal displacement is problematic and rigid use of ISDM should not be encouraged.

It should also be acknowledged that the rationale behind an ISDM is not the only rationale that exists in an organization and during systems development. This has been clearly shown by, for example, Robey and Markus [65] when discussing rituals in information systems development. On a similar note Fitzgerald et al. [17] concluded that ISDMs can have political roles in organizations. This shows that, what is considered rational, irrational, and non-rational depends on the chosen perspective; in our case an ISDM cargo cult analysis is based on the method rationale expressed in the chosen ISDM that an organization is claiming to adhere to.

4   Conceptual Development of ISDM Cargo Cult

As described above, an ISD team might end up in a cargo cult if they perform the wrong activities or perform activities for the wrong reasons. In the context of agile ISDMs, this is often referred to as "doing agile, instead of being agile" [66]. Activities during ISD can be understood as social actions being carried out together with others in the ambition to produce an information system. Cargo cult behavior can thus be related to flawed social actions. One way to understand the concept of social action is through Kalberg's [27] analysis of Weber [26]. This analysis explains the anthropological characteristics that govern the intentions of human behavior and presents a four-fold typology of social action. The typology can be summarized as follows.

Traditional action is defined as behavior governed by habits. A social action that has a traditional foundation does no longer take rational reasons into consideration. The actor, i.e. in our case a systems developer, simply does things in the same manner as he or she has always done and does not think about whether it can be done differently. The reasons for carrying on with a traditional action has faded into the background, as this action has proven to be successful over a long time. As a result, this type of action is no longer carried out for any rational reasons, but only because it is usually done so.

Affectual action is based on the actors' current emotions. This type of social action is founded purely in feelings and emotive responses to internal and external stimuli. A systems developer might become inspired and emotionally embrace ideals without really having fully understood them. Actions taken as a result from this type of stimuli are not due to any rational reasoning, only emotions.

According to Weber [26], these two types of social action do not represent true rationality. However, he rather found them to be non-rational rather than irrational. The difference between irrational and non-rational social actions is that irrational social actions are founded in some type of reasoning when the systems developer's judgment is based on misconceptions or miscalculations of something, for instance an ISDM, whilst the non-rational actions are not founded in any type of reasoning at all.

Value-based actions are founded in a set of values of some sort. This set of values takes the past, the present and the potential future into consideration. The rationality in a certain action lies in the ambition to strive towards and fulfill certain intrinsic motives. As a result of focusing on the intrinsic motives, a systems developer carrying out a value-based action does not think about the consequences of this action. The most important thing is to adhere to the intrinsic values.

Means-end actions can be understood as the focusing of a social action towards specific goals. According to Habermas [67] and Schluchter [68], the means-end rational action involves rational consideration of alternative practical means to an end, relations of the end to secondary consequences and the relative importance of different ends. This means that a systems developer deliberately chooses a certain activity to reach a calculated end.

In order to understand what flawed use of an ISDM really is, we define the misuse as being either irrational or non-rational behavior. According to the typology presented above, irrational behavior are situations where a systems developer has failed in his/her reasoning in relation to the intended value-based or means-end rational actions. Non-rational actions do not have any foundation in reasoning at all, and thus, can only be found in traditional and affectual social actions.

According to Weber [69] affectual and value-based social action are not governed by trying to achievement an ulterior motive, but rather for it's own sake. This type of social action can thus be regarded as intrinsic. Ryan and Deci [28] have put forward the Self-Determination Theory (SDT) where they elaborated on this concept. SDT describes how individuals find motivation by explaining the orientation of that motivation. An intrinsical motivation is founded in interest, belief and enjoyment and is often understood as a free choice. Extrinsically motivated actions have its origins in an intention founded somewhere outside an acting individual. A social action might be carried out not only with different orientation of motivation but also with different amounts of motivation. An extrinsically motivated task can be carried out under protest, with resentment and disinterest, or someone might feel very strongly about the task and follow through with an attitude of willingness that might reflect a rational understanding of the value of the task [28]. Very often, there is a mix of feelings involved in human behavior. For example, a student might play the guitar for the pure intrinsical sake of enjoyment, but at the same time train for the extrinsical motivation of fulfilling the expectations coming from parents who pay for the lessons.

4.1 Cargo Cults in Agile ISD

In the previous section we described flawed ISDM use as malpractices, which can be either irrational or non-rational. To understand how these malpractices can manifest themselves in an ISD organization, we must describe how they can be recognized in an empirical setting. One example of a malpractice in an agile context could be a situation related to the Daily Scrum practice we discussed earlier. Let us assume that actors in an ISD organization decide to implement this part of an agile ISDM, with the intention that this would lead to specific results. If the Daily Scrum meeting does not lead to the expected results in terms of an enhanced feeling of commitment, empowerment, and transparency, something must be wrong. A cargo cult explanation to the lack of expected results is uncontested imitation of a "Daily Scrum" behavior without understanding the method rationale, e.g. the goals and values that motivate this practice and its activities in the first place. This irrationality is the result of deficient reasoning and can lead to uncontested imitation and replication of other successful ISD organizations' use of this particular part of the ISDM. It can also lead to actual malpractice where the ISD organization does not understand why and how they should perform the task suggested by the ISDM.

Two types of irrational behavior can be identified; first, as described in the example above, we have ISD organizations that fail to properly understand the means-end rationality according to Kalberg [27]. For example, they do not understand that only reporting the status of their assigned task during a "Daily Scrum" will not lead to ISD team members' feeling empowered. In order for the team members to feel empowered a Daily Scrum needs to provide them with the possibility to make decisions. A second type of irrational behavior is the result from ignoring the actual activities and concepts that constitute the chosen agile ISDM. It could be a situation where an ISD organization embraces the values behind an agile ISDM but lack the understanding of how to transform these values into the desired outcomes. They like the ideas, but do not have the know-how to apply them. An example of this could be to start planning an agile adoption without really understanding what you need to change. An ISD organization might decide to re-organize staff, change nomenclature, hire agile coaches and send people into training even though this might not be what is actually needed to improve how they conduct ISD. They fool themselves that they have a sound strategy but do not comprehend the strategic requirements.

Turning to non-rational behavior, an ISD organization could act on the basis of collective emotive reasons. Being emotive or affectual, interpreting Kalberg [27], a cargo cult scenario could be to embrace the "hype" and to "jump on the bandwagon" just because others seem to do so. This decision is not founded on any rational analysis. It rather just "feels right". Usually, this does not lead to major practical changes, but rather tend to only temporarily affect the mindsets of those involved.

The second non-rational behavior, traditional social action, can also lead to malpractices; keeping parts of old ways of working can manifest this. It is often hard to change behavior and the saying "old habits are hard to kill" is well known for a reason. A typical cargo cult example of a traditional social action is to unintentionally keep old organizational roles, keep structures according to function, or keep project management processes intact even though these things might be detrimental in the ambition to achieve a successful agile ISDM implementation [25].

4.2 A Definition of ISDM Cargo Cult

Proper understanding of the ISDM's goals and values is fundamental for the ISDM to work efficiently. As shown earlier, an ISDM is based on values and principles, and these are important to understand in order to succeed with the method adoption. The ISDMs themselves have several practices available in order to support the implementation of the values. From a social action perspective, an ISD team could temporarily exist in an ISD cargo cult. This is an unconscious dysfunction and a result of their unsuccessful adoption process. The cargo cult phenomenon stems from misconceptions concerning the underlying goals and values of the chosen ISDM and misuse of the suggested activities, notations or concepts. The incorrect use of an ISDM thus results in malpractices, which have their underlying reasons in the ISD teams' flawed attempts to replicate others.

A cargo cult behavior could be seen as either non-rational or irrational. Also, the cargo cult can be performed intrinsically for its own sake, but a cargo cult can just as well have a separable extrinsic outcome as motivation. Based on our discussion above, we propose the following definition of ISDM cargo cult.

An information systems development method cargo cult is a **temporarily** delimited dysfunction that can have a **non-rational** or an **irrational** foundation. It leads to **misconceptions** and/or **malpractices** and can be **intrinsically** and/or **extrinsically** motivated as an information systems development team unconsciously fails in an attempt to **replicate** the circumstances and success of others.

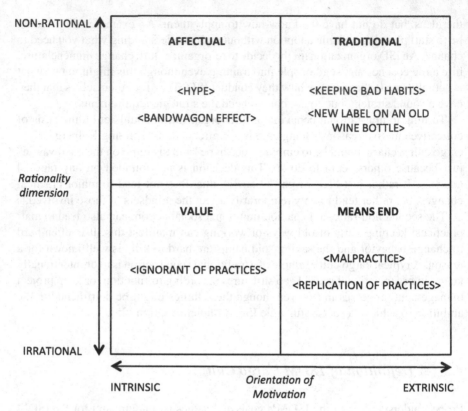

Fig. 1 A framework of ISDM cargo cult type situations

4.3 A Framework of ISDM Cargo Cult Type Situations

In the section above, our conceptual elaboration yielded a definition that can be used to identify different types of cargo cult situations. This definition can be used as a basis for developing an analytical framework to explore this phenomenon. The analytical framework is shown in Fig. 1 and it is aimed to be a diagnostic tool to identify cargo cult situations in ISD.

In the proposed definition, we can identify two distinct dimensions that are used to further clarify the nature of the ISDM cargo cult behavior. The vertical dimension addresses the possible existence of rational thought in relation to the ISDM's method rationale. Remember that cargo cult behavior, in our definition, always refers to some kind of flawed ISDM application with its origins in either a misunderstanding of the reasons behind the ISDM, or no reasoning at all. Thus, being rational in these situations does not apply. Subsequently, the vertical dimension is polarized as "Non-rational" and "Irrational". Non-rational instances of ISDM cargo cult arise because no rational considerations have been done. Irrational instances occur when an ISD organization has tried to reason according to the method's rationale but failed with the ISDM adoption.

The horizontal dimension is the motivation behind why something is done. In line with SDT [50] we suggest "Intrinsic" and "Extrinsic" motivation as the endpoints of this dimension. This serves to explain whether something is carried out for its own sake or with a separable outcome in mind. According to Weber [61], affectual and value-based social actions can be understood as intrinsic by nature. Conversely, extrinsic motivation aligns with both traditional and means-end social actions as they both are performed to achieve some kind of purpose. That said it should be noted that traditional social action is regarded as non-rational since an ISD team would no longer reflect upon the reasons for this action. Systems developers just follow traditions because of habit, regardless the original purposes of the traditions. Based on the above, we suggest two orthogonal dimensions as a basic structure for our analytical framework in Fig. 1.

In Fig. 1 we have included different cargo cult situations that has appeared in, for example, presentations by practitioners. This is done in order to exemplify how the framework can be used to differentiate between such situations. However, it is important to note that these are meant as examples, and that it is based on a convenience-selection; more examples of what has be described as ISDM cargo cults could be out there.

Following Kalberg's [27] interpretation of Weber [69], we can identify four ISDM cargo cult type situations. Continuing with our example of agile ISDMs and starting in the top left corner of our analytical framework, we find an "Affectual" cargo cult situation. Here we have a cargo cult situation where no rationality is at play, and the actions carried out are intrinsically motivated. Conceptually this describes an affectual action [27]. This part of the framework captures situations where an ISD organization would "jump on the bandwagon" [25] or simply follows the "hype" or current trend. Such actions are often done "without considering the reasons" [25] why something is done and/or with a misconception of what really needs to be done and how much effort it would take. Therefore, it seems reasonable to expect that this state only exists for a short period of time. Affectual behavior must evolve into something else, otherwise, the idea would disappear, for example, when realizing the effort needed to accomplish an end.

In the lower left corner of Fig. 1 we find the "Value" cargo cult situation. It draws on the idea of value-based actions [27]; although this situation is irrational as the ISD organization is not able adhere to the values in practice. In this situation an ISD organization embraces the true meaning behind the values of the agile ISDMs. To embrace the true meaning behind the agile values, the ISD organization would need to create a vision based on their understanding of them. They are intrinsically motivated and ignorant of how the values expressed in agile ISDMs really could and need to shape their work. In this situation, they want to be agile, but lack the necessary know-how. The considerations they make are not founded in proper analysis of their actual potential for improvement in various ISD activities, but rather in an intrinsic desire to become agile. Their ignorance of how to adopt agile activities, concepts and notations, and which ones that could actually help them improve, leads to problems in their adoption of the agile ISDM. This situation shares characteristics with the "ignore how the practice actually works" discussed by Soria [25] and Shore [23].

The right lower corner of Fig. 1 contains the "Means-end" cargo cult situation. Conceptually it draws on the means-end action [27], however the ISD organization ends up with irrational actions. In this situation an ISD organization considers how to reach identified agile ISDM goals, such as faster deliveries, less documentation, and better communication with customers. In their adoption process they might try to understand how a proper operationalization of these goals could change how they act and start performing tasks extrinsically aligned with the agile ISDM. The irrationality leads to either malpractices, for example based on wrongful interpretations of how something is supposed to be done, or imitation and replication of practices, for example mimicking the behavior of other successful ISD organizations with the intent to achieve the same outcomes. The ISD organization might believe they are true to the agile goals, values and practices, but in reality, they make misconceptions and turn them into malpractices.

The last cargo cult type situation, "Traditional" cargo cult, is found in the upper right corner of Fig. 1. It is anchored in traditional actions [27] and represents an instance where an ISD organization has adopted several agile practices in their ISD process, however not everything they are doing is agile. Some old habits have unintentionally been kept and/or have not been replaced by new parts from the chosen agile ISDM. As these kept method parts are based on tradition, no one in the organization is questioning them, as they have proved useful before. This is similar to Tranter's [70] description of a "new label on an old wine bottle". The idea of adopting an ISDM comes from the idea of improving what needs to be improved [5]. The reasons for using activities, concepts and notations, in various ISDMs that have previously not been understood as problematic, can be forgotten, just because they "worked fine" earlier. One of these traditional practices—or parts of them—might actually impede efficient agile ISD and result in a cargo cult behavior.

5   Discussion and Conclusion

The aim of this conceptual paper is twofold: (a) to define the concept of information systems development method cargo cult, and (b) to suggest an analytical framework that could be used to identify information systems development method cargo cult situations in information systems development organizations. To this end we employed the original definition of cargo cult by Worsley [21], Weber's [26] typology for social action as interpreted by Kalberg [27], and Self-Determination Theory [28].

The proposed definition of information systems development method (ISDM) cargo cults was used for developing an analytical framework describing four different cargo cult type situations, found in Fig. 1. The framework addresses how an ISDM cargo cult can be understood as the result of irrational considerations or non-rational actions, and whether a certain action is being carried out for intrinsic or extrinsic reasons. The analytical framework transcends the original cliché-type metaphor of cargo cults, as used in the consultancy industry, and provides possibilities for further theoretical and empirical studies to identify, and as a next step, understand and explain ISDM cargo cults in information systems development (ISD).

The proposed definition and our analytical framework define and conclude that by adopting an ISDM, an ISD team could risk ending up in a cargo cult situation, which we view as a temporarily dysfunctional situation resulting in misconceptions and/or malpractices. This occurs if the ISD team is intrinsically and/or extrinsically motivated and has a non-rational or an irrational behavior; the team will, by consequence, most likely not meet the intended goals and values that the ISDM aims to fulfill.

Previous research has addressed ISDMs' claimed use and adoption, and some of these studies have addressed difficulties in such adoptions. However, they have not addressed these difficulties from a cargo cult perspective. For example, deviations from the original agile ISDMs have been categorized as different Anti-patterns [37]. Still, Gregory et al. [14] identified a need for more research on failure in adoption of agile methods. Although not only targeting adoption of agile methods, we provide a response to this call and an alternative view to problematize flawed ISDM adoptions. The analytical framework presented in this paper, is a potential tool for researchers and practitioners to investigate pitfalls in ISDM adoption.

First, the concept of ISDM cargo cults contributes with a group-focus to ISDM-analysis, as cults can only exist on a group level. This can be compared with ISDM-analysis using rationality resonance [60–63] that seems to focus on the individual systems developer's perceived usefulness of the ISDM or some of its parts. Such an analysis centers on the overlap between the rationale expressed in the method and the system developer's rationale. We contribute to ISDM research by focusing on irrational and non-rational use of ISDMs, aspects that have been addressed to a limited extent.

Second, a cargo cult analysis can assist in refining observations in existing research, such as the use of ISDMs based on wrong assumptions and/or with wrong interpretations [58] or in slavish adherence [64]. That does not mean that previous observations are not valuable. However, distinguishing between rational, irrational and non-rational use of ISDMs, or parts thereof, could add an extra dimension to the understanding of, for example, slavish adherence to a method.

Third, the analytical framework does not prescribe a certain analytical level. It means that it can be used to analyze ISDM adoption at different group levels in an organization; ranging from an entire organization, to departments and individual ISD teams. Furthermore, the framework allows ISDM analysis at different levels of method granularity. For example, it could be used to analyze an entire ISDM, such as Scrum, or to target parts of a method, such as individual practices. From a practitioner's perspective it means possibilities to identify areas for improvement in an organization.

This paper is, to the best of our knowledge, the first attempt to frame the original socio-anthropological concept of cargo cults in the field of ISD. The obvious limitation of the analytical framework is the lack of empirical validation. Henceforth, the framework and its underlying definition need to be studied further, both conceptually and empirically, in order to turn them into useful tools for researchers and practitioners. Having said that, it opens avenues for future research. First, we suggest empirical studies trying to identify flawed ISDM adoptions as cargo cults. This would not only give interesting results concerning the validation of the ISDM cargo cult definition and evaluation of the analytical framework, but also results concerning the different types of ISDM cargo cult situations. It can help our understanding and possibilities to explain flawed ISDM adoptions. Second, in order to carry out empirical studies there is a need to connect the analytical framework with useful data collection and analytical procedures. In other words, there is a need for a scientific inquiry method to go with the analytical framework. Of course, proposing such an inquiry method is not without challenges. Based on the definition provided, at least four aspects need particular attention (a) what is considered the reference point for deciding rational, irrational, and non-rational behavior?, (b) what does "replication of success" mean?, (c) how to capture the orientation of motivation which is often a hidden aspect of social actions?, and (d) to correctly capture the group level of an analyzed ISDM adoption or part thereof. Third, if the analytical framework is found useful, future empirical work can include finding possible solutions for how to overcome different cargo cult situations. As stated in the ISDM cargo cult definition, this is a temporal phenomenon. Thus, identifying and understanding ISDM cargo cult situations using the analytical framework, or something similar, should be seen as one step towards finding a remedy for such situations, i.e. the framework should be viewed as tool for organizational development.

References

1. Standish Group: CHAOS Report 2000 (2000)
2. Standish Group: CHAOS Report 2008 (2008)
3. Standish Group: CHAOS Report 2012 (2012)
4. Brooks, F.P.: The Mythical Man-Month. Addison-Wesley, Reading (1995)
5. Avison, D.E., Fitzgerald, G.: Where now for development methodologies? Association for computing machinery. Commun. ACM **46**, 78 (2003)
6. Jayaratna, N.: Understanding and Evaluating Methodologies. McGraw-Hill, London (1994)
7. Introna, L.D., Whitley, E.A.: Against method-ism: exploring the limits of method. Inf. Technol. People **10**, 31–45 (1997)
8. Williams, P.A.H.: When trust defies common security sense. Health Inf. J. **14**, 211–221 (2008)
9. Beck, K.: Extreme Programming Explained: Embrace Change. Addison-Wesley, Reading, MA (2000)
10. Inglehart, R., Welzer, C.: Modernization, Cultural Change, and Democracy: The Human Development Sequence. Cambridge University Press, Cambridge, UK (2005)
11. Boehm, B.W.: A spiral model of software development and enhancement. IEEE Comput. **21**, 61–72 (1988)
12. http://www.agilemanifesto.org
13. El-Haik, B.S.: A Software Design for Six Sigma: A Roadmap for Excellence (2010)
14. Pahnila, S., Siponen, M., Mahmood, A.: Which factors explain employees' adherence to information security policies? An empirical study. In: Pacific Asia Conference on Information Systems 2007, pp. Paper 73. AIS Electronic Library (AISeL), (Year)

15. Avison, D., Pries-Heje, J.: Designing an appropriate information systems development methodology for different situations. In: Filipe, J., Cordeiro, J., Cardoso, J. (eds.) International Conference on Enterprise Information Systems, vol. 12. Springer, Berlin, Heidelberg, Funchal, Madeira, Portugal (2007)
16. McConnell, S.: Cargo cult software engineering. IEEE Softw. (March/April), 11–13 (2000)
17. Fitzgerald, B., Russo, N.L., Stolterman, E.: Information Systems Development—Methods in Action. McGraw-Hill, Berkshire, UK (2002)
18. Päivärinta, T., Sein, M.K., Peltola, T.: From ideals towards practice: paradigmatic mismatches and drifts in method deployment. Inf. Syst. J. **20**, 481–516 (2010)
19. Avison, D., Shah, H.U., Powell, R.S., Uppal, P.S.: Applying methodologies for information systems development. J. Inf. Technol. **7**, 127–140 (1992)
20. Karlsson, F., Hedström, K.: Negotiating a systems development method. In: The 17th International Conference on Information Systems Development (ISD2008). (Year)
21. Worsley, P.: The Trumpet Shall Sound—A Study of 'Cargo' Cults in Melanesia. Macgibbon & Kee, London (1957)
22. Calteches library: http://calteches.library.caltech.edu/51/2/CargoCult.htm
23. Shore, J.: Cargo Cult Agile (2008)
24. Daemons, M.: Cargo Cult Agile (2007)
25. Soria, J.L.: Cargo Cult Agile (2012)
26. Weber, M.: Economy and Society. University of California Press, Berkeley, CA (1978)
27. Kalberg, S.: Max Weber's types of rationality: cornerstones for the analysis of rationalization processes in history. Am. J. Sociol. **85**, 1145–1179 (1980)
28. Ryan, R.M., Deci, E.L.: Instrinsic and extrinsic motivations: classic definitions and new directions. Contemp. Educ. Psychol. **25**, 54–67 (2000)
29. Jarvie, I.C.: Theories of cargo cults: a critical analysis. Oceania **34**, 1–31 (1963)
30. Williams, F.E.: The Vailala madness and the destruction of native ceremonies in the Gulf Division. In: Schwimmer, E. (ed.) The Vailala Madness' and Other Essays. The University Press of Hawaii, Honolulu, HI (1979)
31. Dalton, D.: Cargo cults and discursive madness. Oceania **70** (2000)
32. Guiart, J.: John Frum movement in Tanna. Oceania **22**, 165–177 (1952)
33. Grünschloss, A.: Waiting for the "big beam": UFO religions and "ufological" themes in new religious movements. In: Lewis, J.R. (ed.) The Oxford Handbook of New Religious Movements. Oxford University Press, Oxford, England (2009)
34. Fernaeus, Y., Jacobsson, M., Ljungblad, S., Holmqvist, L.E.: Are We living in a robot cargo cult? In: HRI'09 Proceedings of the 4th ACM/IEEE International Conference on Human Robot Interaction, pp. 279–280. ACM (Year)
35. Holmquist, L.E.: Prototyping: generating ideas or cargo cult designs? Interact.—Robot. **12**, 48–54 (2005)
36. Cerf, V.G.: Cargo cults and information technology development. IEEE Internet Comput. **14**, 96 (2013)
37. Eloranta, V.-P., Koskimies, K., Mikkonen, T.: Exploring ScrumBut—an empirical study of Scrum anti-patterns. Inf. Softw. Technol. **74**, 194–203 (2015)
38. Heikkila, V.T., Paasivaara, M., Lassenius, C.: ScrumBut, but does it matter? A mixed-method study of the planning process of a multi-team scrum organization. In: 2013 ACM/IEEE International Symposium on Empirical Software Engineering and Measurement, ESEM 2013, pp. 85–94, Baltimore, MD, USA (2013)
39. Brown, W.J., Malveau, R.C., McCormick, H.W., Mowbray, T.J.: AntiPatterns: refactoring software, architectures, and projects in crisis. Wiley, New York, NY, USA (1998)
40. Karlsson, F., Ågerfalk, P.J.: Method configuration: adapting to situational characteristics while creating reusable assets. Inf. Softw. Technol. **46**, 619–633 (2004)
41. Ågerfalk, P.J., Wistrand, K.: Systems development method rationale: a conceptual framework for analysis. In: Camp, O., Filipe, J., Hammoudi, S., Piattini, M. (eds.) Proceedings of the 5th International Conference on Enterprise Information Systems (ICEIS 2003), pp. 185–190. Escola Superior de Tecnologia do Instituto Politécnico de Setúbal, Setúbal, Portugal (2003)

42. Russo, N.L., Stolterman, E.: Exploring the assumptions underlying information systems methodologies: their impact on past, present and future ISM research. Inf. Technol. People **13**, 313–327 (2000)
43. Brinkkemper, S.: Method engineering: engineering of information systems development methods and tools. Inf. Softw. Technol. **38**, 275–280 (1996)
44. Oinas-Kukkonen, H.: Method rationale in method engineering and use. In: Brinkkemper, S., Lyytinen, K., Welke, R.J. (eds.) Proceedings of the IFIP TC8, WG8.1/8.2 Working Conference on Method Engineering on Method Engineering, pp. 87–93. Chapman & Hall, Atlanta, USA (1996)
45. Avison, D., Fitzgerald, G.: Information Systems Development: Methodologies, Techniques and Tools. The McGraw-Hill Companies, London, England (1995)
46. Iivari, J., Maansaari, J.: The usage of systems development methods: are we stuck to old practice? Inf. Softw. Technol. **40**, 501–510 (1998)
47. Iivari, J., Rudy, H., Klein, H.K.: A dynamic framework for classifying information systems development methodologies and approaches. J. Manag. Inf. Syst. **17**, 179–218 (2001)
48. Schwaber, K., Beedle, M.: Agile software development with Scrum. Prentice Hall, Upper Saddle River, NJ (2001)
49. Jayaratna, N., Holt, P., Wood-Harper, T.: Criteria for methodology choice in information system development. The J. Contemp. Issues Bus. Gov. **5**, 30–34 (1999)
50. Goldkuhl, G., Lind, M., Seigerroth, U.: Method integration: the need for a learning perspective. IEE Proc.—Softw. **145**, 113–118 (1998)
51. Rossi, M., Ramesh, B., Lyytinen, K., Tolvanen, J.-P.: Managing evolutionary method engineering by method rationale. J. Assoc. Inf. Syst. **5**, 356–391 (2004)
52. Ågerfalk, P.J.: Towards better understanding of Agile values in global software development. In: Krogstie, J., Halpin, T.A., Proper, H.A. (eds.) Eleventh International Workshop on Exploring Modeling Methods in Systems Analysis and Design (EMMSAD'06), pp. 375–382. Namur University Press, Namur, Belgium (2006)
53. Rolland, C., Prakash, N.: A proposal for context-specific method engineering. In: Brinkkemper, S., Lyytinen, K., Welke, R. (eds.) Proceedings of the IFIP TC8, WG8.1/8.2 Working Conference on Method Engineering on Method Engineering, pp. 191–208. Chapman & Hall, Atlanta, United States (1996)
54. Ralyté, J., Deneckère, R., Rolland, C.: Towards a generic model for situational method engineering. In: Eder, J., Missikoff, M. (eds.) Advanced Information Systems Engineering, 15th International Conference, CAiSE 2003, vol. 2681, pp. 95–110. Springer, Berlin (2003)
55. Harmsen, A.F.: Situational Method Engineering. University of Twente, Utrecht, The Netherlands (1997)
56. Gonzalez-Perez, C., Giorgini, P., Henderson-Sellers, B.: Method construction by goal analysis. In: Barry, C., Conboy, K., Lang, M., Wojtkowski, W., Wojtkowski, G. (eds.) 16th International Conference on Information Systems Development (ISD2007), pp. 79–92. Springer, Galway, Ireland (2007)
57. Karlsson, F., Ågerfalk, P.J.: Towards structured flexibility in information systems development: devising a method for method configuration. J. Database Manag. **20**, 51–75 (2009)
58. Conboy, K.: Agility from first principles: reconstructing the concept of agility in information systems development. Inf. Syst. Res. **20**, 329–354 (2009)
59. Stolterman, E.: How system designers think about design and methods: some reflections based on an interview study. Scand. J. Inf. Syst. **4**, 137–150 (1992)
60. Stolterman, E., Russo, N.L.: The paradox of information systems methods—public and private rationality. In: British Computer Society 5th Annual Conference on Methodologies (1997)
61. Wistrand, K.: Method rationale revealed—communication of knowledge in systems development methods. School of Business, vol. Ph.D. Örebro University, Örebro (2009)
62. Karlsson, F.: Longitudinal use of method rationale in method configuration: an exploratory study. Eur. J. Inf. Syst. **22**, 690–710 (2013)
63. Karlsson, F., Ågerfalk, P.J.: Exploring Agile values in method configuration. Eur. J. Inf. Syst. **18**, 300–316 (2009)

64. Fitzgerald, B.: Formalised systems development methodologies: a critical perspective. Inf. Syst. J. **6**, 3–23 (1996)
65. Robey, D., Markus, M.L.: Rituals in information system design. MIS Q. **8**, 5–15 (1984)
66. Zieris, F., Salinger, S.: Doing Scrum rather than being Agile: a case study on actual nearshoring practices. In: IEEE 8th International Conference on Global Software Engineering (ICGSE). IEEE, Bari, Italy (2013)
67. Habermas, J.: The Theory of Communicative Action. Reason and the Rationalization of Society, vol. 1. Polity Press, Cambridge (1984)
68. Schluchter, W.: The Rise of Western Rationalism: Max Weber's Developmental History. University of California Press, Berkeley, CA (1981)
69. Weber, M.: The Theory of Social and Economic Organization. The Free Press, New York, NY (1947)
70. Tranter, L.: (2017). https://www.extremeuncertainty.com/cargo-cult-agile/

Design and Prototyping of an Interactive Virtual Environment to Foster Citizen Participation and Creativity in Urban Design

Barnabé Faliu, Alena Siarheyeva, Ruding Lou and Frédéric Merienne

Abstract Public Participation encounters great challenges in the domain of urban design concerning decision making and citizens' appropriation of a future place. Many tools and methods have been proposed to ease the participation process. In this paper we are targeting artefacts used in face-to-face workshops, in which citizens are asked to make design proposals for a public space. We claim that current state of the art can be improved (i) by better articulating digital artefacts with participatory processes and (ii) by providing interfaces that enhance citizen's spatial awareness and comprehension as well as collective creativity in urban design projects. We present the design and prototyping of an interactive virtual environment that follow the design-science research guidelines.

Keywords ICT-enabled citizen participation · Co-creation · Urban design · Interactive virtual environment · Design-science

A prior version of this paper has been published in the ISD2018 Proceedings (http://aisel.aisnet. org/isd2014/proceedings2018).

B. Faliu (✉)
ISEN Yncréa Méditerranée, LiSPEN, Arts et Métiers, UBFC, HeSam, Institut Image, Toulon, France
e-mail: barnabe.faliu@yncrea.fr

A. Siarheyeva
ISEN Yncréa Méditerranée, Aix-Marseille University, CNRS, LEST, Toulon, France
e-mail: alena.siarheyeva@yncrea.fr

R. Lou · F. Merienne
LiSPEN, Arts et Métiers, UBFC, HeSam, Institut Image, Chalon-sur-Saone, France
e-mail: ruding.lou@ensam.eu

F. Merienne
e-mail: frederic.merienne@ensam.eu

55

1   Introduction and Context

Public Participation (PP) has imposed in the last decades as one of the key factors of successful urban design and development projects. Lack of communication and collaboration between citizens and urban design experts can generate conflictual situations, leading to substantial delays and cost overheads, and eventually to project cancelation and political crisis as in Stuttgart 21, Notre-Dame-des-Landes or EuropaCity projects. To summarize:

> Design is not just for designers and their acolytes. Urban design, like all design, should involve a dialogue with the customer, whether the existing people within an area or those likely to move in. [59], (p. 11)

The stakes of these projects are generally too critical to leave citizens voices apart. Urban designers and local authorities should not forget end users when designing public places in order to respect their quality of life and their 'ownership', in the sense of [35], whom define it as *"the right to act upon an issue..., a sense of belonging to a collective place"* (p. 94). Moreover, in most European countries, participatory processes are mandatory in urban projects aiming to modify the living environment of citizens, in line with the Aarhus Convention[1] and Council of Europe Recommendation 1430 (1999).[2] As a result, a vast number of methodologies and toolkits have been developed lately, applicable to different steps of urban design and planning projects. Among these methodologies, an increasing number are focused on ICT-mediated PP in urban issues, which are: *"technology being addressed in such areas as governance, urban planning, information systems and interaction design, geography, citizen activism and community development"* [44] (p. 1). The ambition of an ICT tool for urban design is to provide a digital interface between experts and citizens to let them collaborate and benefit from each other's knowledge.

Urban design is a process that aims to define the shape of a city, district or public place and connect it to the surrounding environment (people or nature). It defines the spatial configuration and functionalities of a future urban area, but also considers civil society needs and financial aspects to define an attractive and sustainable area. The term urban design is different from urban planning, which is a long-term process focused on urban development, for instance land use plans, environment protection, infrastructures for transportation or job creation strategies. In other terms, urban planners diagnose macro-problems and urban designers manage to solve those problems.

Public authorities can decide to apply a certain degree of citizen involvement in the decision-making process. Wates et al. [55] divided the urban design process in four different steps: initiation, planning and design, implementation and maintenance. For each of these steps, citizens can be highly involved in the process and

---

[1] 1998 UNECE Convention on Access to Information, Public Participation in Decision-making and Access to Justice in Environmental Matters, adopted by the fourth "Europe for Environment" conference in Aarhus, Denmark, on 25 June 1998.

[2] Council of Europe Recommendation 1430 (1999) of the Parliamentary Assembly on access to information, public participation in environmental decision-making and access to justice.

work in autonomy, or just be informed of the decisions without being consulted. The four different degrees of involvement are, from lowest to highest: information, consultation, collaboration and autonomy. This paper will be focused on design and prototyping of a digital artefact to enhance collaborative and creative design of non-trained participants. By non-trained we mean people not having particular skills in 3D design and/or urban design. More particularly, we consider face-to-face creative participatory sessions in which professionals and citizens work together to define the future of a public space such as a public park. We'll also pay attention to the definition of a process facilitating collaboration and co-creation of urban design proposals, and its articulation with the digital artefact.

The paper will be organized as follows. Section 2 will review existing literature and identify eventual gaps. Section 3 will present the research approach. Section 4 will present the main results: a process for collaborative and creative PP in urban design (4.1), specifications of a digital artefact rooted in field observations (4.2), and software architecture as well as user interfaces of a first prototype (4.3). Section 5 will discuss the results, highlight the contributions and acknowledges the limits of the current research, evaluate the research process with regards to design-science guidelines, and lay out directions for further investigations. Section 6 will conclude.

2 Literature Review

In the late 60's, S. Arnstein tackled the problem of citizen implication with her well-known ladder of citizen participation [9]. She edified the fact that most citizen participation processes are limited to information and consultation, where partici-pants have less implication and impact upon the concerned project and are really close to manipulation. In contrast, collaboration and autonomy provides a true level of citizen power. In the same time, the spirit of participatory planning, which is par-ticipatory design [52] applied to urban planning, emerged from the Scandinavian influence. The philosophy is to ensure a bottom-up approach to participation process by providing adequate methodologies and tools. Since then much work has been done on the subject, and participation methods can be various from focus groups to idea competitions and interactive displays in public spaces [55]. Our research is focused on a collaborative way of participation giving consequent decision power to citizen, in the form of iterative design workshops.

During the last decade, a large variety of methods and tools has been proposed to facilitate PP in urban design and planning [55]. Most of those tools traditionally rely on materials such as printed images, printed 2D maps, prepared 3D models, foam, pencils and paper. More recently, effort has been made to benefit from the advances in computer-aided tools to enhance citizen's interaction and engagement in the decision-making process [5]. We selected publications published between 2004 and 2018 that address the topic of a 3D artefact supporting PP in city making process.

Many research projects have demonstrated the value added of digital 3D environments for citizen participation [2–5, 23, 37, 56]. This new form of interaction helps participant to better understand the future of a place and support dialogue.

Based on the reviews presented by [13, 23, 31], we can conclude that most of existing tools are focused on 3D visualization and feedback, which fall into information and consultation degree of participation according to [9]. That is, participants can only see professional proposals, give a feedback, or vote for a design proposal.

Few papers are eager to provide a higher degree of participation, namely collaboration and co-creation. In other words, efforts to define a digital artefact helping non-professional participants to express their ideas through the creation of urban design proposals can be increased. Such artefact shall also enhance collaboration between citizens and experts. A citizen-made design proposal shall be used to inspire urban design experts, so they can create comprehensive designs that take into account citizens opinions. As a result, such professional designs are more likely to be accepted.

The second observation of the reviews is that there is a divide between two main areas of research. Research led from Urban Studies standpoint generally defines PP processes and discusses eventual impacts of ICT-mediated participation, without implementing a digital artefact or considering eventual technological gaps [29–31, 44, 53, 54]. On another hand, research led in Information Systems or in Computer Science fields presents a digital artefact without taking into account its articulation around a participatory process, or without rigorous knowledge of the studied environment [12, 14, 17, 20–22, 32, 38, 47–49, 58, 60]. Furthermore, the above-mentioned contributions mainly propose solutions falling into the space of urban planning, not urban design.

A tentative to address either urban design processes and the artefact design is [39], which describes "*a new strategy of urban design with the purpose to overcome the technological perspective of current urban planning methods towards a participatory planning approach*" (p. 187). However, the paper neither presents specifications and evaluation of the tool, nor its articulation with a participatory urban design process. The main function of the tool is to let users explore an urban design scenario, by changing position of 3D objects, or rotate them. Additionally, objects cannot be edited in terms of geometry, which limits creativity of participants. Moreover, this web tool is well adapted for massive participation but does not cover face-to-face workshop settings. The latter is usually facilitated in a manner to allow direct interaction, collaboration and co-creation between citizens and professionals and thus lead to more qualitative and comprehensive results. The analysis made by [23] confirms our diagnosis: "*The projects verify available technical possibilities and do not match real actions connected with social participation in planning [...] Most of examples show how computer tools may be used for visualizing the new development and not for constructive process of continuous public participation*" (p. 303).

Research Problem

To address the identified gaps-lack of collaboration and co-creation tools, articulated around a well-defined participation process-we are eager to design and prototype a digital artefact to foster collaboration and collective creativity in participatory urban design projects. More particularly, we aim to bring Sander's concept of make tools for co-design [45] in the design process of our artefact. The artefact will be tailored to the settings of face-to-face workshops gathering professionals and non-professionals. Furthermore, it will be designed considering the essential rules and steps of a benchmarked participatory urban design process. Finally, we aim at using cutting-edge immersive and interactive interfaces for the prototype instantiation.

Our overall research question is the following:

How to integrate generative design concepts into an Interactive and Immersive Virtual Environment (IIVE) in order to enhance the creativity of participants to a collaborative workshop for public participation in urban design?

More specifically, we divide the question into 2 sub-questions as following:

RQ1: What are the specifications of an IIVE to foster citizen participation in urban design?

RQ2: What approach can be used for design and development of generative IIVE?

3 Research Approach

In order to bridge the approach from Urban Studies with that of Computer Science and Information Systems, while addressing the complexity of the Environment, design-science [26] seems to be an appropriate methodology. The research design and process along with presented results are expected to contribute to knowledge by theory testing and to practice with effective techniques to produce usable human computer systems in the context of PP in urban design.

3.1 Methodological Framework

In line with the guidelines of design-science research [26] to design, develop and evaluate the immersive collaborative digital artefact, we consider both the Environment of the research problem and its Knowledge Base. The study of the Environment, namely citizen participation in urban design, brings information about problems and needs of end-users and will help us to derive relevant functionalities afforded by virtual environment. To ensure research rigor, we build on the current state-of-the-art empirical contributions, available methodologies and place our research in a well-defined epistemological tradition. Figure 1 synthesizes the way our research is conducted. Environment analysis and Knowledge Base study feed the design, development and evaluation phase. Iterative development loops enable us to refine the digital artefact to bring it to the Environment. During the iterative design, development and assessment we are able to theorize the IT artifact [41] to further feed the Knowledge Base.

Peffers et al. [42] described a process for carrying out design science research (DSR) in information systems consisting of six steps: problem identification and motivation, objective of a solution, design and development, demonstration, evalua-

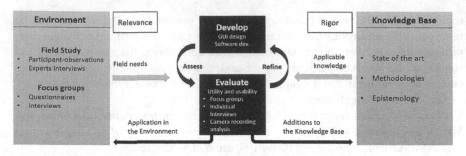

Fig. 1 Research approach overview inspired by design-science research [26]

tion and communication. This process fits well with the Human-Computer Interaction (HCI) discipline focusing on design, evaluation and implementation of interactive systems, as explained Adikari [1].

3.2 Epistemological Position

Since the design of the digital artefact draws on study of humans within their social setting and on their experiences and interpretations, interpretivist epistemological stance and qualitative research seem to be well-suited for our research problem [7, 40]. According to the interpretivist tradition, any individual, researcher or an ordinary citizen, interprets the observed reality. Interpretations are conditioned by her/his life experience. For researcher, to know means to try to understand the ordinary sense that subjects assign to reality, considered as unknowable in its essence. To succeed in its mission of understanding the meaning given by subjects of the research, researcher should be capable of empathy. Understanding is situated at two levels: at the day-to-day life of the field investigator and at the level of researcher who tries to derive meaning assigned by the subjects. Research is thus dependent on double subjectivity: that of the subjects of the research and that of the researcher. In contrast to positivism stipulating exteriority and neutrality vis-à-vis of the subject of the research, interpretivist researcher is engaged in her/his relation to the subjects of the research who transform themselves and retro-act on the researcher. Therefore, researcher has to take into account her/his position: she/he is part of the reality under investigation and cannot be outside of the interpretation process [34].

3.3 Environment

Our research project is informed with participant observation of a participatory design process of an urban park, as a part of a large urban renewal project in Marseille from

April 2016 to March 2018. We adopted an ethnographic approach to discover the facilitation process and study in situ interactions between citizens and professionals during participatory workshops. We engaged in over participatory observation to become familiar with participants and the place and understand individual and collective issues at stake [18, 19]. In addition, we had an opportunity to run ethnographic observations of a participatory design of a sport and cultural community area near Marseille in March 2018. We combined the direct observations with in-depth semi-structured interviews of professional urban designers and planners to collect rich data. The ethnographic study of the participatory workshops offered an enriching empirical perspective that helps to understand the process of collective sense-making, creative expression and negotiation of the future of the place. It uncovers the role of facilitation methods that support these collective processes.

Last, to deepen our understanding of how participants engage with make tools [46] to express their ideas about the future of a place, we organized two simulations of participatory design workshops. The participation methodology employed was closed to the one we observed in Marseille and is described latter in this paper. We complemented our direct observations with semi-structured interviews with the participants of the simulations and analysis of video recordings.

3.4 Research Design

Our research design rests upon a variety of data sources including: (1) participant-observation of participatory urban design workshops; (2) interviews with professionals; (3) simulation of participatory workshops; (4) interviews of the participants of the simulations; (5) reports from the participatory workshops of the design of the public park in Marseille.

We started the investigations by attending the participatory workshops in Marseille. We were active at the workshops and interacted conversationally with various workshop participants: residents, activists, representatives of local associations, etc. We took photographs and notes during the participatory sessions. In a first phase, we interviewed the facilitator of the workshop, a person in charge of relations with citizens, and a professional urban designer managing the design of the park. We attended an alternative event focused on the future design of Marseille organized by city activists and interviewed the leader of the initiative. We triangulated this data with information about the urban renewal project of Marseille collected on Internet (press, blogs, social media).

In order to place the participatory design of the park in a broader professional practice context, we run semi-structured interviewed with two professional urban designers and a creative facilitation professional.

To obtain more information about collective creation practices and processes during participatory urban design workshops we conceived and run two simulations of co-creation workshops. The objective of the simulation was the same as that of the real workshops, envision together the future of a public space. The facilitation process borrowed the steps of the design of the park in Marseille, and an additional step was added asking participants to craft their own design proposal with make tools (see Fig. 2). Each simulation workshop gathered 5–7 participants. They had diverse profiles: knowledge of urban design ranging from non-professional to professional level, knowledge of digital technologies ranging from beginners to skillful users, age ranging from 20 to 60 years old, half of them were female. We did not apply any kind of selection process. Building on the analysis of the simulation workshops, we defined a list of questions for semi-structured interviews of the participants and interviewed them.

The simulations were video recorded. The interviews were recorded and transcribed. Quotes have been translated from French to English for this paper.

This research design, combining observation of real participatory urban design workshops, simulations and interviews enabled us to gather rich data. A thematic content analysis of the collected qualitative data was conducted with NVivo software (version 10). Following the inductive qualitative method [6], we generated representative units and categories of analysis of the phenomenon from the environment data. We can thus shed light on the collective negotiation and co-creation processes during participatory workshops. We can describe how boundary objects support these collective processes [46]; and derive requirements for design and development of the immersive interactive digital artefact.

We are convinced that this methodological approach, mixing the analysis of real case studies and simulated scenario workshops, with feedbacks from professionals of urban design, supplemented with our observations, is particularly suited to the research problem.

3.5 Design Process

Based on our research design, we derived the design of a digital artefact in a user-centered and iterative way. This methodology is commonly used in HCI and Interaction Design research projects. Iterative design is a process-based design research methodology in which designers create and test concepts in various basic forms prior to completing a full prototype (Fig. 2). User-centered design is an iterative process that begins with stakeholder interviews and observational studies of activities prior

Fig. 2 User-centered design cycle

to the typical design activity of brainstorming and generating ideas [43]. Interviews allow participants to talk about their experiences and provide more detailed, qualitative data, along with quantitative usability questionnaires. First, through observational studies, interviews and focus groups, we created knowledge in the form of personas, sketches and story-telling videos. Then, we made technological choices which we though were most adequate to the situation, in line with our interpretivist epistemological stance. Each material was used to define the requirements of an ICT tool and support an iterative software development process, linked with an evaluation process.

Software Development Process

The development-evaluation loop rests on the agile methodology spirit [11]. We currently implemented a first version of the prototype and plan to evaluate its utility and usability following the guidelines of [10]. Each future version of the prototype will consider user feedback (citizens, urban design professionals, immersive and interactive technologies professionals, etc.) gathered during the evaluation phase. In terms of organization, we followed Kanban methodology to follow up 3 different sub projects in a flexible manner [33], by translating requirement to user stories, tasks and sub tasks. Kanban allows the goal of a work in progress change during the development process, which is particularly convenient with our design process [36].

The benefits we see in the design-science approach are flexibility regarding the specification of the artefact, through repeated user tests, which result in the end in a user-defined software meeting the needs of the Environment; and a meaningful contribution to the Knowledge Base for future work in the form of a research design and process, combined with requirements of a digital artefact suited for our Environment.

Evaluation Process

To be in line with design-science research methodology and bring knowledge to IS field, we plan to run an evaluation of the designed artefact. We will focus the process on two points: usability and utility.

Usability evaluation will be a unipersonal evaluation made by different profile of users in terms of age, gender and ease with technology. We will gather quantitative data from following questionnaires: Immersive Tendencies Questionnaires & Presence Questionnaire [57], NASA TLX [24], QUESI [27] and an additional satisfaction questionnaire. Data will be completed with qualitative data through video analysis and coding as described by [8]. After each evaluation, feedbacks (bugs, additional feature, feature update, etc.) will be gathered and directly considered in the software development process.

To evaluate utility, we will organize four simulated workshops based on a real urban design project without any selection process. Participants will have to act as citizens and make a design proposal answering to few requirements using the given artefact. Two workshops will be done with generative design concept integration, and two without. At the end of the process we will gather answers to the Creativity

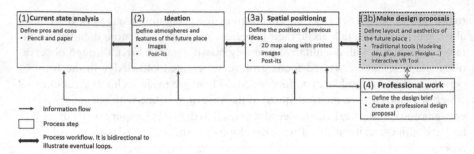

Fig. 3 Participation process inspired by the field observation. Dotted gray square highlights novelty from the observed process

Support Index (CSI) [15, 16] in order to evaluate support to creativity for a particular task. We will collect qualitative data from video recording an ask open questions to participants at the end of the workshop. Finally, we will organize a vote about the four design proposals in terms of novelty (originality, uniqueness), resolution (logic, useful, valuable, understandable), elaboration and synthesis (the product is organic, well-crafted, and elegant) and see which configuration (with or without generative design concepts) supported best creativity of participants. This evaluation will be made by students from our university.

Evaluation of the artefact is an integral part of our research project but is not covered in the current paper due to space limitations.

4   Results

4.1   A Process for Collaborative and Creative PP in Urban Design

A Participatory Process to Support Collective Negotiation

Participant-observation of the early design phase of the urban park in Marseille enabled us to identify a generic sequence of participatory workshops to ensure citizen's expression, negotiation, consensus finding, and a convincing translation between expert's and citizen's language. Figure 3 illustrates the different stages starting from (1) the analysis of the current state of the place, followed by (2) an ideation session without spatial constraints, and finally (3a) refining of the previous step by spatially positioning the ideas. The results are used to feed professional work (4). Each step can be composed of several workshops and the global sequence can be repeated iteratively, as many times as needed.

For example, in the project under observation in Marseille there were two iterations, each composed of five workshops. The first iteration was to establish global specifications about the atmospheres and features of the park, along with the definition of separate zones. It resulted in the definition of requirements, and a competition to select an urban designer team proposing the most suited solution. The second iteration, involving the winning team of urban designers, was to define precisely the content of each zones and assess a final professional design proposal. The tools proposed to citizens during the different workshops were limited to 2D printed maps, printed images representing global features and atmospheres of public parks, pencils, post-its, scissors and printed questionnaire templates to give feedback.

The analysis of the collective negotiation process has been constructed through several workshops observations and enables to derive an initial set of requirements for the definition of a digital artefact:

(a) Reading of scales and distances must be easy
(b) Possibility to define zone with associated surfacing, atmosphere, uses and street furniture
(c) Transparency about technical, political and financial constraints
(d) Precise definition of zones opened to collective negotiation, and zones not opened to public discussion due to technical, financial or other constraints
(e) Necessity of a very rich library of visual representation of atmospheres, uses and street furniture, to unlock participants' imagination
(f) Expert's proposals should not be communicated too early not to lock participant's ideation
(g) Expression of local knowledge (culture, uses of the place, heritage, history, ...) needs to be facilitated.

The participant-observation lead to the conclusion that creativity of participants can be further enhanced. The use of printed images certainly fed the expression of participants by means of various combinations of atmospheres and furniture. Nevertheless, current literature on co-creation highlights the need to improve the process by integrating the use of make tools [45].

Towards Creative Workspaces

Make tools support citizens' creativity by enabling them to express their latent and tacit level of experience, in addition to explicit and observable knowledge that can be expressed with words [45]. To access the explicit layer, well-known narration and visualization techniques are sufficient (the ones used in the observed urban design project). To access the tacit and latent level of knowledge, people should manipulate objects. This implies the integration of a new step (3b in Fig. 3) in the observed process with the help of make tools, focused on the creation of urban design proposals by citizen. Most used tools to achieve this step are 'pencil and paper' tools, meaning participants manipulate paper, scissors, glue, cardboards and pencils to represent elements such as a house, a fountain, basketball field, etc.

In order to identify additional requirements of the digital artefact and better understand how people express with make tools, we organized two simulated scenario workshops relying on traditional tools. The process embraced steps from (1) to (3b) in Fig. 3 and the result of their work is visible in Fig. 4.

Fig. 4 A design proposal realized with traditional tools during one of the workshops we organized

By analyzing the camera/audio recording as well as the individual post-workshops interviews, we derived the following additional requirements:

(h) Participants need a way to add contextual information in order to locate themselves and get a better understanding of the place
(i) Participants need to have access to different types of materials/ground surfaces
(j) Participants need to see reliefs on the map
(k) Proposed prefabricated objects must be on scale
(l) Participant need common objects to better understand spaces (a bus, a bench, a football field…).

We intend to support the presented process with the help of an interactive and immersive environment that will embrace requirements (a) to (l).

4.2 Specifications of a Virtual Environment for PP in Urban Design

In this section we define the specification of a digital artefact meeting the process and requirements presented above (Sect. 4.1). Based on field observations, we assume most users will have low skills in software manipulation and a good awareness of urban design constraints. Hence, using this artefact, a user (expert or amateur) shall be able to easily create a design proposal and associate information to it. Moreover, professionals need an interface to extract useful information from citizen's ideas and implement professional design proposals. Therefore, we propose a conceptual framework composed of three parts, as shown in Fig. 5: a creation workspace, a visualization and feedback workspace and a professional workspace.

WS1: Creation Workspace

This workspace is the transposition in a virtual environment of a traditional creative workshop using prepared 3D models (basic shapes and city furniture), pencil and paper. Therefore, we propose to give users the opportunity to manipulate 3D models as freely as they would using scissors through a "cut and paste" metaphor.

We define the creation workspace as an interactive virtual environment where users can work in collaboration. This means that multiple users can interact with the interface concurrently, as they would do around a 2D map in currently observed configurations. The workspace is representing the future construction zone of the project with surrounding streets and infrastructures represented in 3D, with a predefined scale. To manipulate the environment, users are given multiple tools:

A categorized 3D model database. The categories may be straightforward as "houses" or "bridges" but also grouped by more abstract keywords as "Asian style garden" or "games for children".

A creation toolbox, which is the virtual representation of the manual actions used in standard creative workshops (hands manipulation to rotate, move, cut & assemble) and additional actions as 3D model scaling, cancel previous action, save current work.

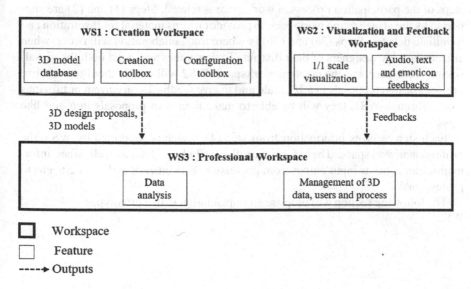

Fig. 5 Conceptual Framework of the Virtual Environment for PP in urban design

A configuration toolbox allowing to add constraints and information to the workspace. For instance, define unmodifiable zones, associate metadata to objects or associate behaviors to preselected zones.

In other terms, this workspace can be seen as multiple layers with associated interactions. The first layer is a map with streets and infrastructure. The second layer gathers additional 3D models and constraints assigned to the first layer. The layer contains sematic information associated to the previous layers.

WS2: Visualization and Feedback Workspace

This is the place for immersive visualization and support of decision-making. The aim is to let the user explore its design proposal in a 1/1 scale, to fully understand the impact of his/her work and feel the atmosphere of the place. This workspace shall be used iteratively with the creation workspace to refine the design proposal. In this workspace, no modification of the current work is possible, the user can only explore the place and associate feedbacks or comments to specific zones.

WS3: Professional Workspace

This workspace allows professionals to visualize and analyze citizen's proposals and access feedbacks gathered during workshops. From this interface, they also have access to management features regarding 3D data, users and process. The aim is to help them in decision-making and inspire their future work.

Articulation with Participation Process

Finally, we synthetize our design process by introducing an articulation of the extended participation process with the conceptual framework (Fig. 6). For each steps of the participation process, a workspace is related. Steps (1) and (2) are supported by the visualization workspace to provide citizens material for inspiration and to initiate debates. Steps (3a) and (3b) is where true collaboration will occur, when citizens become designers of their district. To do so, they will need both the visualization workspace and the creation workspace. WS2 will enable them to visualize previous design proposals in a 1/1 scale and to give feedbacks on current or previous work. Through WS1, they will be able to make their own proposals in a god like view.

Each step receives information from step (4); which is supported by WS3, the professional workspace. The information flow is bidirectional as well, since information can come as input/output from professionals to citizens and from citizens to professional.

The following section will propose an implantation with a prototype for WS1 and WS2.

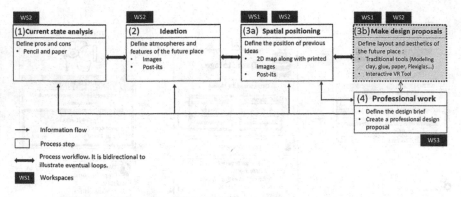

Fig. 6 Articulation of participation process with the conceptual framework

4.3 Software Architecture and User Interface

To follow on the design-science methodology, we propose the implementation of the artefact through a prototype. The aim of the prototype is to demonstrate the artefact's suitability with current context [51]. Figure 7 presents the software architecture of the interactive and immersive artefact, which rests on Unity3D software along with a touch table and a head-mounted device. Unity is a widespread game engine which can easily support 3D visualization and interaction definition by scripting, and is well suited for an urban design tool [28]. The usage of table for the creation workspace seems well-suited to engage discussion and exchange ideas. It supports a circular configuration of multiple subgroups [38], collaboration and parallel problem solving [50]. Well-defined tactile interactions offer a more fluid and intuitive experience than the combination of a mouse and a keyboard [50]. Therefore, we chose to build a touchscreen-based solution for the creation workspace [(1) in Fig. 7]. Moreover, we believe this technological choice is the best suited to support collective creativity in urban design compared to the solution of augmented reality and tangible interfaces [14, 48, 60, 61] that support collective negotiation.

To generate the initial map along with streets and infrastructures, we use a Unity plugin called MapBox, which gathers data from the Open Source platform OpenStreetMap to generate a 3D environment with the provided geocoordinates. Image (1) of Fig. 8 illustrates the user interface developed with Unity3D editor. The camera point of view is a bird-eye view. From this interface, a user has access to the following interactions:

- Move camera (one finger drag)
- Zoom camera (two fingers)
- Select/unselect object (double tap)
- Move a selected object (one finger drag)
- Scale a selected object (two fingers pinch)
- Rotate a selected object (tree fingers drag)

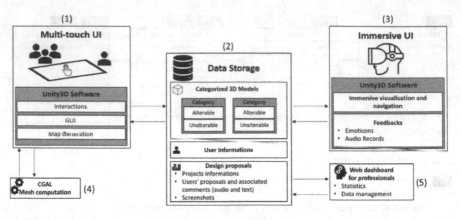

Fig. 7 Overview of software architecture

- Edit a selected object: edition consists in slicing a 3D element in two different parts. It is the implementation of the "cut and paste" metaphor. To do so, the user need to draw a line over the model to extract the desired part.

To implement the slicing operation, we developed a C++ plugin using CGAL Open Source library [(4) in Fig. 7], which receives as input two. *off* files: the model and the line drawn by the user and two transformation matrixes extracted from Unity. The plugin then returns the two slices of the object.

Additional interactions are available through touch buttons: delete, duplicate, change color, change metadata (title and description) of a selected object. The user also has access to a 3D model database, allowing to add additional elements to the environment. Finally, each user can save its work in order to continue later if needed.

To instantiate the immersive visualization workspace [(3) in Fig. 7], we propose to use a Head Mounted Display, such as a low-cost cardboard or a high-end device as

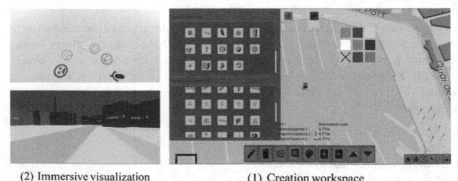

(2) Immersive visualization   (1) Creation workspace
    and feedback workspace

Fig. 8 Snapshots of the different workspaces

an HTC Vive. Our prototype uses a Cardboard, hence we are currently limited with interactions. Through this environment [(2) of Fig. 8], a user can explore his/her or someone else's proposal, either with an 1/1 scale view or with a bird-eye view. The available interactions are only feedback actions:

- Associate an emoticon to a selected object
- Associate an audio record to a selected object

The professional workspace [(5) in Fig. 7] is accessible via a web interface, as presented in the third image of Fig. 8. From this interface a professional can study all feedbacks, in the form of emoticons or audio recordings.

Finally, all the data (3D models, User information and saved Design proposal) are stored in a central database system [(2) in Fig. 7].

5 Discussion and Future Work

To situate our contribution with respect to identified literature (presented in Sect. 2), we compare our work against 8 criteria defined on the basis of the requirements (a) to (l) (Sect. 4). Each criterion contains a needed characteristic for the definition of a collaborative ICT tool for PP in urban design. Table 1 provides an overview of each criterion with associated characteristic and requirement.

Table 2 shows our differentiation compared to the state of the art. The comparison clearly highlights that little attention is payed to co-creation by providing necessary tools, metaphors and interactions (criteria 5–7). The proposed artefact fills this gap. Furthermore, compared to the majority of the contributions in Computer Science and Information Systems, we are placing the artifact in articulation with a well-defined participatory process.

Regarding social sustainability research field, our work contributes to strengthen citizen's impact in the collective negotiation process by providing them an appropriate tool during the different steps of the participation process.

5.1 Evaluation of Research

This section applies the Design Science evaluation guidelines from Hevner et al. [26] to the research project. The goal is to show how the research (including the process and the product) satisfies each of the criteria. This exercise also clarifies our contribution to knowledge in Information Systems.

Problem Relevance

> The objective of design-science research is to develop technology-based solutions to important and relevant business problems. [26], p. 7–8

Table 1 Comparison criteria derived from the analysis of the Environment

Criterion number	Definition	Supported characteristic(s)	Associated requirement(s)
1	Reconstitutes the surrounding area of the future place: streets, buildings, contextual information (street names, building names, ...)	Spatial awareness and comprehension	a), c), d), j)
2	Offers the opportunity to explore the future place with bird's eye view (zoom in/out, move camera)	Spatial awareness and comprehension	a), c), d), j)
3	Offers the opportunity for immersive visualization (scale 1:1 with a Head Mounted Display)	Spatial awareness and comprehension	a), c), d), j)
4	Offers the opportunity to annotate/categorize 3D elements (metadata)	Idea expression and feedback	g), h)
5	Offers the opportunity to manipulate 3D elements (move, scale, rotate, delete, change color/material)	Idea expression and feedback, Creativity	b), e), i), l)
6	Offers the opportunity to add new 3D elements in the virtual site (both abstract and complex shapes)	Creativity	e), k), l)
7	Offers the opportunity to edit 3D elements: cut and assemble	Creativity	e), l)
8	Offers an interactive and collaborative interface via touch screen	Collaboration, Co-creation	a)

Table 2 Evaluation of existing artefacts for PP in urban design

Reference	Criterion number							
	1	2	3	4	5	6	7	8
[47]	N	N	P	P	N	N	N	N
[39]	P	Y	N	N	P	P	N	N
[32]	Y	Y	P	Y	Y	Y	N	N
[58]	Y	Y	P	Y	N	N	N	N
[22]	N	N	N	Y	N	N	N	N
[21]	P	Y	Y	N	Y	P	N	N
[38]	Y	Y	N	N	N	N	N	Y
[20]	N	Y	Y	N	Y	Y	P	N
[17]	N	N	P	Y	Y	P	N	N
Our artefact	Y	Y	Y	Y	Y	Y	Y	P

Y criterion is respected, *N* criterion is not respected, *P* criterion is partially respected

Problem relevance is exposed in Sects. 1 and 2. Professional interviews and observational studies enabled us to identify the need for new ways of interaction for citizen during public participations in urban design. The analysis of previous research also show that work needs to be done to support generative design concepts in ICT tools for PP.

Research Rigor

> Design science research requires the application of rigorous methods in both the construction and evaluation of the design artifact. Often empirical methods are needed to evaluate the artifact as part of a complete human-machine system. [26], p. 8–9

Our artifact is based on past research in the field of ICT-mediated citizen participation. This research area has a long history of formal, rigorous results that have been applied to the design of many artifacts.

We acknowledge the limitations of the interpretivist epistemological stance: interpretations of the observed environment are bound with our subjective experience. We attempted to control our own subjectivity by combining the field observations with recommendations collected from theoretical and methodological literature.

Design as a Search Process

> The search for an optimal design is often intractable for realistic information systems problems. Heuristic search strategies produce feasible, good designs that can be implemented in the business environment. Decomposition of complex problems is an effective heuristic in the search for effective designs. [26], p. 10–11

A clear step by step process is used to design the presented artefact. First, we realized a survey in the literature to identify essential requirements for the artefact. We then enhance the requirements with an ethnological process composed of observational studies of a real project, interviews and focus groups. An evaluation process is defined in terms of usability and utility of the artefact. A conceptual framework is presented and articulated with an extended participation process and finally, a first instantiation of the artefact through a prototype (architecture and user interface).

Design as an Artifact

> Design-science research must produce a viable artefact in the form of a construct, a model, a method, or an instantiation. [26], p. 11–13

As outlined in Sect. 4, the artefact is a *framework* comprising of a conceptual model, a method (the participation process) and an instantiation. The viability of the artefact is claimed in the fact that it can be expressed and applied to a problem domain. Further, its feasibility is argued from the prototype itself.

Design Evaluation

> The utility, quality, and efficacy of a design artefact must be rigorously demonstrated via well-executed evaluation methods. [26], p. 13–16

An evaluation process is described but has not been conducted yet. This is a strong drawback of the paper that will be fixed in future work.

Research Contributions

> Effective design science research must provide clear contributions in the areas of the design artifact, design construction knowledge, and/or design evaluation knowledge. [26], p. 16–17

We presented the design process and results of an IIVE to support citizen participation in urban design as well as its instantiation through a first prototype. Such contribution is considered as an improvement to knowledge in Information Systems through design-science research, as we proposed a new solution to a known problem: *The goal of DSR in the improvement quadrant is to create better solutions in the form of more efficient and effective products, processes, services, technologies, or ideas …Situated instantiations (Level 1) are often constructed to evaluate the level of improvements in comparison with instantiations of the existing solution artifacts.* [25], *p. 346.*

5.2   Future Work

Our future work will be focused on a qualitative and quantitative evaluation of the artefact through simulated scenario workshops to evaluate its utility regarding creativity support. To ensure that the artefact is easy to handle for non-trained participants, another evaluation will be focused on the artefact's usability by running unipersonal tests along with questionnaires and video recordings. We will follow the "Prototyping Pattern" of DSR defined by [51], which consists in 4 steps: specification of the artefact design, implementation of the artefact, realization of a test case with "real users" accomplishing a "real task" within our organizational context, and assessment of whether the task could be solved as intended by using the prototype.

We'll also follow the guidelines for collaborative interfaces from literature since our artefact instantiation doesn't fully respect yet the multi user interactions (criterion 8). Finally, we'll deepen our work on data extraction and visualization for professionals.

6 Conclusions

In this paper we presented the design and software architecture of an interactive virtual environment to support citizen participation and creativity in urban design. We payed particular attention to define an artefact intended for face-to-face workshops, helping citizens to creatively express their explicit and latent expectations of future public spaces. The advantage of our contribution is to bridge knowledge from urban design field about participatory processes in the form of an extended participation process, with knowledge from Computer Science and Information Systems fields about digital artefact design in the form of a design process and requirements. Gathering these two fields enabled us to propose a digital solution to different steps of a PP process. We also considered guidelines from generative design research in our functionalities to ensure creativity of participants. Finally, we proposed an implementation of the artefact by presenting our work in terms of user interface and software architecture.

We built our solution considering current advances in immersive and interactive technologies such as touch screens and head mounted displays.

Acknowledgements This work is part of the U_CODE project. This project has received funding from the European Union's Horizon 2020 research and innovation programme under grant agreement No. 688873.

References

1. Adikari, S., McDonald, C., Collings, P.: A design science approach to an HCI research project. In: Proceedings of the 20th Conference of the Computer-Human Interaction Special Interest Group (CHISIG) of Australia on Computer-Human Interaction: Design: Activities, Artefacts and Environments—OZCHI'06, p. 429. ACM Press, New York, New York, USA (2007)
2. Al-Kodmany, K.: Combining digital and traditional visualisation techniques in community-based planning and design. Digit. Creat. **10**(2), 91–103 (1999)
3. Al-Kodmany, K.: Public Participation: Technology and Democracy. https://www.tandfonline.com/doi/full/10.1162/104648800564635 (2000)
4. Al-Kodmany, K.: Using visualization techniques for enhancing public participation in planning and design: process, implementation, and evaluation. Landsc. Urban Plan. **45**(1), 37–45 (1999)
5. Al-Kodmany, K.: Visualization tools and methods in community planning: from freehand sketches to virtual reality. J. Plan. Lit. **17**(2), 189–211 (2002)
6. Allard-Poesi, F. et al.: Coder les données. Conduire un Proj. Rech. une Perspect. Qual., 245–290 (2003)

7. Allard-Poesi, F., Perret, V.: Conduire un projet de recherche. Une approche qualitative, HAL (2004)
8. Alrashed, T., Almalki, A., Aldawood, S., Alhindi, T., Winder, I., Noyman, A., Alfaris, A., Alwabil, A.: An observational study of usability in collaborative tangible interfaces for complex planning systems. Procedia Manuf. **3**, 1974–1980 (2015)
9. Arnstein, S.R.: A ladder of citizen participation. J. Am. Plan. Assoc. **35**(4), 216–224 (1969)
10. Assila, A.: Une approche et un outil pour l' évaluation subjective et objective de l' utilisabilité des systèmes interactifs : application à un système d' aide à l' information voyageurs Ahlem Assila To cite this version : HAL Id : tel-01411235 (2016)
11. Beck, K., Beedle, M., Bennekum, A. van, Cockburn, A., Cunningham, W., Fowler, M., Martin, R.C., Mellor, S., Thomas, D., Grenning, J., Highsmith, J., Hunt, A., Jeffries, R., Kern, J., Marick, B., Schwaber, K., Sutherland, J.: Manifesto for Agile Software Development (2001)
12. Ben-Joseph, E., Ishii, H., Underkoffler, J., Piper, B., Yeung, L.: Urban simulation and the luminous planning table: bridging the gap between the digital and the tangible. J. Plan. Educ. Res. **21**(2), 196–203 (2001)
13. Billger, M., Thuvander, L., Wästberg, B.S.: In search of visualization challenges: the development and implementation of visualization tools for supporting dialogue in urban planning processes. Environ. Plan. B Urban Anal. City Sci. **44**(6), 1012–1035 (2017)
14. Broll, W., Lindt, I., Ohlenburg, J., Wittkämper, M., Yuan, C., Novotny, T., Fatah Gen Schieck, A., Mottram, C., Strothmann, A.: ARTHUR: a collaborative augmented environment for architectural design and urban planning. J. Virtual Real. Broadcast. **1**(1), 1–10 (2004)
15. Carroll, E.A., Latulipe, C.: The creativity support index. In: Proceedings of the 27th International Conference Extended Abstracts on Human Factors in Computing Systems—CHI EA'09, p. 4009. ACM Press, New York, New York, USA (2009)
16. Cherry, E., Latulipe, C.: Quantifying the creativity support of digital tools through the creativity support index. ACM Trans. Comput. Interact. **21**(4), 1–25 (2014)
17. deVries, B., Tabak, V., Achten, H., De Vries, B.: Interactive Urban Design using integrated planning requirements control. Autom. Constr. **14**(2), 207–213 (2005)
18. DeWalt, K.M., DeWalt, B.R.: Participant observation: a guide for fieldworkers. Walnut Creek (2002)
19. DeWalt, K.M., DeWalt, B.R.: Participant observation. In: Bernard, H.R. et Gravlee, C.C. (éds.) Handbook of methods in cultural anthropology, pp. 259–300. Rowman Littlefield, Walnut Creek (1998)
20. Fatah, A., Schieck, G., Penn, A., Mottram, C., Strothmann, A., Ohlenburg, J., Broll, W., Aish, F.: Interactive space generation through play exploring form creation and the role of simulation on the design table. Int. J. Archit. Comput. **3** (2005)
21. Drettakis, G., Roussou, M., Reche, A., Tsingos, N.: Design and evaluation of a real-world virtual environment for architecture and urban planning. Presence Teleoperators Virtual Environ. **16**(3), 318–332 (2007)
22. Gaborit, N., Howard, T.: A collaborative virtual environment for public consultation in the urban planning process. In: IEEE Proceedings—Theory and Practice of Computer Graphics 2004, pp. 104–111 (2004)
23. Hanzl, M.: Information technology as a tool for public participation in urban planning: a review of experiments and potentials. Des. Stud. **28**(3), 289–307 (2007)
24. Hart, S.G., Staveland, L.E.: Development of NASA-TLX (Task Load Index). Adv. Psychol. **52**, 139–183 (1988)
25. Hevner, A.R., Gregor, S.: Positioning and presenting design science: types of knowledge in design science research. MIS Q. **37**(2), 337–355 (2013)
26. Hevner, A.R., Park, J., Ram, S., March, S.T., Park, J., Ram, S.: Design science in information systems research. Des. Sci. IS Res. MIS Q. **28**(1), 75–105 (2004)
27. Hurtienne, J., Naumann, A.: QUESI—a questionnaire for measuring the subjective consequences of intuitive use. Interdiscip. Coll. 2010. Focus Theme Play. Act Learn 539 (2010)
28. Indraprastha, A., Shinozaki, M.: The investigation on using Unity3D game engine in urban design study. ITB J. Inf. Commun. Technol. **3**(1), 1–18 (2009)

29. Jutraž, A., Moine, J.Le: Breaking out: new freedoms in urban (re) design work by adding immersive environments. Int. J. Archit. Comput. **14**(2), 103–118 (2016)
30. Jutraz, A., Zupancic, T.: Digital system of tools for public participation and education in urban design exploring 3D ICC. In: ECAADE 2012, Digital Physicality, vol. 1, pp. 383–392 (2012)
31. Jutraz, A., Zupancic, T.: Virtual worlds as support tools for public engagement in urban design. In: Planning Support Systems and Smart Cities, pp. 391–408. Springer (2015)
32. Khan, Z., Ludlow, D., Loibl, W., Soomro, K.: ICT enabled participatory urban planning and policy development. Transform. Gov. People, Process Policy **8**(2), 205–229 (2014)
33. Kniberg, H., Skarin, M.: Kanban and scrum-making the most of both. Lulu. com (2010)
34. de La Ville, V.I.: others: La recherche idiographique en management stratégique: une pratique en quête de méthode? Financ. contrôle Strat. **3**(3), 73–99 (2000)
35. De Lange, M., De Wall, M.: Owning the city: new media and citizen engagement in urban design. First Monday **18**, 11–14 (2013)
36. Lindell, R.: The craft of programming interaction and engineering market. In: Proceedings of International Workshop on the Interplay Between User Experience Evaluation and Software Development (I-UxSED 2012), pp. 26–30 (2012)
37. Luigi, M., Massimiliano, M., Aniello, P., Gennaro, R., Virginia, P.R.: On the validity of immersive virtual reality as tool for multisensory evaluation of urban spaces. Energy Procedia. **78**, 471–476 (2015)
38. Maquil, V., Leopold, U., De Sousa, L.M., Schwartz, L., Tobias, E.: Towards a framework for geospatial tangible user interfaces in collaborative urban planning. J. Geogr. Syst. **20**(2), 185–206 (2018)
39. Mueller, J., Lu, H., Chirkin, A., Klein, B., Schmitt, G.: Citizen design science: a strategy for crowd-creative urban design. Cities **72**, 181–188 (2018)
40. Orlikowski, W.J., Baroudi, J.J.: Studying information technology in organizations: research approaches and assumptions. Inf. Syst. Res. **2**(1), 1–28 (1991)
41. Orlikowski, W.J., Iacono, C.S.: Research commentary: desperately seeking the «IT» in IT research—a call to theorizing the IT artifact. Inf. Syst. Res. **12**(2), 121–134 (2001)
42. Peffers, K., Tuunanen, T., Gengler, C.E., Rossi, M., Hui, W., Virtanen, V., Bragge, J.: The design science research process: a model for producing and presenting information systems research. In: The Proceedings of Design Research in Information Systems and Technology DESRIST 2006, pp. 83–106 (2006)
43. Preece, J., Rogers, Y., Sharp, H.: Interaction Design: Beyond Human-Computer Interaction. Wiley (2015)
44. Saad-Sulonen, J.C., Horelli, L.: The value of Community Informatics to participatory urban planning and design: a case-study in Helsinki. J. Community Informat. **6**(2) (2010)
45. Sanders, E.B.-N., Stappers, P.J.: Co-creation and the new landscapes of design. CoDesign **4**(1), 5–18 (2008)
46. Sanders, E.B., Stappers, P.J.: Convivial Toolbox (2012)
47. Van Schaik, P.: Using interactive 3-D visualization for public consultation. Interact. Comput. **22**(6), 556–568 (2010)
48. Seichter, H.: Augmented reality and tangible interfaces in collaborative urban design. In: Computer-Aided Architectural Design Futures (CAADFutures) 2007, pp. 3–16. Springer Netherlands, Dordrecht (2007)
49. Seichter, H.: Sketchand+ a collaborative augmented reality sketching application. In: Proceedings of the Conference on Computer-Aided Architectural Design Research, pp. 209–219. Bangkok (2003)
50. Shen, C., Ryall, K., Forlines, C., Esenther, A., Vernier, F., Everitt, K., Wu, M., Wigdor, D., Morris, M.R., Hancock, M., Tse, E.: Informing the Design of Direct-Touch Tabletops (2006)
51. Sonnenberg, C., Vom Brocke, J.: Evaluation patterns for design science research artefacts. In: Communications in Computer and Information Science, pp. 71–83. Springer, Berlin, Heidelberg (2012)
52. Spinuzzi, C.: The methodology of participatory design. Tech. Commun. **52**(2), 163–174 (2005)

53. Turan, S.Ö., Pulatkan, M., Beyazlı, D., Özen, B.S.: User evaluation of the urban park design implementation with participatory approach process. Procedia—Soc. Behav. Sci. **216**, 306–315 (2016)
54. Voinov, A., Kolagani, N., McCall, M.K., Glynn, P.D., Kragt, M.E., Ostermann, F.O., Pierce, S.A., Ramu, P.: Modelling with Stakeholders—Next Generation. http://linkinghub.elsevier.com/retrieve/pii/S1364815215301055 (2016)
55. Wates, N., Brook, J., De Lange, M., De Waal, M., Salter, J.D., Campbell, C., Journeay, M., Sheppard, S.R.J., Yeang, L.D., others, Jutraz, A., Zupancic, T., Slotterback, C.S., Senbel, M., Church, S.P., Panagopoulos, T., Andrade, R. dos R., Barreira, A.P., Luigi, M., Massimiliano, M., Aniello, P., Gennaro, R., Virginia, P.R., Fonseca, D., Valls, F., Redondo, E., Villagrasa, S., Turan, S.Ö., Pulatkan, M., Beyazlı, D., Özen, B.S., Hanzl, M., Saad-Sulonen, J.C., Horelli, L., Ben-Joseph, E., Ishii, H., Underkoffler, J., Piper, B., Yeung, L., Köninger, A., Bartel, S., Ahn, H.-C., Jacobi, M., Halatsch, J., Kunze, A., Schmitt, G., Turkienicz, B.: The Community Planning Handbook: How People Can Shape Their Cities, Towns and Villages in Any Part of the World. Springer (2000)
56. Westerberg, P., Von Heland, F.: Using Minecraft for Youth Participation in Urban Design and Governance (2015)
57. Witmer, B.G., Singer, M.J.: Measuring Presence in Virtual Environments: A Presence Questionnaire (1998)
58. Wu, H., He, Z., Gong, J.: A virtual globe-based 3D visualization and interactive framework for public participation in urban planning processes. Comput. Environ. Urban Syst. **34**(4), 291–298 (2010)
59. Llewelyn Davies, Y.: Urban Design Compendium. English Partnerships, London (2000)
60. Changing Places. http://cp.media.mit.edu/cityio/. Consulté le: juillet 01, 2017
61. Everyday Objects as Interface: Collaborative MouseHaus Table, A Physical Interface for Urban Design (2015)

Developing Crisis Training Software for Local Governments—From User Needs to Generic Requirements

Monika Magnusson, John Sören Pettersson, Peter Bellström and Henrik Andersson

Abstract In this paper, we identify, analyze and propose generic requirements for software aiming at supporting crisis management training in local governments. The study builds on a Swedish-Norwegian R&D project based on a quadruple helix model. A design science approach was applied and the artifact presented in this paper is a list of generic requirements. The generic requirements are divided into overall requirements, requirements connected to the trainer's role and requirements connected to the trainee's role. The requirements are also mapped to the problems and opportunities identified in the project. Finally, we present examples of elaborations of the addressed requirements based on software design considerations. The presented requirements and the systems development process that was used provide guidelines for systems analysts and developers in future systems development projects aiming at constructing new software for crisis management training.

Keywords Crisis management training · Crisis exercises · Design science research · Requirements engineering · User needs analysis

A prior version of this paper has been published in the ISD2018 Proceedings (http://aisel.aisnet.org/isd2014/proceedings2018).

M. Magnusson (✉) · J. S. Pettersson · P. Bellström · H. Andersson
Karlstad University, Karlstad, Sweden
e-mail: monika.magnusson@kau.se

J. S. Pettersson
e-mail: john_soren.pettersson@kau.se

P. Bellström
e-mail: peter.bellstrom@kau.se

H. Andersson
e-mail: henrik.andersson@kau.se

1   Introduction

Despite the fact that it is vital to any society, the digitalization of crisis management in general and of crisis training in particular is still in its early stages. Natural disasters and refugee streams are two examples of crises that are expected to increase in the future. This adds to the wide range of risks already faced by local and regional governments. An important part of crisis preparedness is arranging crisis training, here referred to as both collaborative exercises and training for carrying out individual roles. Collaborative exercises are traditionally performed by gathering personnel ("trainees") from different organizations (municipalities, police, fire department, healthcare, etc.) to handle a fictive crisis scenario. There are several types of exercises, such as tabletop discussions, functional exercises or field exercises (cf. [25]). These traditional time-and-space-dependent methods are often time consuming for the participants (trainees) as well as resource demanding and complex to plan for the trainers (often a security coordinator) (cf. [10]). This is especially the case in smaller municipalities with limited personnel for crisis preparedness.

It has been suggested that computer-based training offers resource-efficient and flexible complements to traditional training (e.g. [16]). However, an earlier study has found few examples of continued usage of such systems [18], perhaps indicating that the spread is limited. One possible explanation is that the systems fail in information or system quality. Despite many examples of the design specification of computer-based training systems, there are only a few earlier studies that present the need elicitation, objectives and requirements specification for the software [18], thus giving little guidance for the design of future solutions. In this paper, we report on the requirement elicitation in a research and development (R&D) project aiming at developing a generic tool for crisis management training in local and regional governments. A design science research (DSR) approach was used, and in this paper we seek to answer the following question: *What are the (generic) requirements of software aiming at supporting crisis management training in local governments?* The focus in this study is on information systems for discussion-based or "tabletop-like" exercises. Next, we describe the research setting of the R&D project, followed by related work. The research method is described in more detail in Sect. 4, and the results from the requirement engineering process are presented in Sect. 5. The paper ends with conclusions and suggestions for further research.

2   Research Setting

The research was primarily performed in the Swedish-Norwegian multidisciplinary R&D project Preparing for Future Crisis Management (abbreviated to CriseIT). The project ran 2016–18 and was financed by the EU/Interreg Sweden-Norway program. The collaboration and preparation for the project started a couple of years earlier. In addition, some members of the Swedish project group had conducted two smaller projects in the same problem area during 2013–2015. The purpose, goals and project group of the CriseIT project were therefore influenced by the results from the earlier projects. Three of the interviews used as empirical data in this study took place in 2015, although the respondents later also participated in the CriseIT project. The aim of the CriseIT project was to develop networks, knowledge, methods and ICT tools that enable cheaper, easier, more efficient and effective crisis training thereby lowering border-region barriers for good crisis preparedness. All of the authors participated in the project. The partnership was based on a quadruple helix model, and included sixteen organizations: two universities (and three disciplines), three businesses, as well as national, regional and local government agencies and Non-Governmental Organizations (NGOs).

3 Related Work

The area of crisis management training is first presented, followed by a review of studies on IS in crisis (disaster, emergency) management training.

3.1 Crisis Management Training

During a major crisis or disaster, the strategic level has a vital role in identifying and prioritizing the critical actions an organization needs to take, and to communicate these to lower levels (e.g. [8]). Decisions are mainly unstructured at this level, and the stressful conditions in a crisis add to the complexity of the tasks. Furthermore, as few crises reach this severity, there are few opportunities for the strategic level to obtain practical experience. Individual crisis training and collaborative exercises are therefore important in improving preparedness. Sinclair et al. [31] claim that "the fact that disasters are infrequent makes training and exercises especially important in emergency management" (p. 508). Exercises permit the testing of the disaster plan and the adequacy of the training of personnel, and provide "hands-on" checks of communication tools [25]. Moreover, exercises can test the viability of the response network [25].

There are several challenges in crisis management training. Before the exercise type and a scenario are chosen, the purpose (*why*) of the exercise and its goals (*what*) need be a defined, as noted in many national crisis training guidelines (e.g., [21]). Furthermore, Bharosa et al. [7] stress the importance of coordination in disaster management. As a result, crisis exercises need to involve a number of actors—otherwise it is hard to train coordination. Another challenge is that local governments with their limited budgets have the primary responsibility both for handling real crisis events and preparing for them. In smaller municipalities, a single security or emergency coordinator may have the sole responsibility for planning, and sometimes also performing, crisis training in the organization [20].

3.2   Information Systems (IS) in Crisis Management Training

Computer-based crisis training could offer a resource-effective complement to traditional training (cf. [16]). Nikolai et al. [23] acknowledge a number of advantages with computer-based (simulation) training:

> [...] simulation-based training allows emergency managers to train new personnel without being in the middle of a disaster. Moreover, simulation-based training allows personnel to train more frequently than they otherwise would be able to in live and face-to-face exercises. In addition, they enable distributed access to data, resources, communication, and even the training itself. Computer simulations also enable teams to train selective portions of the emergency management hierarchy. Finally, whereas feedback has delays in non-computer solutions, feedback can be immediate in a computer-based simulation system.

However, Ahmad et al. [1] concluded from their study of crisis simulation software and decision support systems (DSS) in 2012 (p. 3) that "[...] the literature reports primarily on design specifications, ideas, and 'prototypes'—very little can be found on assessment/evaluations of software-in-use". A few years later, Magnusson and Öberg [18] claimed from their literature review that reports in the research literature on ongoing usage of computer-supported training were still rare. In the wake of the ongoing digitalization and the growing importance of crisis preparedness due to global warming, this is somewhat surprising.

The lack of reports on usage does not seem to stem from a lack of IT solutions. There are several studies reporting on computer-based software for crisis training. Pottebaum et al. [27] (p. 383), for example, present a taxonomy of IT support for training exercises constructed from "a thorough analysis of available commercial IT systems, demonstrators and concepts from research projects and use cases derived from stakeholders and context analysis". The taxonomy takes a trainer's perspective and a phase-driven approach. According to Pottebaum et al.'s taxonomy [27], there are IT systems for planning, controlling, observing, and debriefing during an exercise. Magnusson and Öberg [18], however, found that earlier studies mainly concern systems supporting the execution of training/exercise (and not planning or after-action tasks). Magnusson and Öberg [18] also conclude that design specifications of existing or proposed systems dominate in research while few studies report on usage or regular tests of systems.

Computer-based crisis training may be individual or collaborative [3], distributed or co-located [17], and support different types of exercises. Our literature review identified numerous examples of studies on systems for simulations (e.g. [1, 8, 15, 17]), while studies focusing on IT support for discussion or tabletop exercises seem to be rare. An exception is Araz et al. [4], who report on a tabletop exercise where video clips, digital maps and interactive simulation tools were used to enrich traditional tabletop exercises. Moreover, Asproth et al. [5] present a study where a web-based system for "tabletop-like" collaborative exercises was tried out in two exercises—one co-located and one distributed—to study if it could serve as an exercise platform and an evaluation tool. They conclude that the results were promising. A web-based system has the advantage of enabling usage from different platforms and locations [5].

Another possible explanation for what seems to be a limited adoption of software for crisis training, except for technology resistance as indicated by MacKinnon and Bacon [17], may be that the systems on the market simply fail to meet the needs and prerequisites of the target groups. Magnusson and Öberg [18] found few explicit studies of user needs in their literature review of computer-based crisis training. They conclude: "It is thus not clear from our literature review which (generic) user needs these systems were developed to meet". However, we have found a few studies that discuss development methods and requirements (e.g. [16]), or the need for standardization in components, information models and data interfaces [15]. Further, Nikolai et al. [23] call for the ability to share exercises and simulations in a standardized way.

Some studies identify desirable features of crisis training systems such as logging of exercise data for analysis, reflection or evaluation and the ability to enter new events or changes to a scenario [6, 27, 29]. Also, Greitzer et al. [12] (p. 4) suggest a number of design guidelines to promote active learning in training applications. One such guideline is to manage the learner's cognitive load by organizing material in small chunks and gradually increasing complexity. A frequently cited study in the field of design of emergency response management IS is Turoff et al. [32]. They propose eight generalized design principles, several of which are equally applicable to training systems, such as updated information and support for psychological and social needs. In fact, Turoff et al. [32] (p. 6) suggest that systems for response and training should be the same, because "An emergency system that is not used on a regular basis before an emergency will never be of use in an actual emergency". Reuter et al. [30] present another interesting study. They suggest modules and functionality in a prototype for a collaborative exercise system for training crisis communication management. The modules, e.g. for user, role, event and time management, seem generic enough to be useful in the design also of other crisis training systems. In addition, Reuter et al. [30] briefly describe their development process. However, overall, we have not been able to identify any earlier studies that describe the entire development process from business needs to requirement elicitation and a validated system.

4 Method

The overall research approach used in this study can be described as design science research (DSR) (see [9, 13, 14]). Although growing in the Information systems research field since the 1990s [23], a search in Scopus (January 2019) with the search string TITLE-ABS-KEY ("design science" AND ("crisis management" OR "disaster management" OR "emergency management") AND ("information system*" OR "information technology" OR software)) indicates that DSR is still rare in the IS for crisis management field. The search resulted in fewer than twenty papers. In DSR, the result is always an artifact, more precisely described by Hevner et al. [14] in IS research: "IT artifacts are broadly defined as *constructs* (vocabulary and symbols), *models* (abstractions and representations), *methods* (algorithms and practices), and *instantiations* (implemented and prototype systems)" (p. 77). The relevance of an IT artifact depends on the problems and opportunities, i.e. the business needs for a new IS, in the application domain (cf. [9, 13, 24]). Ahmad et al. ([1]: 3) conclude from their literature review that "[...] the research makes painfully clear that IT/software engineers and crisis scholars do not communicate, i.e. they are clearly unfamiliar with each other's work and key findings of that work. This leads to IT products that crisis managers do not need; it also means that crisis managers are not familiar with the technological possibilities available to them". Thus, a first step is to identify problems and opportunities for the stakeholders.

Components of methods for change analysis [11] and work system analysis [2] were utilized to identify, analyze, and describe problems and opportunities in our project. This involved mapping organizations and people involved in planning and performing exercises, the organizational strategies and processes applied, the use of technology etc. (cf. [13]). Examples of system development modelling that could support this step are (static) snapshots of the work system [2], problem or goal diagrams [11] and business process models. However, only goal lists and problem lists were used for evaluation with the target group. The reason for this was that it was not considered feasible to obtain the time required for introducing and performing joint modelling from the practitioners. After having identified problems and opportunities, the next step was to define objectives or (meta-)requirements for the solution (cf. [9, 24]). In this paper, we strive to identify generic requirements, i.e. generic issues that a (groupware) designer of collaborative crisis training systems should consider when designing a system (cf. [19]). Several iterations following the seven guidelines of DSR [14] were conducted to reach the list of generic requirements presented in Sect. 6.

4.1 Elicitation, Data Collection, and Continuous Evaluation

Several requirement elicitation methods were used during the data collection phase, such as interviews, screen-sharing prototyping activities, workshops, walkthroughs as well as evaluations "in the wild" (see Table 1).

Due to the nature of the present study, with stakeholders separated by long distances and spread widely across the border region of Sweden and Norway, different data collection methods were employed in different cases.

Nineteen qualitative and semi-structured interviews were held to gain an initial foundation regarding the objectives, requirements and expectations for the project, such as the project aim, project outcomes and degree of participation. The interviews were also valuable for gaining an initial knowledge of the business processes/workflows. The interviews were held in 2015 (3) and in 2016 (16). All of the respondents were active in planning and/or performing crisis management training at different levels of government, or in companies or NGOs. All but one interview were recorded and transcribed. Seven interviews were conducted via video-conferencing or telephone, and the rest face-to-face. On the respondents' requests, two interviews included two and three participants respectively. The interview questions concerned,

Table 1 Requirement engineering methods used during the project

Method/technique	Purpose	Stage in the project cycle	Data collection method
Background interviews	Collecting data related to the needs and expectations of the users, project aim, outcomes etc.	Early	Sound recording and note-taking
Screen-sharing prototyping activities	Collecting data related to users' needs and expectations related to the prototype and the final artifact (the crisis management training system)	Early	Screen recording with voice and the GUIs
Sequence of work interviews	Collecting data related to the business process/sequence of work tasks to be performed with the crisis management training system	Early	Sound recording and note-taking
Workshop(s)	Identifying problems, needs and objectives and later collecting general systems requirements from project stakeholders. Evaluation of the project up to now. Evaluation and validation of requirements. Future heading. Validation of progress this far	Early-Mid	Note-taking, power point files, google docs
Walkthrough(s)	Evaluation and validation of the artifact (prototype) and requirements	Mid	Written summaries afterwards
Pilot field testing	Evaluation of the developed artifact when used in natural environment by expected end-users. Collection of proposed changes. Validation of the progress this far	Late	Trainees' input during the sessions, trainees' written evaluation of the system when finishing the exercise, workshop discussions with written summaries

for example, the current situation regarding training methods, frequency of training, problems, IT usage, and attitudes towards IT-based training.

During the study, several workshops took place. In a participatory design sense, workshops "are often held to help diverse parties ("interested parties" or "stakeholders") communicate and commit to shared goals, strategies, and outcomes (e.g. analyses, designs, and evaluations, as well as workplace-change objectives" [22] (p. 20). Some of the early workshops were held to identify problems and opportunities. Later the workshops served to evaluate and refine the problems and objectives in an iterative process.

In total, 17 screen-sharing prototyping sessions were conducted. The first ten sessions were held during April–May 2016. The last seven sessions were held during the autumn of 2016. As for the interviews, all respondents were active in planning and/or performing crisis management exercises in their organizations. All interviews were held with the aid of the web collaboration tool Ozlab, developed at Karlstad University. For oral communication, some kind of communication tool like Skype was used. All sessions were recorded, both screen and audio. During the first ten interviews, the interviewees were presented to fairly empty mockups (content wise). During the last seven interviews, the interviewees were presented to a more complete mockup. During the sessions, the interviewees were asked to "suggest contents in addition to what had been jointly defined in workshops, or to comment on existing content including interaction design" [26] (p. 156).

Mainly for budgetary reasons, the implementations were later conceived in WordPress. The project had already a prototype WordPress site for shorter, individual training for crisis management. Therefore, the tool for conducting collaboration exercises was thought to be implementable in WordPress. As WordPress provides the means to edit sites published with it, the parts for constructing the collaboration exercises have now (partly) been developed in WordPress.

Walkthrough is one kind of expert evaluation [28]. In our study, domain experts, together with the designer/facilitator "walk through" a specific (or complete) part of the prototype. This was done three times before the pilot field testing started. The purpose of this technique was twofold. First, the designer got the chance to validate and evaluate the prototype to ensure compliance with the requirement specification. Second, new requirements could arise. In contrast to screen-sharing prototyping based on mockups, such requirements could take a little longer to implement, and sometimes costs had to be balanced with benefits.

For the pilot field testing, some key users took part in a series of walkthroughs, where they acted as "exercise managers" and created or validated the exercises to be tested in the pilot field tests. In 2018, the first three pilots were run. These pilots were small, sometimes with security coordinators or similar, sometimes with researchers and professionals. In order for everyone involved to understand problems connected with building an exercise as well as problems connected with being a participant in an exercise, the roles were shifted through these pilots, and one pilot was carried out with people not involved in the project.

As noted, the walkthroughs constitute in themselves a kind of evaluation, as feedback from stakeholders was immediate even if not all suggestions could be accommodated. Workshops and requirements lists also accompanied the walkthroughs and pilot field tests.

5 Results

We found that most of the organizations in the study used the nationally provided systems WIS (Sweden) and its equivalent CIM (Norway) for logging and sharing information during actual events. However, while there are exercise modes in both systems, the usage of these were less common. One explanation was that few in the (trained) organizations were familiar with the system(s). Another explanation was that the functionality for training was perceived as (too) limited. In terms of other IS, mainly regular office software, such as Word or PowerPoint, was used for planning the crisis management training. Some mentioned having considered different commercial systems but found them too expensive. The early empirical grounding thus indicated a need for, and an interest in, complementary IS. The identified problems and opportunities served as basis for systems requirements. The resulting requirements are here sorted into three categories: overall, trainers, and trainees. We start by presenting the problems and opportunities found in interviews and early workshops.

5.1 Grounding in Interviews and Early Workshops

Here we present the problems and opportunities in current crisis training practices that were most frequently mentioned and/or considered most important by the stakeholders. Problem (P) and opportunities (O) are numbered to ensure traceability to requirements later in the paper.

Problems

A frequently mentioned problem in interviews and workshops was that *too few exercises* (P1) took place. Almost all of the respondents in the nineteen interviews believed that their organizations did not carry out enough exercises and *few organizations carried out any training* (P2) for the individual role. Some of the respondents referred to specific problems such as *failing to involve relevant internal and external actors* (P3), or *lacking particular types of exercises* (P4), but there was also a desire to train/exercise more in general. Among the problems that result in few exercises was *time-consuming and complex planning* (P5). Constructing a scenario takes time, as does finding a date that suits all or most of the intended trainees. In addition, most organizations had *scarce resources* (P6) in budget and personnel (e.g. security coordinators). Some of the organizations even lacked a dedicated role responsible for planning training. Furthermore, the trainers/security coordinators found it *difficult to design exercises that are realistic, varied, and provides learning* for all trainees

(P7). Some also mentioned the problem of *"having to reinvent the wheel"* every time (P8) a new exercise was planned, partly because most of the organizations were *lacking dedicated IT support* (P9) for exercise planning (and execution). At the same time, several trainers/security coordinators claimed they *were lacking a structured approach for planning* (P10) where the purpose and goal of an exercise are defined first, as recommended by the national authority.

Exercises were also *time-consuming for the trainees* (P11), as they often needed to devote somewhere between half a day to 24 h and more and in rural areas and sometimes needed to travel long distances (P12). This is problematic, as participants at the strategic level tend to have busy agendas. Furthermore, *keeping up the organizational knowledge in-between exercises* (P13) was seen as problematic as was *employee turnover* (P14), as it severely affected P13.

Opportunities
The respondents identified two primary target groups: the strategic level/crisis management team (as trainees) and the security/emergency/safety coordinators (as trainers). Several opportunities with IT-supported training were identified for these two groups. IT-supported training/exercises were thought to enable *more frequent exercises* (O1), in *short sessions* (O2) and with *more actors/trainees* (O3). In addition, digitalization was considered to allow high *flexibility* (O4) such as both *asynchronous and synchronous* (O5) exercises and *distributed exercises* (O6) with participants at different locations. The latter would enable participants to take part in training/exercises from their regular workplaces or "on the go", using either a *computer, tablet or smartphone* (O7). Moreover, IT was believed to contribute to *simplified, and more structured planning* (O8) and to *provide a holistic process* (O9), from training needs to (implemented) improvements. Furthermore, several respondents saw great potential in being able to *collaborate and reuse exercise/training* (O10) planning and content between organizations. Another opportunity that was mentioned was automatic logging to get *richer data from exercises/training* (O11) (e.g. who participated, the discussions underpinning decisions, etc.). Yet other opportunities identified included *better overview* (O12) of an ongoing exercise, for both trainers and trainees, and the ability to *use multimedia* (O13) to "color" a scenario and make the training/exercise more fun or realistic. Moreover, IT was seen as having the potential not only to serve as a complementary training/exercise type but also to *enrich traditional exercises* (O14), and *support individual training* (O15). In addition, IT was considered as enabling *role-based access* and *adaptation of content* (O16) to functions, roles or individual training needs.

5.2 Initial Requirements

A needs analysis of problems and opportunities was used as a starting point for discussing the (initial) requirements or objectives (cf. [24]) of the system to be built.

Table 2 Requirements derived from interviews and workshops

No	Requirement	Problems and opportunities	Early design choices
Overall			
R1	(Integrated) support of the entire process from planning, invitation, execution, and evaluation to bringing back identified needs for improvement to the organization	P5, P9, P10, P13, P14, O9	Web-based system(s) (as it will be accessible to all involved parties in all stages)
R2	Enable inter-organizational (and cross-sector) exercises	P3, O3, O10	Open web-based solution
R3	Mobile access	P11, P12, O3, O4, O6, O7	Responsive design
R4	Low cost	P6, P9, O3, O10	Free access, user organizations set up instances of exercise and user accounts, tabletop exercises (no simulations/virtual environments)
R5	Role-based system	P2, P4, P7, O16	
R6	Timeline of exercise/events	O8, O12	(Prototype dependent)
R7	Support short, module-based exercises	P1, P5, P11, P13, O1, O2	
Requirements connected to trainers' role			
R8	Enable reuse, and collaboration in planning, of exercises	P4, P5, P6, P7, P8, O1, O10	Copy function included in planning view
R9	Support trainer's overview of, and intervention in, an ongoing exercise	P7, P10, O11, O12	Progress report aligned to timeline (R6)
R10	Support both collaborative exercises and individual training	P1, P2, P3, P4, P7, P12, P13, P14, O1, O3, O14, O15	Two separate systems
R11	Support both synchronous and asynchronous exercises	P1, P3, P5, P11, P12, O1, O3, O4, O5	

(continued)

Table 2 (continued)

No	Requirement	Problems and opportunities	Early design choices
R12	Support knowledge progression	P7, P13, P14, O16	
R13	Logging of training/exercise data incl. participants and their "results"	P7, P13, O11	
R14	Ordered planning process for quality checking	P10, O8, O9	Enter goals and indicators when creating a new exercise module
R15	Possible to send out invitations to an exercise	P5, P9, O9	
Requirements connected to trainees' role			
R16	Accessible independent of platform	P1, P2, P3, P12, O4, O6, O7	Responsive web
R17	Ease-of-use	P1, P2, P3, P11, P13, P14, O1, O3, O15	
R18	Support Multimedia content	P2, P3, P7, P13, O13	Web supports multimedia content
R19	Possible to pause, repeat/replay an exercise	P11, O2, O4	
R20	Flexibility in time and place	P1, P2, P3, P4, P11, P12, O1-O7	Asynchronous and distributed

The initial sets of requirements identified in the spring of 2016 are presented in Table 2.

5.3 Elaboration of Requirements

The initial requirements were further elaborated (refined or redefined) (see Table 3) through co-design activities on distance in screen-sharing prototyping sessions with some interactivity. After a year, a CMS (Content Management System) publishing system (WordPress) was selected on which to base the prototyping, instead of developing the tool from scratch. The requirements were then further specified through pilot trials in which exercise modules were built and then ran for a few days according to the stakeholders' idea of suitable pace for asynchronous but collaborative exercises.

Prototyping can lead to specifications that make software easy to use but may at the same time result in very specific solutions that are dependent on the system

Table 3 Examples of elaborations

Req.	Requirement	Problems and opportunities	Design choice
R17a	Preview of the trainees' views when building a new exercise module	Trainers need support in their design roles	Prototype-dependent but for CMS the trainer needs to be familiar with web editing
R6a	Overview of the whole exercise process	Trainers commonly use timelines with callouts; not suitable for simple web design	Exercise with few steps may suffice with accordion design
R8a	Supporting search function for easy reuse of excrcises within and between rescue organizations	Lack of generally accepted terminology. Vocabulary might differ inside and between organizations	Continuous trimming of the classification scheme(s)
R11a	Guiding trainers to design short (=few steps) exercises	Many steps in an exercise makes it hard to managed asynchronous processes	This is pedagogical awareness that trainers should have, not that the tool itself should limit the number of submodules
R11b	Possibility to set times for when a module in an exercise opens and closes	Possibility to plan "automated" processes	Submodules are made visible according to a time scheme
R1a	Entering/selecting quality planning parameters (goals and indicators) must be easy	Pre-defined goals and indicators, common for different organization, are difficult to find at present	Simple text boxes to fill in; no automatic prompts. This reduces entry cost for new trainers

emerging. We here try to highlight emerging requirements that can qualify as generic aspects of a tool for defining and executing exercises.

R1, R8: It is important to define the purposes and goals of an exercise in order to plan it, and later the exercise should also be evaluated to determine whether further exercise(s) should be conducted to develop the same skills. In the shared-screen prototyping sessions, some participants mentioned the risk of incoherent classification schemes, for example of exercise goals/skills to achieve. They knew of shared file systems where each user could set their own classification terms, which had resulted in guessing how other people had classified documents. How exercise modules should be classified, not only according to the general skills as seen by the national coordinating bodies, but also to support crisis training in local organizations, was not resolved in the prototyping sessions. However, they clearly pointed to the necessity of defining and maintaining a process required to trim the classification schemes. In addition, as concerns R1, prototyping showed that indicators for goal measurement have to be simple.

R17: The two primary target groups defined above would typically have very different views on the desired functionality of the tool. The trainers would build exercise modules and oversee the exercises when these are run. The other group, the trainees, would typically only login to participate in a collaborative exercise or for individual training. In the first prototyping phase, it was deemed necessary for the trainers to use computers to define ("building") exercises. Later on, it was found that trainers also needed to see the exercise from the future participants' view, especially the view provided by a small-screen device.

The second phase, when WordPress had been selected, gave further insights into the requirements. WordPress has a preview function, and any publisher (here, trainers who publish exercise modules) can use a second web browser to check their websites while making changes. However, this is perhaps not so obvious for our stakeholders, especially if it has to be done on another device (namely a mobile phone).

R11: In the second phase, modularization (R7) appeared as a very important requirement. As it was hard for the experts on collaborative crisis training to foresee how an exercise would flow in a real asynchronous and distributed environment, they lowered their ambitions and agreed that this tool (admittedly a prototype) should primarily be used for very short/decomposed exercises. For instance, even if it was envisioned that trainees would spend only 10 min on each session, it turned out that they sometimes spent half an hour, as they would like to read what other trainees had written since the last time they were logged in.

R6: This also lowered the graphic requirements of using a timeline, even if this is the standard procedure for developing an exercise scenario and communicating it. The shorter and more specific the tasks or subtasks in focus for a certain exercise, the less demanding are the overview requirements. In the second phase, the WordPress (blog) posts could possibly suffice; in this project we used a plug-in called LearnPress from ThimPress where each task (or bundle of tasks) was put in a "lesson". These are accordions that open when the user wants. The trainer composing the exercise can keep them open in order to have an overview.

Reflection on the Iterative Development Process and Stakeholders' Participation

When the WordPress version was ready for demonstration to the trainers, it was agreed that one local safety coordinator should use it as a follow-up exercise for city council members who had participated in a county level exercise after which they felt the need for more training on one specific collaborative task. After an initial walkthrough by one of the IS researchers, the coordinator continued planning the exercise but was gravely disappointed. It was hard to work with the tool and the coordinator had the feeling that the busy city council people would be annoyed with a clumsy IT tool. This attempt to plan an exercise resulted in a lot of feedback, but also provided reason for questioning our process: the developers should have assisted the local coordinator more in the initial steps. Also, proceeding quickly to a real field test left this person critical of the impression the prototype would make. The plans changed to several pilot tests with researchers and trainers on both sides, and only a limited field test with people outside the project (we classified also this as a "pilot test" in the Method section).

6 Conclusions and Discussion

In this study, we strive to answer the question *What are the (generic) requirements of software aiming at supporting crisis management training in local governments?*

From our need analysis and later requirement elicitation, we have identified a set of generic requirements or issues that we believe are valuable to consider for any designer of information systems for "tabletop-like" crisis management training in local government:

- *Support an integrated training/exercise process* from planning to execution and evaluation of training/exercise to follow-up of identified improvements
- *Support multi-actor collaboration/exercises and single user training* as real-life events demand a number of collaborating actors while requiring each participant to have good knowledge of their individual responsibilities
- *Provide synchronous and asynchronous exercises*
- *Support co-located and distributed training/exercises*
- *Support reuse/copying of exercises/training* content
- *Provide functionality for searching* for existing exercises/training
- *Support built-in control* e.g. to ensure that purpose and goals are defined before the scenario in the planning process, or ensure that the trainer can intervene in or change the content of an ongoing exercise
- *Provide easy overview*, e.g. of the entire exercise with its modules and steps as well of how many and who have participated in different exercises/training
- *Support module-based training/exercises*
- *Use business models that ensure low costs* for public organizations and/or demonstrable cost savings as the resources are limited in most tax-funded organizations

- *Provide easy access and low entry barriers*
- *Support a wide range of interaction methods, multimedia and data formats* for import/export—to increase "the fun factor" and thus encourage more training, and facilitate integration with other IS/open resources
- *Support role-based content* to enable custom made content/assignments that "mirror" real-life organization of crisis management teams
- *Support logging of exercise/user data* to support trainers' monitoring and evaluation of an exercise/training session and to support analysis of organizational preparedness.

We believe that a "tabletop-like" digital crisis management system based on these generic requirements is valuable in supporting the planning process as well as complementing traditional (non-digital) training. Such a system could decrease the time spent on planning and increase the variation in and learning from training. Perhaps most importantly, it could enable increased crisis training. Obviously, there are also risks and limitations with such systems, for example in terms of integrating a new type of exercise and tool in the organizations. These "high level" requirements need to be complemented with functional and non-functional requirements. Some of these will follow naturally from the requirements above, such as a need for functionality for creating groups of trainees. Moreover, it should be noted that these requirements are mainly from a trainer's/planner's view, as the respondents primarily belonged to this group. Further studies are needed of the trainees' requirements. Our pilot field tests showed for example that the trainees wanted notifications from the system, e.g. when a new module is opened in an exercise, and to be able to create new chat rooms.

Furthermore, many of the identified problems, opportunities and requirements (e.g. R7 & R12) point to the need for accompanying digital training tools with new methods (documented in handbooks, checklists, help texts, etc.) for planning and executing. As in any other e-learning situation, digital crisis training also needs to rest firmly on pedagogies and theories for (groupware) learning. By creating very small chunk modules that fit into other demanding tasks during a workday, one would fulfil the requirements pertaining to the organizations adopting this tool, such as familiarizing themselves with asynchronous exercises both as concerns planning as well as participating in them. Establishing inter-organizational training databases is a promising goal, but blending national training standards, local needs and organizational terminologies still requires a great deal of collaboration—which such tools indeed will pave the way for if they allowed the multi-actor collaboration desired for effective crisis management.

While more studies are needed to confirm and complement the requirements presented here, we believe them to be valuable as a starting point for system analysts and developers as well as practitioners purchasing software for crisis management training. Our contributions to the research in the field are twofold. First, we believe this to be an early example of a DSR study in the field of IS/IT for crisis management (training). The study thus presents an operationalization of (the early stages of) DSR in the field. Second, our study contributes to the research on user needs for and requirements of discussion-based/"tabletop-like" training systems. Earlier research are largely focused on simulation software and few present the user needs behind the systems. The novelty of this study does not so much lie in the individual requirements as in the compiled list and the detailed description of the requirement elicitation process. The latter may serve as inspiration for early phases in future DSR projects.

Acknowledgements This research was partly funded by EU/Interreg, Sweden-Norway program (20200721). Professional language check has been provided by Elisabeth Wennö and Marinette Grimbeek.

References

1. Ahmad, A., Balet, O., Boin, A., Brivio, P., Ganovelli, F., Gobbetti, E., Himmelstein, J., Pintore, G., De la Rivière, J.B., Schaap, M.: Interactive simulation technology for crisis management and training: the INDIGO project. In: Proceedings of the 9th International Conference on Information Systems for Crisis Response and Management (2012)
2. Alter, S.: The Work System Method: Connecting People, Processes, and IT for Business Results. Work System Press, Larkspur, CA (2006)
3. Arafa, Y., Boldyreff, C., Dastbaz, M., Liu, H.: A framework for developing a collaborative training environment for crisis management. In: Proceedings of the First International Conference on Advanced Collaborative Networks, Systems and Applications (2011)
4. Araz, O.M., Jehn, M., Lant, T., Fowler, J.W.: A new method of exercising pandemic preparedness through an interactive simulation and visualization. J. Med. Syst. **36**, 1475–1483 (2012)
5. Asproth, V., Borglund, E.A., Öberg, L.M.: Exercises for crisis management training in intraorganizational settings. In: Proceedings of the 10th International Conference on Information Systems for Crisis Response and Management (2013)
6. Bacon, L., Windall, G., MacKinnon, L.: The development of a rich multimedia training environment for crisis management: using emotional affect to enhance learning. Assoc. Learn. Technol. **19**, 67–78 (2011)
7. Bharosa, N., Van Zanten, B., Zuurmond, A., Appelman, J.: Identifying and confirming information and system quality requirements for multi-agency disaster management. In: Proceedings of the 6th International Conference on Information Systems for Crisis Response and Management (2009)
8. Cesta, A., Cortellessa, G., De Benedictis, R.: Training for crisis decision making—an approach based on plan adaption. Knowl.-Based Syst. **58**, 98–112 (2014)
9. Drechsler, A., Hevner, A.: A four-cycle model of IS design science research: capturing the dynamic nature of IS artifact design. In: Parsons, J., Tuunanen, T., Venable, J.R., Helfert, M., Donnellan, B., Kenneally, J. (eds.) Breakthroughs and Emerging Insights from Ongoing Design Science Projects: Research-in-Progress Papers and Poster Presentations from the 11th International Conference on Design Science Research in Information Systems and Technology, pp. 1–8 (2016)
10. Field, J., Rankin, A., Lemmers, A., Morin, M.: Instructor tools for virtual training systems. In: Proceedings of the 9th International Conference on Information Systems for Crisis Response and Management (2012)
11. Goldkuhl, G., Röstlinger, A.: The significance of workpractice diagnosis: socio-pragmatic ontology and epistemology of change analysis. In: Proceedings of Action in Language, Organisations and Information Systems pp. 27–50 (2003)
12. Greitzer, F.L., Kuchar, O.A., Huston, K.: Cognitive science implications for enhancing training effectiveness in a serious gaming context. J. Educ. Resour. Comput. **7**(3), 2 (2007)
13. Hevner, A.R.: A three cycle view of design science research. Scand. J. Inf. Syst. **19**(2), 87–92 (2007)

14. Hevner, A.R., March, S.T., Park, J., Ram, S.: Design science in information systems research. MIS Q. **28**(1), 75–105 (2004)
15. Jain, S., McLean, C.R.: Components of an incident management simulation and gaming framework and related developments. Simulation **84**(1), 3–25 (2008)
16. Lukosch, H., van Ruijven, T., Verbraeck, A.: The participatory design of a simulation training game. In: Proceedings of the 2012 Winter Simulation Conference (2012)
17. MacKinnon, L., Bacon, L.: Developing realistic crisis management training. In: Proceedings of the 9th International Conference on Information Systems for Crisis Response and Management (2012)
18. Magnusson, M., Öberg, L.M.: Crisis training software and user needs: research directions. In: Proceedings of the 12th International Conference on Information Systems for Crisis Response and Management (2015)
19. Mandviwalla, M., Olfman, L.: What do groups need? A proposed set of generic groupware requirements. ACM Trans. Comput.-Hum. Interact. **1**(3), 245–268 (1994)
20. Meum, T., Munkvold, B.E.: Information infrastructure for crisis response coordination: a study of local emergency management in Norwegian municipalities. In: Proceedings of the 10th International Conference on Information Systems for Crisis Response and Management (2013)
21. MSB—The Swedish Agency for Civil Contingencies: Metodhäfte - Simuleringsövning med motspel, https://www.msb.se/RibData/Filer/pdf/27422.pdf
22. Muller, M., Druin, A.: Participatory design: the third space in human-computer interaction. In: Jacko, J.A. (ed.) The Human-Computer Interaction Handbook: Fundamentals, Evolving Technologies, and Emerging Applications. CRC Press, Boca Raton (2012)
23. Nikolai, C., Prietula, M., Madey, G., Becerra-Fernandez, I., Johnson, T., Mooney, M., Bhandari, R.: Experiences and Insights Using A Virtual Emergency Operations Center. http://www3.nd.edu/~veoc/resources/Papers/Experiences-and-Insights-Using-A-Virtual-Emergency-Operations-Center-v5.pdf
24. Peffers, K., Tuunanen, T., Rothenberger, M.A., Chatterjee, S.: A design science research methodology for information systems research. J. Manag. Inf. Syst. **24**(3), 45–77 (2007)
25. Peterson, D.M., Perry, R.W.: The impacts of disaster exercises upon participants. Int. J. Disaster Prev. Manag. **8**(4), 241–254 (1999)
26. Pettersson, J.S., Wik, M., Andersson, H.: GUI interaction interviews in the evolving map of design research. In: Paspallis, N., Raspopoulos, M., Barry, C., Lang, M., Linger, H., Schneider, C. (eds.) Advances in Information Systems Development. Methods, Tools and Management. Springer LNISO, vol. 26, pp. 149–167 (2018)
27. Pottebaum, J., Marterer, R., Schneider, S.: Taxonomy of IT support for training emergency response & management. In: Proceedings of the 11th International Conference on Information Systems for Crisis Response and Management (2014)
28. Preece, J., Rogers, Y., Benyon, D., Holland, S., Carey, T.: Human Computer Interaction. Addison-Wesley, Wokingham (1994)
29. Reuter, C., Pipek, V., Müller, C.: Avoiding crisis in communication: a computer-supported training approach for emergency management. Int. J. Emergency Manage. **6**(3/4), 356–368 (2009)
30. Reuter, C., Pipek, V., Müller, C.: Computer supported collaborative training in crisis communication management. In: Proceedings of the 6th International Conference on Information Systems for Crisis Response and Management (2009)
31. Sinclair, H., Doyle, E.E., Johnston, D.M., Paton, D.: Assessing emergency management training and exercises. Disaster Prev. Manag. **21**(4), 507–521 (2012)
32. Turoff, M., Chumer, M., van de Walle, B.A., Yao, X.: The design of a dynamic emergency response management information systems (DERMIS). The J. Inf. Technol. Theory Appl. **5**(4), 1–35 (2004)

Digital Services Development and the Dynamics of Transformation by Service Providers

Ahmad Ghazawneh

Abstract Service providers are increasingly depending and using digital infrastructure and tools provided by digital platforms to transform their services and develop digital ones that meet the needs of heterogeneous end users. However, while there is an emerging literature of developing digital services, little is known about the dynamics of transformation. Using multiple cases of firms that develop digital services, the digital service taxonomy was synthesized to understand the dynamics of transformation in developing digital services. This study identifies five main dynamics: the services experience, the service process, the service capabilities, the service environment and the service delivery. Each of those dynamics and their associated factors are explored under the objectives of business, interaction and technology. This enables us to extend the existing literature on digital service development in particular and contributes to the research of digital innovation in general.

Keywords Digital services · Service transformation · Platforms · Ecosystems · Development

1 Introduction

The last few years have witnessed a tremendous increase in the value of digital services in the form of 'applications' or 'apps' [1–3]. This value is recognized by various stakeholders within digital ecosystems such as owners of digital platforms, developers, partners and users [4]. These digital services have a very significant role in building the business around digital platforms [4–6]. They will address the needs of

A prior version of this paper has been published in the ISD2018 Proceedings (http://aisel.aisnet.org/isd2018/proceedings2018).

A. Ghazawneh (✉)
Halmstad University, Halmstad, Sweden
e-mail: ahmad.ghazawneh@hh.se; agha@itu.dk

IT University of Copenhagen, Copenhagen, Denmark

the heterogeneous end users [7, 8], and build a competitive advantage over platform competitors [9, 10].

Digital transformation of services involves the digitalization of services from analogue to digital and the change of the actual process generated by digitization [11]. In so doing, the provider of services is applying new technologies that improves the performance of their provided services and increasing their reach to new potential markets and customers [12]. This is a challenge for service providers and their ability to renew the way they make use of digital resources. Thus, service providers must develop and build new methods to develop digital services in the form of 'applications' or 'apps' [2]. This will involve a new envisioning of the customer needs and experiences [8], and operational processes [7] as well as other strategic assets. Although digital technologies are significant for digital service transformation, the processes, knowledge and experience of developing these digital services are equally important which is facilitated by the adoption of digital platforms and ecosystems [1, 13].

The subject of digital services in general and in platforms in particular has been discussed in a growing body of literature [14, 15], such as the evolution of digital services [16], the design of digital services [17], and challenges of in designing digital services [18]. However, little has been done to understand the dynamics of transformation when developing digital services by the service provider. To this end, the focus of this paper is identifying and discussing those dynamics associated with developing digital services. Hence, the research question is: *What are the dynamics of transformation for developing digital services by the service provider?* To address this research question, we have studied fourteen firms from Sweden, Denmark, Norway, Finland, Germany, UAE, Egypt and Jordan.

The paper was initiated with an overview of related literature and a conceptual discussion on the subject of digital platforms and ecosystems as well as the evolution of digital services. Then, this was followed by illustrating the research method, multiple case studies, data collection and analysis. Later the findings are presented in five different dynamics: the service experience, the service process, the service capabilities, the service environment and the service delivery. After that, the analysis and discussion of the dynamics of transformation in developing digital services were presented. Finally, the paper sums up the contributions as well as main conclusions.

2 Related Literature and Conceptual Basis

2.1 Digital Platforms and Ecosystems

The concept of 'platform' has been investigated by researchers in multiple domains [19]. In product development, researchers use this concept to illustrate products that are developed to meet core customers' needs within product family projects [20], while at the same time enable its ability to be changed and modified into derivatives

[21]. This concept of 'platform' enables firms that are not essentially part of the supply chain to build, develop and design complementary assets [20], which is often observed in software development [13, 22–25]. This concept of 'platform' is labelled as "digital platform" and is defined as "the extensible codebase of a software-based system that provides core functionality shared by the modules that interoperate with it and the interfaces through which they interoperate" [16, p. 676].

The platform functionality is extended by incorporating digital modules [19, 26]. These modules are the developed digital services in the form of applications "apps" [27]. The developed digital services mainly contribute to the platform innovation by network effects reinforcement [28], growing the users installed base [29] and by addressing the requirements and specifications of the heterogeneous users of the platform [7, 8] and by enriching the digital ecosystem is formed to serve the digital platform [12].

The digital ecosystem is the functional unit around the digital platform that consist of actors (such as platform owners, development firms and users), and technology elements (such as software platform, boundary resources) which are mutually interdependent [18]. The different actors within these ecosystems are "inter-linked by a common interest in the prosperity of a digital technology for materializing their own product or service innovation" [29, pp. 184–185].

The owner of digital platform provides a digital marketplace or "appstore" to facilitate the exchange of digital services between users and development firms within digital ecosystems [10]. The digital marketplace is described as "a platform component that offers a venue for exchanging applications between developers and end-users belonging to a single or multiple ecosystems" [5, p. 200]. It has a prominent role in matching the development firms, who aim to market and sell their digital services to users who pursue to use these services and enhance their smart devices with new functionalities [12]. These marketplaces also enable the digital transactions features such as service delivery, payments and trust [30, 31].

2.2 The Evolution and Development of Digital Services

Digital services are code-based software modules that are attained and communicated through digital transactions [17]. These services are delivered to the users with the use of the Internet-Protocol (IP) and supported by technological infrastructure [16]. Digital services usually involve parallel transactions that are executed and implemented by the digital service providers. These transactions involve three main activities that include identifying, negotiating and handling the submitted requests from the users of these digital services [12]. Digital services are classified based on the type of users and service providers engaged and has three classifications: (1) business-to-consumer (B2C) (e.g., Netflix, Apple Music), (2) business-to-business (B2B) (e.g., SAP applications, Tableau), and (3) consumer-to-consumer (C2C) (e.g., Popcorn Time, Napster).

There is a dramatic grow of digital services the last few years in the form of applications "apps". They are referred to as platform digital services which are executable pieces of software that are offered as services to the end-users of digital platforms [1]. The development of these digital services aims at extending the digital platform functionality [19, 26], which is a significant innovation element besides their deployment in digital marketplaces "appstores" where these services are exchanged [5, 32, 33]. It is argued that the institutionalization of such digital services is a major success factor in the success of Apple's and Google's digital platforms. This kind of progression is labelled by [34] as "combinatorial evolution" of digital services. It includes the technological development in the form of digital service innovation "applications", technological development "platforms", market innovation "appstores" and hardware innovation "smart devices" [12].

The development of digital services is scientifically different from the development of other types of services. This is due to the availability of digital infrastructure [35]. Consequently, the development of such services goes beyond software development where engaged to 3rd party developers deal with multiple needs and specific requirements to develop digital services. To understand this, we have adopted [17] design taxonomy as in Fig. 1.

There are four fundamental dimensions for the taxonomy: service delivery, service maturity, malleability and pricing/funding. The service delivery describes how the developed service is provided to the users and what is required from the users to be able to use the service. The second dimension, is the malleability, which explains the ability of the developed digital service to be malleable enough when market needs change and user requirements altered. Third is pricing/funding which considers the value associated with the developed digital services and the various revenue capturing approaches. The last dimension service maturity tackles the various developed phases and the technical skills that are required. Service maturity tackles the various developed phases and the technical skills that are required.

This taxonomy is useful for digital service providers and 3rd part developers when developing digital services [17]. The taxonomy provides a general understanding of the science of developing digital services and helps in maintaining a structured view of the development process. It also helps in understating how the development choices

Fig. 1 Digital service design taxonomy (Williams et al. [21])

Design Dimensions	Objectives		
	Business	**Interaction**	**Technology**
Service Delivery	Reducing costs	Mobility Scalability	Efficiency Bandwidth
Malleability	Adaptability opening new markets	Customization	Evolution
Pricing/ Funds	Value-added services	Optimizing Revenue	Commoditization
Service Maturity	Adoption & Scale	HCI standards	Towards full automation

have direct impacts on the business, interaction and technical objectives of the digital service [17].

There are three objectives of the service provider on this taxonomy: business, interaction and technological objectives. First is the business objective, which concerns the financial side of the digital service, customer loyalty and brand establishment and marketing. The second objective is interaction objective, which concerns the user experience part of the digital service and the interaction design process. The third objective is the technology objective, which tackles the technology choice and the associated technical components when developing digital services [17].

3 Research Method

3.1 Research Context and Case Selection

The research reported in this article is based on multiple case study methodology [36] of fourteen firms from Sweden, Denmark, Norway, Finland, Germany, UAE, Egypt and Jordan. The use of multiple case study is suitable for descriptive research studies, theory building and testing [37]. In addition, it is of a great value to extend theoretical perspectives and working with cross-case analysis [38]. In so doing, general research results can be achieved [37]. It is worth mentioning that evidences from the use of multiple case studies can lead to an overall vigorous and compelling generalized results [36]. Table 1 illustrates general information about the studied cases.

3.2 Data Collection and Analysis

Data for this research study was collected through several interviews, meetings, and secondary data sources in the form of documentations which is informed by the case study and the qualitative research approach studies [36]. The number of interviews collected was 27 from 14 different cases which range from at least 1 interview and at most 3 interviews per case as indicated in Table 1. All interviews were face-to-face, semi-structured with an average time of 80 min. The interviews were also recorded, transcribed and verified.

For this study, we have followed the inductive analysis approach [39]. This helped us in understanding the studied subjects without being forced to have pre-conceptions on data while at the same time having scientific integrity [38]. First, we established relations between codes and the current digital service development approaches by the studies case studies. Then, the various events in the studies cases were folded chronologically [40]. This was done during the process of understating the development procedures of digital services in each case [41]. Last, we analyzed the views

Table 1 Case studies and data collection

#	Origin	Headquarter	Founded	Employees	#Digital services	Interviews	Industry
1	Sweden	Stockholm	2007	14	2	2	Finance
2			2016	5	5	3	News
3		Malmö	2011	12	2	2	Entertainment
4		Gothenburg	2001	14	3	1	Health
5	Denmark	Copenhagen	2011	19	5	2	Education
6			2016	7	1	1	Travel
7	Norway	Oslo	2007	21	3	3	Finance
8			2014	8	2	2	Health
9	Germany	Berlin	2016	4	1	2	Education
10			2009	25	7	2	Finance
11	Finland	Helsinki	2008	12	3	1	Real Estate
12	UAE	Dubai	2012	16	3	2	Finance
13	Egypt	Cairo	2014	7	3	2	Shopping
14	Jordan	Amman	2014	10	1	2	Travel

of development teams, how they worked with the development constructs and dealt with them from a development perspective.

4 Results

4.1 The Service Experience

Data from our studied cases revealed that the service experience of customers when interacting with the provided services is very crucial when transforming services into digital interacting ones. This experience forms the perception and feelings of customers when using and with the provided services. Our study identified five types of interactions that shape the service experience. First, the Website Service Experience, a CEO in our studied case "3" explained:

Customers still visit our service website and explore it and they expect all content to be relevant and all information to be there and accurate. We are aware that we must provide two versions of our website, desktop one and mobile one so we can make sure we address all our users.

This was also clarified by another CEO in our studied case "7" pointing out:

Websites are still relevant and they will stay exactly as email services that a lot thought will demolish after the introduction of smart mobile devices. We even have one our services that is only based on a website.

Second is the App Service Experience. Data from all our studied case indicated that between 65 and 85% of their users access the provided service via the digital service application or "app", a product manager at our studied case "8" stated:

At the beginning in 2010 we thought we could live by only providing the service in a mobile friendly website. We were wrong, the native app that we developed late 2011 was a hit as most of our customers are using it and it gives another type of experience.

Third is the Social Media Experience. Using various social media channels become essential for businesses. We have found that all of our studied cases user at least three different social media channels to cope up with customers. A marketing manager from our studied case "9" illustrated:

Listen, I'm serious, we use, Facebook, Linkedin, Twitter, Snapchat, Instagram and YouTube. To form the whole experience of our service customers we must be wherever our customers are. Simply, they have to find us where they go.

Fourth is the Internet Bot Experience. Seven of our studied cases reported the use of Internet Bot or Web Robot when interacting with their customers at some level. This enables them to perform simple interaction or structurally repetitive tasks that can save time, efforts and resources. A CIO at the studied case "14" explained:

Over the last three years, we studied all our customers' requests and develop some categories. We programmed our web bot and are able to deal with a lot of customers interactions without any physical intervention from our staff here.

4.2 The Service Process

The service process refers to the flow of activities and their mechanisms in which a service is delivered to the customer. We have identified three varieties of service processes while firms transform to provide digital services to their customers. We have found that the three identified services processes are experienced by all of our studied firms. First, is the *Standardized Service Process*. This type of service process includes a set of standardized activities that are performed the service customer. This type of service process allows the service provider to act and perform their operations with high efficiency. A COO at our studied case "9" explained:

> We have been operating since 2000 in the insurance business. We experience those processes for example, initiating an incident claim. But when you go digital its totally different, old processes might differ, new processes that are not standard can become standard.

Our study also revealed that the *Standardized Service Process* has three properties: (a) its identical (b) occurs frequently, and (c) easy to accomplish. This was explained by a manager at the studied case "3":

> These service processes occur in a daily base when our customer interact with our app and they are accomplished in a matter of minutes. If we are unable to develop them in a that manner we risk losing customers satisfaction as they are the core of our service.

Second, is the *Semi-Standardized Service Process*. We have found that the second type of service process has the following properties: (a) semi-identical, (b) occurs less frequently, and (c) more complex than the *Standardized Service Process*. A product owner at our studied case "7" explained:

> We have service processes that look similar to some extent but they are not. For this reason, we have to be able to handle them differently in our digital service while finding a common ground.

Third, is the *Non-Standardized Service Process*. This type of service process is new to the digital service owners and they vary accordingly based on users' needs and behaviors. Our data analysis revealed that this type of service process is very complex and require a lot of attention by the service provider and it needs human intervention at some point during the service execution. This was emphasized by a manager at the studied case "3":

> These are the most complex ones, imagine you have 50,000 daily users who have changing activities.

4.3 The Service Capabilities

The service capability refers to the potential of a particular service to be developed and used. We have identified three main service capabilities that are significant for service providers and users in digital service transformation. First, is the *Technology*

Capability. This type of capability considers the technology that is used to design and develop the service. Our data analysis revealed that the type of technology affects the user perception, interaction and behavior. A CTO from our studied case "12" explained:

> I want to say that users are clever, many of them know if our used web-technology is old or new, slow or quick, secure or not. Thus, we are very selective when selecting a technology for our digital services.

Second is the *Platform Capability*. We have found that the type of platform that the digital service integrates to is very essential in digital transformation. There are multiple platforms that are used and each of those platforms has its own capabilities and features. Our data analysis shows that all of our studied case designs their services to be integrated to at least two platforms. A CTO at out studied case "10" illustrated:

> You know in UAE and Dubai in particular our user base is fragmented. This means we have iOS users, Android users and also a large amount use BlackBerry OS. So, we have to accommodate all users and work with three different platforms.

Third is the *Hardware-Device Capability*. There are fragmentation of hardware and devices across platforms. For example, Apple's iOS has 25 devices, Google's Android 8600 devices, Blackberry's OS 33 devices and Microsoft's Windows Mobile 132 devices. Findings based on our studied cases revealed that they have dealt with this differently to accommodate user needs. A CEO at our studied case "12" explained:

> We are with a limited budget and we have to prioritize, we can't develop services for all Android devices, different screen sizes, resolutions, CPUs, etc. So, we have to pick up the most used devices by our users and accommodate them.

4.4   The Service Environment

The service environment signals the intended digital market segment and the positioning of the service. For example, a digital bank app indicates it is serving clients between 18 and 34 years old. Our data analysis identified three factors that determines the service environment. First, is the *User Experience*, which is determined by the user group, their skills and needs. We have found that 10 of our studied cases focus on one particular user group while the rest have several user groups and deal with multiple *User Experiences*. A marketing manager at our studied case "7" explained:

> We are focused on Millennials, so we develop a user experience strategy for those between 18 and 26. We studied them, what they like what they hate and design accordingly.

Second, is the *Service Integration* which corresponds to the ability of the service to integrate other services from multiple suppliers. Our data analysis shows that the ability to integrate other services in the main provided service can determine the degree of adoption and amount of usage of a particular service. This was emphasized by an informant, from our studied case "14":

Once we integrate social services in our app, the growth of user increased dramatically.

This was also emphasized by a CIO from our studied case "11":

It goes beyond Facebook or Twitter integration, there are many services that we have to consider integrating to our digital provided services when we design them. We take into consideration the types of users we deal with and their current and future needs. So, I can tell you, the integration and the way we integrate is a very big deal to our growth and success.

Third, is the *Service Customization,* which corresponds to the ability of the service to be customized by its users. Our data analysis indicates that the degree of customization varies based on two factors which are the service industry and users. A CTO, from our studied case "17" emphasized:

We deal with a complex user group that needs everything to be customized based on their need or even moods. We thought that's difficult but we have to deal with it.

4.5   The Service Delivery

The service delivery signals the set of configuration and organizational networks that are developed to deliver services to end user that satisfy their needs. We have found that the service delivery of digital services is focused on digital application marketplaces as the main delivery channel and interaction point between digital service provider and digital service users. We have identified three main factors that play considerable role in the delivery of digital services. First, is the *Service Delivery Cost,* which determines the cost of the service after being delivered by the end user. The factor that we have found which is added to this cost is the commission rates or cut that is taking by the digital application marketplaces such as Apple's Appstore of Google Play. A marketing manager is our studied case "5" explained:

When we develop our services, we have to always increase the price to end customers because there is this huge cut that is taken by Apple and Google, add to this also the transaction cost when we receive our payments at the end of each month from them. In addition, sometimes we have to set our service free for Android users and paid for iOS users which might makes things complex little bit.

The second identified factor is *Service Delivery Review*, which corresponds to the ability of end users to interact directly with the digital service provider and the other users via the digital application marketplace. This was explained by a manager at our studied case "8" illustrated:

Users can try our digital services or buy them. They have the ability to leave their reviews and rate us. This is very sensitive as these users are verified by the appstore and they are real users which are trusted by the other future users of our service.

The third identified factor is *Service Delivery Infrastructure*, which identifies the set of technology infrastructure that are supporting the delivery of the digital service to end users. This was clarified by an IT expert from our studied case 6:

Pus notifications is one of the most important issue in our app business. It will let us send notifications to users via the platform and keep them updated. It is complex and cost a lot of money to maintain but it's very essential.

5 Results

There are several dynamics that digital service providers work and consider with when developing services for their end users within digital platforms. Our empirical based understanding help in identifying five major dynamics at a service level: the service experience, the service process, the service capabilities, the service environment and the service delivery. Set of actors for each dynamic were also identified. These actors were classified and illustrated under three objectives: business, interaction and technology based on the digital services taxonomy [17]. In the discussion below, each dynamic was thoroughly discussed and all of the associated factors were explained (Table 2).

5.1 The Service Experience

Digital services providers are required to consider the experiences of end users when developing digital services. There are four main factors that have to be taken into consideration. Two of those factors are *Interaction* factors: first is the *Social Media Experience*. This identifies the degree of integration between the developed digital service and the various social media tools, technologies and networks that became a core part of the overall users' experience. The variety of the integrated social media

Table 2 The dynamics of transformation in development of digital services

	Dynamics	Objectives		
		Business	Interaction	Technology
1	The service experience	*N/A*	*– Social media Experience* *– Internet Bot Experience*	*–Website Service Experience* *– App Service Experience*
2	The service process	*– Semi Standardized Service Process*	*– Standardized Service Process*	*– Non-Standardized Service Process*
3	The service capabilities	*– Platform Capability*	*– Hardware-Device Capability*	*– Technology Capability*
4	The service environment	*– Service Integration*	*– User Experience*	*– Service Customization*
5	The service delivery	*– Service Delivery Cost*	*– Service Delivery Review*	*– Service Delivery Infrastructure*

channels and the degree of interaction using those channels will affect the use and the degree of adoption of the digital service by the end users. Second, is the *Internet Bot Experience*. It is found that this is an essential factor for interaction between service providers and service users within the digital service. Its importance lays in its ability for prompt feedback handling and follow up compilations.

The other two factors are *Technology* based. First is the *Website Service Experience*. It clearly indicates that the service provider has to address the needs of users based on the technology they used, for example, desktop web browsing and mobile web browsing. The second factor is the *App Service Experience,* which explains the necessity of developing an application based digital service in addition the web-based ones. This is due to the fact to the large number of end users who tend to use mobile devices for the consumption of their used digital services.

5.2 The Service Process

The second dynamic that providers of digital services has to consider while developing their services in a transformation context is the *Service Process*. It entails the flow of activities and their mechanisms in which a service is delivered to the customer. Three factors have been identified. First, is the *Interaction* objective which considers the *Standardized Service Process,* that allows the provided service to be performed high efficiency due to its standardized manner that allows common and stable interaction with the end users. Second, is the *Business* objective, that corresponds to the *Semi Standardized Service Process* which is semi-identical, occurs less frequently which entails new business opportunity for the service provider. Third, is the *Technology* objective which entails the *Non-Standardized Service Process.* This type of service process is new to the digital service owners and they vary accordingly based on users' needs and behaviors. It needs the service provider to use an advanced technology to develop its services in accordance to this factor.

5.3 The Service Capabilities

The third dynamic is the *Service Capabilities* which refers to the potential of a particular service to be developed and used. The *Business* objective for this dynamic regards the *Platform Capability* that determines to which platforms the service provider is integrating its digital services. For example, iOS, Android, Blackberry and Windows Mobile. These multiple platforms are used and each of those platforms has its own capabilities, features and business objectives. The second factor is *Hardware-Device Capability* which is associated with the *Interaction* objective which refers to the fragmentation of hardware and devices across platforms in which the digital services to be developed for and integrated in. The more hardware-device the digital service is integrated in the more the interaction between the end users and the service provider.

The last factor is the *Technology Capability* which considers the technology that is used to design and develop the service. For example, XCode, Java, to name a few. The service provider has to determine the robustness, the performance, the adaptability and the efficiency of the used technology in developing the digital services.

5.4 The Service Environment

This is the fourth dynamic and it signals the intended digital market segment and the positioning of the service. The *Business* objective for this dynamic regards the *Service Integration* factor that corresponds to the ability of the service to integrate other services from multiple suppliers which is very essential for the service provider to expand the growth of their user base and to entail to different options of business models. The *Interaction* objective regards the *User Experience* factor which is determined by the user group, their skills and needs and is highly connected to the *Business* objective at the user growth level. Providers of digital services has to identify to what user group(s) they are developing their services in advance as this determination might affect the development processes and is recommended at early stages. The *Interaction* object regards the *Service Customization* which corresponds to the ability of the service to be customized by its users. In this regard, providers of digital services analyze their correspondent service industry and their end-users to develop and customize their digital service accordingly.

5.5 The Service Delivery

The *Service Delivery* dynamic is a set of configuration and organizational networks that are developed to deliver services to end user that satisfy their needs. Its *Business* objective is mainly regarding the *Service Delivery Cost* factor that determines the cost of the service after being delivered by the end user. Providers of digital services have to take into consideration not only the cost of their digital service delivery but also the cost of the after-delivery cost. For example, in Apple's Appstore, there is the commission rates or cut that is taking by the digital application marketplaces to deliver the service and there is the In-App purchase to deliver other features after the digital service has been deployed for the end users.

Then the Interaction objective that regards the *Service Delivery Review* which is the ability of end users to interact directly with the digital service provider and the other users. Digital service providers have to be aware to develop interaction features that facilitate the review process by the end users of their digital services. Last is the *Technology* objective that details the *Service Delivery Infrastructure* which identifies the set of technology infrastructure that are supporting the delivery of the digital service to end users. Digital service providers have to work at different level of

Infrastructure for example, platform level, ecosystem level and digital marketplace level to assure the delivery of their digital services to the end users as designed.

6 Conclusions

The research study reported in this article has a number of contributions. First, the perspective on digital services innovation extends the existing literature on digital service development in particular [14, 17, 35] and contributes to the research of digital innovation in general [10, 16]. Second, the reported results provide a new understanding on the development of digital services and illustrates new study agenda in digital ecosystems. This study identifies the four main dynamics that developers and providers of digital services has to take into consideration when developing digital services. Finally, this research contributes to the overall research stream in digital innovation and development [4] by identifying the dynamics and their associated factors that affect the process of developing digital services by service providers [12].

In this paper, we studied the dynamics of transformation for developing digital services by the service providers by synthesizing the digital service perspective [14, 17, 35] while designing digital services for digital platforms [1, 10, 16]. The study was based on studying fourteen firms from Sweden, Denmark, Norway, Finland, Germany, UAE, Egypt and Jordan. We have developed an empirically grounded understanding of the dynamics. In addition, we have identified set of dynamics and associated factors and classified them under three objectives: business, interaction and technology. There are several opportunities to our work that could be addressed through future studies. For example, studying develop digital services for specialized industries such as health-care or banking by focusing on one single unique case or multiple cases within the same industry.

References

1. Ghazawneh, A., Henfridsson, O.: Balancing platform control and external contribution in third-party development: The boundary resources model. Inf. Syst. J. **23**(2), 173–192 (2013)
2. Kim, H. J., Kim, I., Lee, H.G.: The success factors for App store-like platform businesses from the perspective of third-party developers: an empirical study based on a dual model framework. In: Proceedings of Pacific Asia Conference on Information Systems (PACIS) (2010)
3. Ghazawneh, A., Mansour, M., Bergquist, M.: Strategizing in digital application marketplaces. In: The 29th Australasian Conference on Information Systems (ACIS2018), Sydney, Australia (2018)
4. Eaton, B.D., Elaluf-Calderwood, S., Sørensen, C., Yoo, Y.: Distributed tuning of boundary resources: The case of Apple's iOS service system. MIS Q.: Special Issue on Service Innovation in a Digital Age **39**(1), 217–243 (2015)
5. Ghazawneh, A., Henfridsson, O.: A paradigmatic analysis of digital application marketplaces. J. Inf. Technol. **30**(3), 198–208 (2015)

6. Messerschmitt, D.G., Szyperski, C.: Software Ecosystem: Understanding an Indispensable Technology and Industry. MIT press (2003)
7. Adomavicius, G., Bockstedt, J.C., Gupta, A., Kauffman, R.J.: Technology roles and paths of influence in an ecosystem model of technology evolution. Inf. Technol. Manage. **8**(2), 185–202 (2007)
8. Evans, D.S., Hagiu, A., Schmalensee, R.: Invisible engines: how software platforms drive innovation and transform industries. MIT Press, Cambridge, MA (2006)
9. Meyer, M.H., Seliger, R.: Product platforms in software development. Sloan Manag. Rev. **40**(1), 61–74 (1998)
10. West, J., Mace, M.: Browsing as the killerapp: explaining the rapid success of Apple's iPhone. Telecommun. Policy **34**, 270–286 (2010)
11. Agarwal, R., Guodong, G., DesRoches, C., Jha, A.K.: The digital transformation of healthcare: current status and the road ahead. Inform. Systems Res. **21**(4), 796–809 (2010)
12. Ghazawneh, A.: The challenges of designing digital services for multiple mobile platforms. In: Proceedings of European Conference on Information Systems, ECIS 2016. Istanbul, Turkey, June 2016
13. Baldwin, C.Y., Woodard, C.J.: The architecture of platforms: a unified view. In: Gawer, A. (ed.) Platforms, Markets and Innovation, pp. 19–44. Edward Elgar, London, UK (2009)
14. Barrett, M., Davidson, E., Prabhu, J., Vargo, S.L.: Service innovation in the digital age: key contributions and future research". MIS Q. **39**(1), 135–154 (2015)
15. Saarikko, T.: Digital platform development: a service-oriented perspective. In: ECIS 2015 Completed Research Papers. Paper 152 (2015)
16. Tiwana, A., Ramesh, B.: E-services: problems, opportunities, and digital platforms. In: Proceedings of 34th Hawaii International Conference on System Sciences, 2001
17. Williams, K., Chatterjee, S., Rossi, M.: Design of emerging digital services: a taxonomy. Eur. J. Inf. Syst. **17**, 505–517 (2008)
18. Ghazawneh, A., Henfridsson, O.: Micro-strategizing in platform ecosystems: a multiple case study. In: Proceedings of International Conference on Information Systems, ICIS 2011, Shanghai, China, Dec 2011
19. Baldwin, C., Clark, K.: Design rules: the power of modularity. MIT Press, Cambridge, MA (2000)
20. Gawer, A.: Platforms, Markets and Innovation. Edward Elgar, Cheltenham, UK (2009)
21. Wheelwright, S.C., Clark, K.B.: Creating project plans to focus product development. Harvard Bus. Rev. **70**(2), 67–83 (1992)
22. Franke, N., von Hippel, E.: Satisfying heterogeneous user needs via innovation toolkits: the case of Apache security software. Res. Policy **32**(7), 1199–1215 (2003)
23. Gawer, A., Cusumano, M.: How companies become platform leaders. MIT Sloan Manag. Rev. **49**(2), 1–28 (2008)
24. Morris, C., Ferguson, C.: How architecture wins technology wars. Harvard Bus. Rev. **71**(2), 86–96 (1993)
25. West, J.: How Open is open enough? Melding proprietary and open source platform strategies. Res. Policy **32**, 1259–1285 (2003)
26. Sanchez, R., Mahoney, J.: Modularity, flexibility, and knowledge management in product organization and design. Strateg. Manag. J. **17**(1), 63–76 (1996)
27. Tiwana, A., Konsynski, B., Bush, A.: Research commentary: platform evolution: coevolution of platform architecture, governance, and environmental dynamics. Inf. Syst. Res. **21**(4), 675–687 (2010)
28. Katz, M., Shapiro, K.: System competition and network effects. J. Econ. Perspect. **8**(2), 93–115 (1994)
29. Selander, L., Henfridsson, O., Svahn, F.: Capability search and redeem across digital ecosystems. J. Inf. Technol. **28**(3), 183–197 (2013)
30. Amberg, M., Thiessen, I., Lang, M. and Belkius, B.: Mobile application Q4 marketplaces—an investigation from customers' perspective. In: Proceeding of MKWI (2010)

31. Kazan, E., Damsgaard, J.: A Framework for analyzing digital payment as a multi-sided plat-
    form: a study of three european NFC solutions. In: Proceedings of European Conference on
    Information Systems, ECIS 2013, Utrecht, The Netherlands, June 2013
32. Sako, M.: Globalization of knowledge-intensive professional services. Commun. ACM **52**(7),
    31–33 (2009)
33. Vargo, S.L., Lusch, R.F.:. Chapter 1: Service-dominant logic foundations of E-novation. In:
    Pattinson, H.M., Low, D.R. (eds.) E-Novation for Competitive Advantage in Collaborative
    Globalization: Technologies for Emerging E-Business Strategies, pp. 1–15. IGI Global, Her-
    shey, PA (2011)
34. Arthur, W.B.: The nature of technology: what it is and how it evolves. Free Press, New York
    (2009)
35. Lyytinen, K., Yoo, Y., Varshney, U., Ackerman, M.S., Davis, G., Avital, M., Robey, D., Sawyer,
    S., Sorensen, C.: Surfing the next wave: design and implementation challenges of ubiquitous
    computing environments. Commun. Assoc. Inf. Syst. **13**(14), 697–716 (2004)
36. Yin, R.: Case study research: design and methods. Sage Inc., London (2009)
37. Benbasat, I., Goldstein, D.K., Mead, M.: The case research strategy in studies of information
    systems. MIS Q. **11**(3), 368–386 (1987)
38. Eisenhardt, K.: Building theories from case study research. Acad. Manag. Rev. **14**(4), 532–550
    (1989)
39. Strauss, A., Corbin, J.: Basics of qualitative research. Grounded theory procedures and tech-
    niques. Sage, Newbury Park (1990)
40. Langley, A.: Strategies for theorizing from process data. Acad. Manag. Rev. **24**(4), 691–710
    (1999)
41. Kirsch, L.J.: The management of complex tasks in organizations: controlling the systems
    development process. Organ. Sci. **7**(1), 1–21 (1996)

How Do Practitioners Understand External Platforms and Services? A Grounded Theory Investigation

Anar Bazarhanova, Jesse Yli-Huumo and Kari Smolander

Abstract In this article, we investigate how practitioners understand external platforms, whose core offering is shared and utilized by a number of heterogeneous and interconnected organizations in an ecosystem. We especially look into situations where organizations wish to extend their own capability instead of building services that extend the functionality of the platform. Such dependencies to external platforms can be envisioned as the contemporary evolution from traditional outsourcing service models. We interviewed twenty-four practitioners from eight IT organizations and discovered a considerable ambiguity in understanding of what are the external platforms utilized by the organizations. We further elaborate that the diversified meanings that various stakeholders give to the concept of external platforms, can hinder efficient communication and may have implications on important strategic decision making.

Keywords External platform · Industry platform · Ecosystem · Dependency · Integration

A prior version of this paper has been published in the ISD2018 Proceedings (http://aisel.aisnet. org/isd2014/proceedings2018).

A. Bazarhanova (✉) · J. Yli-Huumo
Aalto University, Espoo, Finland
e-mail: anar.bazarhanova@aalto.fi

J. Yli-Huumo
e-mail: jessey187@gmail.com

K. Smolander
Lappeenranta University of Technology, Lappeenranta, Finland
e-mail: kari.smolander@lut.fi

© Springer Nature Switzerland AG 2019
B. Andersson et al. (eds.), *Advances in Information Systems Development*,
Lecture Notes in Information Systems and Organisation 34,
https://doi.org/10.1007/978-3-030-22993-1_7

1 Introduction

There is a growing interest on platform thinking [1, 2], which has resulted in a cumulative knowledge on platform ecosystems and their governance [3–5]. However, there are fewer attempts to investigate the companies that are not dominant players [6–8], but need to integrate to various infrastructures and platforms to sustain or extend their business capabilities [9]. These non-focal firms, from the viewpoint of platforms, are platform-utilizing businesses that do not develop platform capability extensions, have no influence on the platform whatsoever, but depend massively on it.

Our research focus departs from the majority of contemporary platform ecosystems research in two aspects. First, we position non-focal actors—subordinate ecosystem participants that are not in the position of power and control to influence the changes in the ecosystem, at the center of our attention. Second, we are interested in integrations with external platforms—when the core offering of the platform is shared and utilized by a number of heterogeneous actors to build services that extend not the functionality of the platform, but their own capability. For example, the travel management industry has platforms that are jointly established by one or many large organizations and then opened to other businesses of any size. Various infrastructures and platforms are constantly evolving, proliferating and becoming more integrated [10]. Blockchain and Internet-of-Things will bring integrated platforms that force firms to utilize them without any control of the platforms. As platforms grow bigger and form monopolies, smaller firms are constrained to interact with big players. As scholars [11, 12] put it, the management of an enterprise-wide digital infrastructure is quite impossible to do isolated from wider platform ecosystems. For example a company using Google services will be somewhat dependent on how the Google platform ecosystem evolves. This can be explained as an indirect or cross-side network effect [13], i.e., the more users the platform has, the more valuable it is for platform-utilizing firms. Once firms integrate into a platform ecosystem, they become dependent on the decisions of the platform owner, which is similar to vendor lock-in.

Success of many businesses in the future is dependent on their ability to leverage the power of innovations coming for the outside, which are often global, remote and dynamic. A new breed of outsourcing—the external platform dependency can emerge as a monopoly-like industry platform, integration with which is critical to the thriving of a non-focal actor. An example of public API program shutdown at Netflix shows high volatility of the platform and its boundary resources. The significance of dependencies to external platforms is not yet well understood from the viewpoint of platform users. We address this gap by analyzing how practitioners give meaning to their integrations with external platforms. The objective of our study was to understand how practitioners understand external platforms utilized in their firms. The meanings and definitions of external platforms among stakeholders within and across organizations are interpreted into higher level conceptualizations. Grounded Theory with no a priori hypotheses was used as the inductive research method.

2 Background

2.1 Platforms

The notion "platform" is relative to its design, utility and the environment of its use, which could often cause confusion. There are a number of studies on platforms evolution [14, 15] their governance [16], the leadership [17] of big players like Google [18], Amazon [19], Apple [20] and organizational decisions to adopt platform strategies [21].

We adopt the definition of Parker and Van Alstyne [13] and define a digital platform "as the components used in common across a product family whose functionality can be extended by applications and is subject to network effects" [7, 22]. Gawer and Cusumano [2] categorize platforms in two predominant types: internal or company-specific platforms, and external or industry-wide platforms. The authors define external platforms as "products, services, or technologies developed by one or more firms, and which serve as foundations upon which a larger number of firms can build further complementaries". Throughout the manuscript we imply the aforementioned definition, however, narrowing the focus in two critical areas and discussing about so-called shared external platforms. First, the extant literature tends to focus on challenges of platform leaders and their competitors. In this study, we investigate external platforms from the other end i.e., the perspective of non-focal actors. Non-focal actors are ecosystem participants that do not have any control over the offering of an external platform. The second aspect is in the context of platform utilization. Unlike Gawer and Cusumano [2], that discuss about industry platforms as a base for complementary products development for the platform e.g., solution extensions built on top of SAP platform that can be sold to third parties, we look at non-focal firms that utilize industry platforms for their own needs. An example case is a popular messenger application WeChat, China's App for everything, which operates as a platform for providers of payments, bookings management, transport and other services. There the third-party developers of the platform consciously choose to be non-focal, but their initial business intention is to develop complementary products primarily for their own business.

Double-sided markets where the role of the platform is purely to facilitate exchange or trade, without the possibility for other players to innovate on complementary markets, seem to belong to the supply-chain category. Innovation moves of non-focal actors may be opportunistic at times, due to the need to act fast to tap into new capabilities. Thus, dependencies and long-term consequences created from integrations into platforms are not always fully anticipated. As the relationships between non-focal businesses and platform orchestrators (i.e. owners) can be characterized as asymmetric [23], non-focals are forced to continuously accommodate quick adjustments to changes introduced by platform owners [24]. When the number of reasonable platform choices in the market falls to one or only a few, then that only reasonable choice become the de facto standard, also known as its dominant design [25]. While many scholars study how the dominant design emerges and platforms become industry leaders, in our research we wish to draw attention to the need for the knowledge on how "ordinary" firms interact with them.

2.2 Integrations

The motivation for our work is in line with the problem described by Rolland et al. [11]. They discuss a similar problem in the management of external industry platforms as part of a user organization's (non-focal) digital infrastructure and work processes. The authors suggest that while the studies on platforms utilization from the non-focal perspective are not so prevalent, yet, organizations are increasingly adopting digital platforms, "such as Google's G Suite and Microsoft's SharePoint, as central components of their digital infrastructures to support work processes and innovation efforts" [11]. Organizations can integrate with an external platform to sustain their business when the market is disrupted or to extend their offering by combining various resources. These resources can be attributed to some valuable, rare, inimitable and non-substitutable [26], resources (data), unique competences (knowledge), services (methods and algorithms) and people (customer base). Using the service composability principle software companies might consciously or by chance become dependent on platforms using which they build their innovations.

Semantically, the choice between the concepts of "integrating with" and "integrating into" depend on how equal the two things being integrated are. From perspective of platform owner, all heterogeneous ecosystem participants become part of the ecosystem i.e., integrating the smaller ones into the platform ecosystem. Although non focal ecosystem participants understand their obedient position, zooming in into their innovation habitat, the platform is only one component of their business landscape. When the external platform becomes the infrastructure of the firm, consequently, it might become virtually impossible to substitute or eliminate the integration. Cusumano [27] provides a good illustrative example of actors' integrations with platform ecosystems: real estate agencies or retail shops that build applications that incorporate Google Maps and, therefore, tie their applications to Google's platform. When firms plan to integrate into a global, multinational and remote platform, their relationships can hardly be called a partnership. Agreements and terms of service may include some standard performance metrics like service availability and response time, but rarely assure responsibility, continuity and business decisions-driven changes. Success of non-focal firms is dependent on their abilities to leverage the platform offering and their organizational response strategies. Managing external platforms while organizations are increasingly adopting them as part of their infrastructures is a costly and highly uncertain process [11]. As supported by Rolland et al. [11], the research from non-focal viewpoint is almost non-existent, yet, it has a high potential of gathering important insights for research and practice.

3   Methods

It is important to state that our study commenced with a different research question than we are reporting in this manuscript. Initially, we wanted to investigate how the utilization of external platforms can be explained. We then proceeded with data collection as explained in the paragraph below. During the data collection and analysis we recognized the emerging phenomena—divergent understanding among interviewees. Thus, the findings we report in this manuscript answer the following research question: How do practitioners understand external platforms utilized in their firms? In order to explore the understanding of practitioners on external platforms, we used the Grounded Theory method [28]. We chose this qualitative theory-forming method as the area of interest is complex and the perspective is unexplored. An interpretive research methodology also allows to investigate a phenomenon within its real-life context.

We arranged meetings with interviewees for data collection, formulated initial research objectives and interview themes. We chose an exploratory focus with no specific theory in mind. Most of the interviews were conducted together by the first two authors. While the data analysis and coding were done primarily by the first author, a number of discussions on theoretical concepts elicitation were held together with all authors. We had discussions with 24 industry experts from 8 organizations, see Table 1.

The organizations vary by sectors: telecommunications, finance, software development, research, municipalities and ministries. The company sizes vary from 10 to 40,000 employees operating mostly in Finland and the Nordics. The selection of companies was based on convenience sampling.

3.1   Data Collection and Analysis

We planned the interviews as semi-structured, more in the form of a discussion. We used the interview instrument as a guide to discuss the topics such as "external platform utilization examples in the company", "reasons for the integration with this platform", "problems and benefits of this integration". The interviews were conducted during the period of 6 months and lasted between 35 and 95 min. The interviews followed the funnel model principle [29]—from open to more specific questions. Each interview began by asking general questions regarding the position of the interviewees, their background, experience and the projects they are managing, and then, proceeding to the questions on external platforms identification. The list of interviewees with their corresponding organization and positions is provided in Table 1. The interviews were conducted face-to-face at company facilities, except one video-conference call with A11 and A22.

We analyzed the gathered data with a qualitative data coding and analysis tool, Atlas.ti. The first step of Grounded Theory [28] was open coding, where we went

Table 1 Interviewees

ID	Industry	Position
A1	Telecom	Head of enterprise architecture
A2	Telecom	Director, corporate solutions
A3	Telecom	development manager, corporate solutions
A4	Telecom	Chief digital officer
A5	Telecom	Manager, data services
A6	Telecom	Development manager
A7	Telecom	Head of online performance
A8	Telecom	Vice president, broadband and entertainment business
A9	Finance	Head of point of sale, service engineering
A10	Finance	Head of quality assurance, merchant services
A11	Finance	SVP digital innovation
A12	Finance	Senior manager, digital practices
A13	Ministry	Development manager
A14	Ministry	Main architect
A15	Ministry	Service manager
A16	ISV	Development manager
A17	Research	Main architect
A18	Research	Architect
A19	Research	IT services manager
A20	ISV1	CEO
A21	ISV2	CEO
A22	ISV2	CTO
A23	Municipality	Project manager, head of e-services program
A24	Municipality	Main architect

line-by-line in each of 24 interviews and labelled the pieces of information. For example, we coded the quote "but we have almost all of the platforms somehow in-house"—as attributing the external platform to its physical location outside the premises of the company. We extracted quotes from all transcriptions that we believed were relevant regarding the research topic such as the names of the platforms that interviewees identified as external platforms. The next step was axial coding, where we systematically browsed through the open codes to find the relations between them, merged or disaggregated relevant concepts.

Table 2 presents the examples of what the interviewees identified as "external platform"—open coding data (column 2), labelled with the corresponding axial coding indicative concept (column 3) e.g., physical location, lack of customization, outsourced solution. Our goal was to let the understanding of the phenomenon emerge from the interviews. Finally, in selective coding [30] we selected and described the central phenomenon, "external platforms interpretations" in the light of core categories. The goal was to integrate and refine the degree to which a concept varies in its dimensions. Excerpts in Table 2 are provided as illustrative examples. By merging and recombining the labels from the third column we discuss higher level conceptualizations below.

4 Findings

One of the first striking observations we noticed was that almost each interviewee gave different examples of what they considered to be external platforms. Even the respondents from the same organization suggested different cases: A17 discussed about the services from Google, Microsoft and Dropbox; A18 considered their Platform as a Service (PaaS) for billing as the most suitable case, whereas A19 managed to interpret the external platform phenomenon immediately. Table 2 demonstrates example excerpts. The differentiation between dedicated *aaS models (i.e., a collective term that refers to the delivery of a centrally hosted service over a network and on a subscription basis) and external platforms was particularly challenging for business-unit professionals. Obviously, the difficulties in distinguishing the specifics of deployment and service models may have been due to incomplete technical expertise; yet, most of the interviewees have had managing and executive positions in organizations that operate in technology industry.

An example excerpt below suggests that external platforms are seen as something the organization did not develop, i.e., software products from various vendors. In contrast, tech-savvy professionals could clearly recognize the distinctions of external platforms and the types of dependencies to them.

A2: *"Do you know how many external platforms we have? We do not develop anything ourselves."*

Another response below is from an informed interviewee critically reflecting on the differences between dedicated instances of external platforms (Salesforce, SaaS) and a shared external platform (eBay for merchants).

A5: *"our BSS solutions, is more or less like a cloud service, but more like a dedicated cloud service for us [Telco], and from my point of view it is not a real cloud service [external]."*

To summarize, we identified four categories of disparate interpretations on external platforms. Table 3 presents the mapping of axial coding to selective coding categories and in the section below we explain each category (i.e., dimension) of practitioners understanding on external platforms.

Table 2 Representative excerpts from interviews are presented in column 2. Axial codes in the column 3 are based on the corresponding interpretations and explanations of the interviewees

ID	Position	External platforms identified examples	External platform is primarily a/an
A1	Architect	"We have almost all of the platforms somehow in-house", "Salesforce would be that kind of [external] platform"	Instance physically running externally Instance from big vendors
A2	Director, corporate solutions	"You can name any brand and most likely we have it"	Instance from big vendors
A3	Development manager, corporate solutions	Google Azure	Instance for service development, instance from big vendors
A4	Chief digital officer	SAP CRM solution	Instance from big vendors
A5	Manager, data services	"Our BSS solutions, is more or less like a cloud service, but more like a dedicated cloud service of ours, and from my point of view is not a real cloud service"	Instance for service development, instance that is not under direct control
A6	Development manager	"Because when you have this kind of monopoly as [name] have had, the problem is that there is no driving force to develop it"	The only choice platform
A7	Head of online performance	"Whether that is explicitly external, or, a service that we buy from a company and we integrate into, there is, tons of, different types of providers that we use for, say, uh, order handling, billing systems"	Black box service
A8	VP, broadband and entertainment business	Content delivery platforms	Instance from big vendors
A9	Head of point of sale, service engineering	ECR machines, ERP systems, MasterCard, Visa, hardware i.e. payment terminals	Instance that is not developed/maintained by them, IT outsourcing, Instance from big vendors
A10	Head of quality assurance, merchant services	AWS real-time analytics	Black box service

(continued)

Table 2 (continued)

ID	Position	External platforms identified examples	External platform is primarily a/an
A11	SVP digital innovation	"But we are not using any AWS, not Google for production services or other kind of open platform trends. I think there is a fair question if we want to extend something on top of something, why should we do that. How much value can that bring us?"	Instance for service development
A12	Senior manager, digital practices	"That is not really a platform but a service out of the platform"	Instance from big vendors
A13	Development manager	"What is the role of Facebook in governmental organizations?"	Not under direct control
A14	Main architect	"Security issues, so we do not really buy that as a service or rely on external service providers"	Instance that is not developed by them, Instance from big vendors
A15	Service manager	SAP	Instance from big vendors
A16	Development manager	"Something like that or, or whatever product that is, that is they are using via web"	Instance physically running externally
A17	Main architect	Microsoft, Google, HR platforms, billing, invoicing services	Instance from big vendors,
A18	Architect	Billing platform	Instance physically running externally,
A19	IT services manager	Capability level platforms	Receiving as a service, IT outsourcing
A20	CEO	Google transit	That is not developed and maintained by them
A21	CEO	MailChimp, Trello, Office 360	Instance that is not under direct control
A22	CTO	eID platform	The only choice platform
A23	Project manager, head of e-services program	eID platform	The only choice platform, Instance from big vendors
A24	Main architect	"There is always some learning to do, and some problems usually arise. Suddenly you find that there's some integrations to make and some systems to upgrade, they don't support certain protocols"	Instance with a limited customization

Table 3 Mapping of axial codes to selective coding categories

ID	Axial coding	Selective coding categories
A1	Instance physically running externally	Externally deployed
A2	Instance from big vendors	Externally developed, deployed
A3	Instance for service development, instance from big vendors	Externally developed, deployed
A4	Instance from big vendors	Externally developed, deployed
A5	Instance for service development, instance that is not under direct control	Externally developed, managed, deployed
A6	The only choice platform	Externally {managed + developed + deployed} + shared use
A7	Black box service	Externally managed
A8	Instance from big vendors	Externally developed, deployed
A9	Instance that is not developed/maintained by them, IT outsourcing	Externally developed; managed, deployed
A10	Black box service	Externally managed
A11	Instance for service development	Externally deployed, developed
A12	Instance from big vendors	Externally developed, deployed
A13	Not under direct control	Externally managed, deployed
A14	Instance that is not developed by them, instance from big vendors	Externally developed, deployed, managed
A15	Instance from big vendors	Externally developed, deployed
A16	Instance physically running externally	Externally deployed
A17	Instance from big vendors	Externally developed, deployed
A18	Instance physically running externally,	Externally deployed
A19	Receiving as a service, IT outsourcing	Externally managed, deployed
A20	That is not developed and maintained by them	Externally developed, managed
A21	Instance that is not under direct control	Externally managed, developed
A22	The only choice platform	Externally {managed + developed + deployed} + shared use
A23	The only choice platform, Instance from big vendors	Externally {managed + developed + deployed} + shared use
A24	Instance with a limited customization	Externally {managed + developed + deployed} + shared use

4.1 Different Dimensions of External Platforms

Externally Deployed. The most common understanding of external platform is the physical deployment of the underlying physical infrastructure where the platform is hosted. A platform was understood to be external when it is not running in house, but outside of the organization's premises.

A1: "... *the definition what is the external platform or ecosystem and so on, but we have almost all of the platforms somehow in-house. We have to keep them in-house, we have our own datacenters, and we would like to keep those platforms in our own datacenters as well. So lots of stuff is happening in our own datacenters.*"

Hence, most interviewees assumed any service from the cloud, i.e., with network access, to be external. In a way, it is a valid statement, but in our interviews we explained that *aaS service model may imply a dedicated instance for each user organization, where there is a limited, but some control over the instance. For example, organizations may utilize several cloud service platforms that are remote by definition, but there is a degree of control over the dedicated instance that the utilizing company has. This category reflects one of the characteristics of the cloud computing deployments models—availability over the network and accessing the resources remotely via the Internet.

Externally Developed. The clear majority of practitioners associated any software system with the origin of predominantly big vendors e.g., SAP, Salesforce, Oracle, SAS, as external platform by default.

A2: "*You can almost name whatever brand we probably use it somehow. Because of our large portfolio.*"

The above is an example-reply when the interviewee was asked about the cases of external platforms used in the organization. Partially, the confusion might have been caused by commercial offer descriptions where the terms may be misused for marketing purposes.

A12: "*I really don't think we are using any platforms currently. The thing is every software would like to call itself a software platform. So naturally, if you were using Oracle Database, Oracle would call it a platform. We are using Oracle, but we are using the database. For security reasons we are running all of our product lines all by ourselves.*"

Such concepts misuse may lead to ambiguous understanding among vendors, their customers and management what the offering really is [31].

A17: "*Another problem, our support is confronted basically every three month when users call and ask how to use the functionality ... a new feature in the [platform]. That is setting a dramatic user support problem for user organization. Microsoft is glad to sell us a service... It is not cheap, 80,000 € per year for a subscription, to be notified about new features they are about to release.*"

Externally Managed. This category includes two subcategories which we integrate for simplicity reasons. One abstraction the respondents affiliated with external service platforms were the black box services developed for the organization. Nowadays, organizations prefer to recruit individual developers or small supplier-companies to build and maintain the systems for the organization to solve some specific problems. Interviewees referred to them as something they do not want or/and need to know how it works. Examples include billing, invoicing services and other business intelligence tools.

As a second abstraction is, interestingly, even when only the operation and maintenance of a service was outsourced to a subcontractor or partner firm, the service was mentioned to be external too. Interviewees from medium-sized and large organizations characterized their relations with service providers as "partnerships", regardless the size of partners, implying a horizontal relationship mind-set. When choosing vendors or outsourcing partners they prefer to exploit existing network of partners. Respondents justify these strategic preferences by the degree of the power they are able to impose on long-term partners.

A4: *"For us, the roadmap of a provider is important. Because of single point of failure in a way, if it's going to be Google for example, let's just for fun say we use it. And if everybody integrates to that, you now have to ask who owns the ecosystem? The one who owns it that, owns the API, owns the ecosystem, they can do all the changes. If they want to change the API, they can do it like this and everybody has to, you know, just accept it or stay out of there."*

Externally {Deployed + Developed + Managed} + Shared. Lastly, interviewees acknowledge the existence of some voluntary-compulsory dependencies to certain services provided by other firms. These can be legal enforcements or constraints imposed by industry monopolies [32].

A17: *"If we go outside of this scope: what you refer is our current subscription to Microsoft, Amazon and Google. Where we are in a passenger seat and we don't know where we are going. The challenge is that every 3 months there are new changes coming in, which are not necessarily compliant with Finnish laws."*

Other examples include public digital infrastructures such as X-Road [33], an open source data exchange layer solution that enables organizations to exchange information over the Internet. This metaphor reflects the notion of external platforms we introduce in this article; i.e., the dependencies in business-critical operations that were not possible to avoid. In case of such integrations, all interviewees expressed their preference to have a number of competing platforms than a full-fledged "one-stop shop" platform. The categories we identified are not mutually-exclusive and disconnected. On the contrary, the first three categories emphasize different dimensions of a bigger concept of external platforms.

5 Discussion

External platforms utilization, as well as cloud services adoption or systems maintenance outsourcing, can be seen as a means to manage the complexity [34]. Schneider and Sunyaev [35] define a cloud-sourcing decision as "the decision of the organization to adopt and integrate cloud services from external providers into their IT landscape, that is, the customer organization's assessment of cloud computing offerings from one or more providers in any form of service model (IaaS, PaaS, SaaS) or deployment model (public, private, community, hybrid)".

We commit to the view of IT outsourcing as a predecessor of cloud computing models and extend this continuum with external platforms. Based on their comparison of Cloud Computing with IT outsourcing [35] we reuse the determinant factors (Table 4, Column 1) to contrast Cloud Computing (Table 4, Column 2) and IT outsourcing (Table 4, Column 3) with external platforms. The categories from our findings descriptively correspond to the cloud sourcing models presented in Table 4: externally developed primarily (but not exclusively) refer to cloud computing models, externally managed to IT outsourcing, and externally deployed to all. Inconsistencies in understanding may represent idiosyncratic differences in the perceptions of interviewees and reflect the contextual differences of priorities among key personnel e.g., top management and enterprise architects. The confusion may also be due to lack of comprehensive clarifications and taxonomies.

5.1 Implications

Diversified answers of interviewees point to divergent notions of external platform among practitioners. Moreover, even traditional service models are confused with each other. Our findings indicate the absence of agreement within community of practitioners on various criteria of systems utilized in their organizational operations. The ambiguity is, perhaps, amplified because of difficulties to define what the platform is. The same level of comprehension on the phenomenon of integrations and dependencies with external platforms is crucial in conversations between architects, IT and business unit professionals. Improper differentiation can potentially lead to inaccurate communication of problems and opportunities, their evaluation and cause misleading judgments. One can argue that the dependency to external platforms are rare, because organizations hesitate to outsource business-critical resources or functions [31]. Obviously, no business will take the risk of putting its business-critical applications in the cloud without a very strong assurance of access to those applications and associated data. However, the utilization of intangible resources e.g., technological or managerial knowledge [37] or tangible IT resources i.e., software, data [38] coming from the outside is more common. As scholars note [39, 40], innovation shifts do not "happen teleologically, but rather though gradual and locally emergent evolutions". Cost advantages, flexibility and competitive advantages made

Table 4 External platforms as IT sourcing evolution, adapted and shortened from [35]. In italics are the essential categories from our analysis

	Primarily externally managed; IT outsourcing in [35]	Primarily externally developed; Cloud computing in [35]	Shared external platforms
Decision	Vendor selection prior to decision on degree of outsourcing Top management as decision maker	Vendor selection bound to product selection SaaS by business department, IaaS/PaaS by IT department	The platform is valuable, rare, inimitable and non-substitutable enough to represent nearly the only reasonable choice Top management as decision maker
Asset specificity	Custom-tailored IT-services, may include software development, datacenter or desktop maintenance, help desk	Standardized software (SaaS) or cloud infrastructure (IaaS/PaaS)	Standardized, dynamic platform offering with volatile boundary resources (APIs, SDK, contracts)
Customizability	Individually negotiated configurations	At a minimum, some limited user-specific application configuration settings	Non-existent configurational tuning capability at any of OSI stack layers
User-to-system utilization cardinality	One-to-one relationship between user-organizations and individual system instance, i.e. each user-organization has exclusive access to its own instance		many**one relationship, i.e. all user-organizations reuse the same platform instance
Externally deployed	Outside or in-premises	Usually outside, broad network access and dependence	Outside
Ownership	Varies with the type of outsourcing	Ownership of the data stored in the system and the rights to get it back belongs usually to the customer	The platform, its derivatives and sometimes even the associated data are owned by the provider

(continued)

Table 4 (continued)

	Primarily externally managed; IT outsourcing in [35]	Primarily externally developed; Cloud computing in [35]	Shared external platforms
Contractual mode	Usually long-term strategic partnerships preferred	Standardized terms of use	Non-negotiable SLAs, strategic decisions on platform development or service discontinuity, interfaces availability are made by provider
Substitutability or abandonment options [36]	Moderate to high number of alternatives Outsourcing market is well established with numerous experienced providers	Moderate to high number of alternatives Volatile and immature market	Number of alternatives is non-existent or extremely limited Market in its nascent stage, uncertain legal issues
Examples	Software development subcontracting	SaaS e.g. Salesforce,	CRM integration with Facebook, Google AdWords in marketing business, applications based on distributed ledger technology

IT sourcing, as one of the main strategic decision concepts in modern businesses [35]. In our work, we denote the integrations with external industry platforms as a contemporary emerging service model.

Dynamic capabilities of a firm can be defined as the ways to manipulate resource configurations to gain a competitive advantage [41]. They include strategic decision making, alliancing, and product and service innovation. There are studies on the relation of cloud computing solutions adoption into the internal IT capabilities of the company, and the results call for more research to confirm whether the lack of internal IT capabilities as a driver for SaaS adoption and inhibitor for IaaS/PaaS [35]. Benlian [42] provides evidence on the differences regarding the perceived relative performance of different delivery models among IS managers of SMEs compared to large enterprises [31, 35]. Examples of integrations with shared external platforms seemed to be rarer in larger organizations we interviewed. The mental model of managers in incumbent and large companies may be seen as trying to avoid dependencies they cannot control, preserve power integrity and gain more power and secure their position by carefully establishing alliance partner relationships. Exceptional cases are when established companies allow the use of external platforms for non-critical activities or as complementary solutions. For example, the use of social media platforms for boarding tickets distribution by airline companies where e.g. Facebook's Messenger is only one option among other distribution channels (e.g. email, sms).

Our findings may also be a starting point for further theorizing on external platform adoption tendency. Organizations in nascent highly-dynamic markets often follow entrepreneurial modes of behavior strategies [43], i.e., they are fast decision makers, open to experimenting and value newly acquired knowledge. Studies on cloud computing adoption find that "smaller and medium-sized firms are generally more prone to adopt on-demand outsourcing options for obtaining fast access to valuable IT resources and capabilities" [31, 42]. It is possible that such firms are more pragmatic in leveraging innovations coming from the outside. Small and young firms may understand that they are undisguised to innovation threats from tech giants as they do not possess required capabilities and resources. Such organizations, therefore, can be seen unprejudiced about their power and control disadvantage and, consequently, fast in adopting innovations from global providers. Due to the lack of resources and power they make decisions based on facts and features and what actually the platform capability is. On the other hand, incumbent organizations that operate in moderately-dynamic markets with stable industry structures, tend to follow linear and incremental changes. These organizations usually value and try to leverage existing, cumulative knowledge, and therefore they follow risk mitigation practices [41] to avoid integrations they cannot fully control. These propositions, however, need to be investigated in future research with a larger sample.

5.2 Limitations and Future Research

As with any qualitative inquiry, our study has three potential validity threats. We follow the validity dimensions of Maxwell [44] in qualitative research. First, descriptive validity threat is eliminated by recording and transcribing each interview in true verbatim, to ensure the factual accuracy of the data. As qualitative researchers are not interested in solely describing the reality, but concerned what the phenomenon under study mean, there is an interpretative validity threat. Although there is no "in principle access to data that would unequivocally address this threat to validity", we attempted to construct our findings closely grounded in the language used by interviewees, their own words and concepts [44]. We used mostly open-ended questions to allow respondents to elaborate on answers and avoided using leading questions to get a desired response. In fact, we view non-consistent interpretations among respondents as findings. The next validity threat is theoretical, which is not concerned with factual accuracy and consensus, but rather with the legitimacy of the applications of the concepts to the phenomena and the validity of causal relationships among them. Here, the choice of Grounded Theory with no a priori theory in mind and its continuous interplay of data collection and analysis along with incremental open, axial and selective coding procedure spanning for several months has proved its usefulness. This ensured that the constructs identifications and their application to the data are not biased and the patterns identified were (as much as possible) theoretically saturated and different types of relations between concepts are identified. Next, as with any other qualitative study we cannot claim the internal or external generalizability of the findings as such, but rather their analytical transferability extended to other cases. Moreover, the generalization in qualitative research implies that the phenomenon identified should be also identified in other settings and cases, but, perhaps, with different results i.e., new interpretations on external platforms.

An important future research agenda can be to identify the emergent conditions of external platforms-based dependencies; empirically-valid risks mitigation practices along with benefits realization would form a fundamental understanding of the phenomenon. Another important research direction can be the role of APIs as boundary resources between non-focal actors and platforms, including API ecosystems evolution and what it means for different industries and enterprise strategies [45]. The state of the practice indicates that the external dependencies among more established organizations are at its nascent stage—firms have mostly *aaS types of relations and only few external platforms. Part of the difficulty in distinguishing these approaches is that they often coincide in practice and are neglected in theory. Proper visualization and modelling of enterprise information and IS architecture could improve the practice. Nowadays, organizations seem to be much consumed and involved in transforming their own products into platforms i.e., "platformization", so that the external dependencies might be neglected, which could lead to twisted strategic maneuvers, or missed opportunities.

6 Conclusions

From our interviews with 24 practitioners we found that practitioners across units and sectors perceive the notion of external industry platforms differently, confusing them within service and deployment models. External platforms, from the understanding of practitioners, may primarily refer to the ones which are externally deployed, developed, managed. A combination of three attributes together with a multiple simultaneous use of the platform refers to shared external platform-based dependence, i.e., monopoly-like platforms. We also anticipate that integrations with external platforms could be more common among entrepreneurial firms in nascent markets and that established organizations are less open to have such dependencies and give up the control. However, this proposition needs to be investigated and developed further in future research.

Acknowledgements This research was funded by Academy of Finland (304439).

References

1. Boudreau, K.J., Hagiu, A.: Platform rules: multi-sided platforms as regulators. Platf. Mark. Innov., 163–191 (2009)
2. Gawer, A., Cusumano, M.A.: Industry platforms and ecosystem innovation. J. Prod. Innov. Manag. **31**, 417–433 (2014)
3. Eisenmann, T.R., Parker, G., Van Alstyne, M.: Opening platforms: how, when and why? Platf. Mark. Innov., 131–162 (2009)
4. Huber, T.L., Kude, T., Dibbern, J.: Governance practices in platform ecosystems: navigating tensions between co-created value and governance costs. Inf. Syst. Res. (2017)
5. Tiwana, A.: Platform Ecosystems: Aligning Architecture, Governance, and Strategy. Morgan Kaufmann Publishers Inc., San Francisco, CA, USA (2014)
6. Ghazawneh, A., Henfridsson, O.: Balancing platform control and external contribution in third-party development: the boundary resources model. Inf. Syst. J. **23**, 173–192 (2013)
7. Huang, P., Ceccagnoli, M., Forman, C., Wu, D.: When Do ISVs Join a Platform Ecosystem? Evidence from the Enterprise Software Industry. ICIS 2009 Proceedings, pp. 1–18 (2009)
8. Lindgren, R., Eriksson, O., Lyytinen, K.: Managing identity tensions during mobile ecosystem evolution. J. Inf. Technol. **30**, 229–244 (2015)
9. Selander, L., Henfridsson, O., Svahn, F.: Capability search and redeem across digital ecosystems. J. Inf. Technol. **28**, 183–197 (2013)
10. Evans, P.C., Gawer, A.: The rise of the platform enterprise: a global survey (2016)
11. Rolland, K.H., Mathiassen, L., Rai, A.: Managing digital platforms in user organizations: the interactions between digital options and digital debt. Inf. Syst. Res. (2018)
12. Yoo, Y., Henfridsson, O., Lyytinen, K.: The new organizing logic of digital innovation: an agenda for information systems research. Inf. Syst. Res. **21**, 724–735 (2010)
13. Parker, G., Van Alstyne, M.: Innovation, openness, and platform control. Manag. Sci. (2017)
14. Henfridsson, O., Bygstad, B.: The generative mechanisms of digital infrastructure evolution. MIS Q. **37**, 907–931 (2013)
15. Tilson, D., Lyytinen, K., Sørensen, C.: Digital infrastructures: the missing IS research agenda. Inf. Syst. Res. **21**, 748–759 (2010)
16. Jansen, S., Cusumano, M.A.: Defining software ecosystems: a survey of software platforms and business network governance. Softw. Ecosyst. Anal. Manag. Bus. Netw. Softw. Ind. **13** (2013)
17. Gawer, A., Cusumano, M.A.: How companies become platform leaders. MIT Sloan Manag. Rev. **49**, 28–35 (2008)
18. Karhu, K., Tang, T., Hämäläinen, M.: Analyzing competitive and collaborative differences among mobile ecosystems using abstracted strategy networks. Telemat. Inform. **31**, 319–333 (2014)
19. Venkatraman, V.N., El Sawy, O.A., Pavlou, P., Bharadwaj, A.: Theorizing digital business innovation: platforms and capabilities in ecosystems. Fox Sch. Bus. Res. Pap. **15–80**, 1–36 (2014)
20. Eaton, B., Elaluf-Calderwood, S., Sørensen, C., Yoo, Y.: Distributed tuning of boundary resources: the case of apple's iOS service system. MIS Q. **39**, 217–243 (2015)
21. Ghanam, Y., Maurer, F., Abrahamsson, P.: Making the leap to a software platform strategy: issues and challenges. Inf. Softw. Technol. **54**, 968–984 (2012)
22. Boudreau, K.: Does Opening a Platform Stimulate Innovation? The Effect on Systemic and Modular Innovations. https://ssrn.com/abstract=913402 (2007)
23. Pfeffer, J., Salancik, G.R.: The external control of organizations: a resource dependence perspective. Stanford University Press (2003)
24. Altman, E.J.: Dependency Challenges, Response Strategies, and Complementor Maturity: Joining a Multi-Sided Platform Ecosystem. Working paper (2016)
25. Baldwin, C.Y., Clark, K.B.: Design rules: the power of modularity. Acad. Manag. Rev. **26**, 471 (2000)

26. Barney, J.: Firm resources and sustained competitive advantage. J. Manag. **17**, 99–120 (1991)
27. Cusumano, M.: Cloud computing and SaaS as new computing platforms. Commun. ACM **53**, 27 (2010)
28. Glaser, B., Strauss, A.: The Discovery of Grounded Theory. Weidenfield Nicolson, London (1967)
29. Runeson, P., Höst, M.: Guidelines for conducting and reporting case study research in software engineering. Empir. Softw. Eng. **14**, 131–164 (2008)
30. Strauss, A.L., Corbin, J.: Basics of Qualitative Research: Grounded Theory Procedures and Applications. Sage Publications, Newbury Park, CA (1990)
31. Hoberg, P., Wollersheim, J., Krcmar, H.: The Business Perspective on Cloud Computing-A Literature Review of Research on Cloud Computing (2012)
32. Bazarhanova, A., Yli-Huumo, J., Smolander, K.: Love and hate relationships in a platform ecosystem: a case of finnish electronic identity management. In: Proceedings of the 51st Hawaii International Conference on System Sciences (2018)
33. Anthes, G.: Estonia: a model for e-government. Commun. ACM **58**, 18–20 (2015)
34. Iyer, B., Henderson, J.C.: Preparing for the future: understanding the seven capabilities cloud computing. MIS Q. Exec. **9** (2010)
35. Schneider, S., Sunyaev, A.: Determinant factors of cloud-sourcing decisions: reflecting on the IT outsourcing literature in the era of cloud computing. J. Inf. Technol. **31**, 1–31 (2016)
36. Saya, S., Pee, L.G., Kankanhalli, A.: The impact of institutional influences on perceived technological characteristics and real options in cloud computing adoption. In: ICIS, p. 24 (2010)
37. Teece, D.J., Pisano, G., Shuen, A.: Dynamic capabilities and strategic management. Strateg. Manag. J. **18**, 509–533 (2008)
38. Dreyfus, D., Iyer, B.: Managing architectural emergence: a conceptual model and simulation. Decis. Support Syst. **46**, 115–127 (2008)
39. Boland, R.J., Lyytinen, K., Yoo, Y.: Wakes of Innovation in project networks: the case of digital 3-D representations in architecture, engineering, and construction. Organ. Sci. **18**, 631–647 (2007)
40. Lyytinen, K., Yoo, Y., Boland, R.J.: Digital product innovation within four classes of innovation networks. Inf. Syst. J., 47–75 (2015)
41. Eisenhardt, K.M., Martin, J.A.: Dynamic capabilities: what are they? Strateg. Manag. J. **21**, 1105–1121 (2000)
42. Benlian, A., Hess, T., Buxmann, P.: Drivers of SaaS-adoption–an empirical study of different application types. Bus. Inf. Syst. Eng. **1**, 357 (2009)
43. Santos, F.M., Eisenhardt, K.M.: Constructing markets and shaping boundaries: entrepreneurial power in nascent fields. Acad. Manag. J. **52**, 643–671 (2009)
44. Maxwell, J.A.: Understanding and validity in qualitative research. Harv. Educ. Rev. Camb. **62**, 279 (1992)
45. Evans, P.C., Basole, R.C.: Revealing the API ecosystem and enterprise strategy via visual analytics. Commun. ACM **59**, 26–28 (2016)

How to Design an Interactive System for Data Science: Learning from a Literature Review

Ana Sofia Almeida, Licinio Roque and Paulo Rupino da Cunha

Abstract As part of an ongoing design science research project, this paper presents a systematic literature review and the classification of 214 papers scoping the work on Data Science (DS) in the fields of Information Systems and Human-Computer Interaction. The overall search was conducted on Web of Science, Science Direct and ACM Digital Library, for papers about the design of IT artefacts for Data Science, over the period of 1997 until 2017. The work identifies promising research clusters in the crossroads of IS, HCI and Design, but few studies were found with concrete guidance on how to design a system for DS, when targeting for broader technical and business user profiles and multi-domain applications. In this paper, we propose a DS lifecycle process and a set of design principles to guide the design of such a system to support the whole creative DS lifecycle process.

Keywords Data science · Information systems design · Human computer interaction · Design science research · Design methods · UI/UX design

1 Introduction and Motivation

Solving the "big challenges and opportunities" of Big Data [1, 2] has emerged as an important area of study. With the convergence of Big Data and powerful computational capabilities, Machine Learning (ML) and Artificial Intelligence (AI)

A prior version of this paper has been published in the ISD2018 Proceedings (http://aisel.aisnet. org/isd2014/proceedings2018).

A. S. Almeida (✉) · L. Roque · P. R. da Cunha
University of Coimbra, Coimbra, Portugal
e-mail: asa@dei.uc.pt

L. Roque
e-mail: lir@dei.uc.pt

P. R. da Cunha
e-mail: rupino@dei.uc.pt

© Springer Nature Switzerland AG 2019
B. Andersson et al. (eds.), *Advances in Information Systems Development*,
Lecture Notes in Information Systems and Organisation 34,
https://doi.org/10.1007/978-3-030-22993-1_8

are becoming effectively viable for widespread use. Enterprises need to adapt and combine domain-expertise with DS, to respond with speedier and tailored solutions to demanding markets. This increases the demand for data competences, with a focus on collecting, processing, analyzing and using data to create value. DS is the new needed literacy, regardless of professionals technical background [3, 4].

This paper is a partial result of a Design Science Research project [5–7] with a global company, combining AI and ML for fraud fighting in the Finance sector. The main research goal is to design a supporting system for all DS activities involved. This raises the question of *"How to design such a system, keeping user/consumer perspective in (a) a fast-changing environment/market; with (b) scarce access to end-users, while (c) meeting agile development pace deadlines?"*. In order to approach this problem, we considered a twofold perspective over the underlying process:

1. as the design of an *Information System* (*IS*)—where data, technology and people are involved to deliver a data product or service—and
2. as the design of a system for *Human-Computer Interaction* (*HCI*)—an interactive system, used by different user profiles to perform complex activities.

A third area of *Design* with its actual methods and techniques (e.g. design theories, practices, studies, and approaches) is taken to be transversal to both fields and hence was also mapped, by including relevant search keywords, as tertiary terms of search.

In the next section, we present the systematic literature review effort, detailing the search used to attain a representative list of publications for classification. In Sect. 3, relevant articles were grouped by similar concepts into a set of three main categories and ten sub-categories, outlining the scope of retrieved literature and proposed as major (current and) future research clusters. In Sect. 4, from a narrowed list of papers further inspected, we outline some of the contributions to our understanding about the *process* of DS and about the attributes of the *artefact* to support it, thus proposing a generic workflow of the entire life cycle.

In the last section we discuss the work done and some of the shortcomings of the literature review, proposing found research gaps as opportunities for further work.

2   Research Method and Search Strategy

A systematic literature review is a formal iterative approach of "analyze the past to prepare the future" [8] and locate, select, explore and report [8–10]. Although challenging, systematic literature review provides a means for practitioners to use the evidence provided by previous research to inform their decisions [10]. For theoretical background, we conducted a systematic literature review of papers in the areas of Information Systems, Human-Computer Interaction and Design studies, relevant to the problem of design and evaluate a system for DS.

Table 1 Search query was done using combinations of AND and OR between the terms in each row

Search terms	Keywords used	
Primary terms Searched in metadata of the data sources (WOS, SD, ACM)	'big data'; 'data science'; 'data scientist', 'data analytics'; 'business intelligence'; 'business analytics'	
Secondary terms Searched in *Topic*, *Title*, *Abstract* and *Keywords*, depending of data source (WOS, SD, ACM)	'IS'; 'information systems'; 'information systems design'	'HCI'; 'human computer interaction'
Tertiary terms Searched in *Topic* and also in *Title/Abstract/Keywords* (WOS + SD, ACM)	'design'; 'system design'; 'approach'; 'process'; 'method'; 'tools'; 'solutions'; 'practice'; 'application'	
	'software'; 'system design'; 'artefact'; 'service'; 'lifecycle'	'user interface'; 'usability'; 'user experience'; 'user experience design'; 'UX design'
Conceptual terms	'model'; 'mental model'; 'theory'; 'survey'; 'case study'; 'field study'; 'review'	

An overall search was carried out on Web of Science, Science Direct and ACM Library databases, in November and December of 2017, ranging the period from 1997 to 2017. Table 1 illustrates the search query followed for retrieving the articles from the three databases. The steps followed are:

1. Boolean combinations of the primary and secondary terms were searched, using the search engines of the databases for cross-reference work in the relevant areas.
2. Tertiary terms were used to refine the retrieved results of 1.
3. Boolean combinations of primary and transversal tertiary terms were additionally considered with other tertiary terms, progressively narrowing the scope of results.
4. Transversal tertiary terms (e.g. 'approach') along with discipline specific terms (e.g. 'user experience') were used to capture community's discourse specificities.
5. Conceptual terms were mainly used in manual searches, to capture different discourses over the theme (e.g. 'mental model'; 'survey', 'theory'; 'case study').

We searched papers appropriate for review, not considering: (a) Papers not written in English and (b) Dissertations, lecture notes, reports on tutorials, posters, demos and workshops. We are aware that some articles may have not been retrieved, partially due to the search method and the different technical capabilities of each database.

From the 519 articles that resulted, we selected 214 papers, directly mentioning "Data Science" in *Title*, *Abstract* and/or *Keywords*, for a first paper categorization, revealing rich research clusters and gaps for potential further work.

3 Paper Categorization and Main Research Clusters

Paper categorization was done iteratively, in a process of clarification and refinement. Considering the two aforementioned perspectives adopted (IS development and HCI views over the research work studies) and the blurred frontier of the research in the emerging field of "Data Science", we organized papers into three categories:

1. **CAT1—Data Science and Information Systems**: Considers theories and studies; models, methods from IS applied to DS (e.g. statistics, data analysis, business intelligence, decision making, DS lifecycle, technologies). This category mainly embraces papers about foundational theories and overviews; questions about data production, storage and availability or reports and evaluations of available tools, algorithms and technologies for DS.
2. **CAT2—Data Science and Human-Computer Interaction**: Work being done in the HCI field, related to data-driven research in the area and efforts to user experience understanding and improvement, including papers related to data-driven and data-informed design, implementation and evaluation of systems and services; data visualization and data discovery and DS in multi-domain projects.
3. **CAT3—Emerging Perspectives or Shared Work for DS**: Everything related with cloud computing, machine learning, algorithms, (data, mobile, web, network, text, social media) analytics; privacy; ethics and policy making. This category includes articles proposing conceptual models or methods; discussing emerging trends and future challenges; the impact of potential technologies or how to educate for DS.

Table 2 presents an overview of the three main categories. Albeit not being exhaustive, these categories outline what we found to be known or at least reported, focusing on the consensus and shared perspectives on both fields.

These categories overlap, meaning that one paper can be classified in more than one category. We find that few studies cross IS and HCI disciplines (only seven

Table 2 First paper categorization—three main categories or research clusters relating to data science

Categories by study focus	# of papers	% of papers	Description, according to main research problems
CAT1—Data Science and Information Systems	102	48	Theories, studies, models and methods from IS applied to Data Science
CAT2—Data Science and Human Computer Interaction	54	25	Work in HCI field, related to data-driven research and user experience improvement
CAT3—Emerging Research and Shared Problems	97	45	Work related with cloud computing, machine learning, algorithms, analytics; privacy; ethics and policy making

Table 3 First paper categorization—categories and sub-categories used for classification of selected publications

Categories	Major sub-categories of research
CAT1—DS and Information Systems	1. Theories and Case Studies 2. Production, Storage and Analysis of [Big] Data 3. Data Quality
CAT 2—DS and Human Computer Interaction	4. Application of DS in multi-domains 5. Data Visualization and Data Discovery 6. DS to improve Research and Learning
CAT 3—Emerging Research and Shared Problems	7. Education and Training for Data Science 8. Methods and Systematization of DS lifecycle 9. Regulatory, Ethical and Public Policies Issues 10. Real Life Global Problems with Social Impact

articles are classified in both categories 1 and 2), revealing a somewhat separate investigation, at least, on what relates to data-related and user-centered issues and DS.

The overlapping is stronger between categories CAT1 and CAT3, where twenty papers from IS field are closely related to emerging research trends and gaps, considering the DS context. This is not that surprising, since IS and digital information systems are increasingly responsible for generating data and demanding solutions to extract value from it in order to improve operational, organizational, strategical and societal activities, pushing the boundaries of both related theory and practice.

Surprisingly, we did not found articles reporting user experience studies involving data scientists (as a target group) or about the UI design of tools for both data scientists and non-data scientists. As if, albeit being a complex process and an activity best served by digital tools, usability and a user-centered perspective over the design for DS does not seems to be present or reported, at least in the academic discourse.

An analysis of research problems and main focus of study, lead to further classification of the retrieved papers into ten sub-categories, presented in Table 3.

Some of the sub-categories, such as "2. *Production, Storage and Analysis of [Big] Data*", "5. *Data Visualization and Data Discovery*" or "7. *Education and Training for Data Science*" can be viewed as design goals to be developed into functionalities.

For each category, we further discuss each sub-category and present some examples of articles and how they relate to the found research gaps and potential opportunities. Due to space limitations, only a sample of the categorized papers appear on the references. The full list is available by requesting the first author.

3.1 CAT1—Data Science and Information Systems

A total of 102 (48%) articles, classified in this first category, reveal a body of knowledge pushing the confluence of more traditional disciplines (e.g. statistics, mathematics, data analysis or decision support systems). Among other themes, main research clusters and favorable avenues of work and challenges are related to:

1. **Theories and Case Studies**: relevant scoping literature reviews that organize both research and practice and studies reporting on technologies, tools and techniques, borrowed from other areas, to be applied in DS. Plus, overall research to map the complex phenomena of DS itself. Some exemplary work can be found in the research efforts of [11–14];

2. **Production, Storage and Analysis of [Big] Data**: information systems produce large amounts of data, collecting, storing, managing and distributing it, creating challenges. Organizations struggle to grasp its potential to make decisions, to innovate and to create value for Customers and Citizens. Arguably, this is a fast-pace growing study area, in need of *"tools to deal with variety, velocity and volume of data"* [2, 11, 15] so as to decision-making [16–18]; and

3. **Data Quality**: a fast-growing problem, with research challenges focusing *"on scalability, availability, data integrity, data transformation, data quality"* [19] urging the need to manage identified *"causes for 'bad big data science', focusing primarily on the quality of the input data"* [20], or the *"data quality in supply chain research and practice"*, calling for *"interdisciplinary research topics based on complementary theory"* [21].

Table 4 summarizes major problems found in the retrieved publications, with some examples and quotes, relating the work in the IS field applied to Data Science.

3.2   CAT2—Data Science and Human-Computer Interaction

The 54 articles (25%) classified in this category show the growing application of DS in multi-domain scenarios. How data can improve the user experience and the service design, adding value for clients and citizens is pushing the work on data visualization (for communication and discovery) and crowdsourced research. From a user-centered perspective and DS, the current research clusters mainly relate to:

4. **Application of DS in multi-domains**: DS is fast becoming ubiquitous in multi-domain sectors. Examples range from Health [22, 23], Agriculture [24, 25]; Social Studies [26–28] or Urban Planning [29], urging for the genericity of solutions. There are challenges on structuring the DS practices and effectively democratize its use among professionals and across disciplines of inquiry and practice;

5. **Data Visualization and Data Discovery**: Examples come from research addressing the challenge of *"making sense out of big data using visual analytics"* [30] or to *"allow users to directly interact with the visualization to build combination models"* [31], promising to guide users to extract value in data. Other samples address data visualization courses for sectors as tech industry [32] or citizen science [33], targeting non-experts in DS; and

Table 4 CAT1—Data Science and Information Systems: major research problems in selected publications, with examples

	Main problems/research questions found	Examples/Quotes
CAT 1 **DS and IS**	**Evolution/overview of Big Data** and related research (challenges, trends, future directions) **Production, storage and analysis of [big] data** **Efficiency of systems** through data, in particular, in Industry 4.0 **Call for methods, approaches and systematization** of practice **Tools and technologies** (design and development of tools to deal with data problems) **Data quality** (integrity, security, availability)	*"big data over the past 20 years"* [11–14] *"increasing open source tools to deal with variety, velocity and volume of data"* [2] and a need to *"process large real-time streams of data"* [14] *"research challenges ..., with focus on scalability, availability, data integrity, data transformation, data quality"* [19] *"how to align [organizations'] decision-making and organizational processes to data that could help them make better-informed decisions"* [35] *"big data has resulted in the development and applications of technologies and methods aimed at effectively using massive amounts of data to support decision-making and knowledge discovery activities"* [12] *"apply multiple technologies, carefully select key data for specific investigations, and innovatively tailor large integrated datasets ... All these actions will flow from a data value chain"* [16] *"causes for 'bad big data science', focusing primarily on the data quality of the input data, and suggests methods for minimizing"* [20]

6. **DS to improve Research and Learning**: ML combined with large datasets can improve research in different fields, *"converting data to actionable knowledge"* [34] and creating *"new opportunities for researchers to achieve high relevance and impact"* [28]. DS is also important "in an educational context", a field where studies "related to outcome measurement and prediction, to be linked to specific interventions" [26] are needed. This can be considered yet another domain of DS application, lacking a much-needed framework and agile tools.

Table 5 CAT2—Data Science and Human-Computer Interaction: major research problems and examples

	Main problems/research questions found	Examples/Quotes
CAT 2 **DS and HCI**	**Context of use**: several domains for DS application (e.g. health, heritage, urban cities, social, manufacturing, finance, research and learning) **Tools** for data manipulation, understanding, discovery and visualization **Data availability as enabler**: data is used to enable HCI projects or research with a user-centered perspective (e.g. user data is collected to improve UI/UX design or UI/UX studies that involve diverse users' profiles are becoming possible)	Multi-domain examples of HCI projects with DS application range from Health [22, 23], Agriculture [24, 25]; Social Studies [26–28] to Urban Planning [29] "making sense out of big data using visual analytics" [30] or "*allow users to directly interact with the visualization to build combination models*" [31] "*interactive visualization over data sets*" [36] "*converting data to actionable knowledge*" [34] "*yet to fully harness the potential of visualization when interacting with non-scientists.*" [37] "*new opportunities for researchers to achieve high relevance and impact*" [28] DS to improve studies "*related to outcome measurement and prediction, to be linked to specific interventions*" [26]

Table 5 recaps some current challenges and growing work from researchers and practitioners, to withdraw the value of the increasing data availability in various fields, with individual, economic and societal impact.

3.3 CAT3—Emerging/Shared Research Problems

Ninety-seven articles (45%) report on emerging challenges and trends [2]. Industry 4.0 and Internet-of-Things with Cloud Computing, ML, AI and other technologies urge for interdisciplinary collaboration to create effective DS solutions for the data-related challenges societies face. Ongoing research and practice will grow in:

7. **Education and Training for Data Science**: shortage of data-professionals is a reality and "*we're missing the boat again*" [38]. Calls as "*towards data science literacy*" [39] effectively organize the body of knowledge while industry urges for fast-forward training pipelines and shorter processes for demanding markets.
8. **Methods and Systematization of DS Lifecycle**: in data-driven societies, DS is "*significant for business strategies, operations, performance, efficiency and*

Table 6 CAT3—Emerging Research and Shared Problems: major research problems and some examples

	Main problems/research questions found	Examples/Quotes
CAT 3 **Emerging and Shared Work**	**Education for Data Science** (enhance skills and competences) **Emerging Technologies** and how to use them (e.g. ML, AI, IoT, Industry 4.0, Cloud Computing) **Case studies** and Contextual Surveys **Legal and regulatory issues**. **Ethics** and **public policies** concerns	*"DS increasingly significant for business strategies, operations, performance, efficiency and prediction ... little work on this to provide a detailed guideline."* [40] *"how we might design effective methods for systematizing such practice and research"* [41] *"Data science literacy = computational literacy + statistical literacy + machine learning literacy + visualization literacy + ethical literacy."* [39] *"we identified four types of DS projects, and ... some of the sociotechnical challenges"* [44]

prediction" [40] but *"there is little work on this to provide a detailed guideline"*. *"Additional sociotechnical challenges"* [38] and how we might *"design effective methods for systematizing such practice and research"* [41] eventually automatizing tasks or the parts of the ML pipeline are worth for further work.

9. **Regulatory, Ethical and Public Policies Issues**: a fast growing topic concerns legal ethical, privacy and security issues, with studies outlining data problems *"that could result in invalid conclusions and unsound public health policies"* [42].

10. **Real Life Global Problems with Social Impact**: DS is increasing the hope to solve global problems such as understanding *"the evolving global economy"* [2] or the *"open collaboration ecosystems"* [43] phenomena, with data-driven designed or data-informed solutions to human and society benefit.

Table 6 recaps some of the emerging problems, with examples from the retrieved literature. The emergent work is increasingly interdisciplinary, urging for methodologies for process organization and a more effective way to spread the literacy needed across disciplines, enhancing the skills of people of diverse technical backgrounds.

Plus, we are scratching the surface of understanding the potential impact, inherent to the difficulty people sometimes have to understand 'what the data is saying' and how that is informing and influencing private and public decision-making.

4   Second Paper Categorization

Being an iterative process of clarification and keeping in mind our research question, we further tried a thematic analysis, resorting to the tertiary terms to select papers for a second paper categorization. The original list of 214 papers, relating to "data science" work in the fields of IS and HCI (categorized on Sect. 3), was narrowed to a list of 80 papers explicitly mentioning "design" (e.g. 'design methods', 'design approach', 'user-centered design') in *Title*, *Keywords* or *Abstract*.

Doing the best effort to avoid bias, this list was narrowed to a final list of 23 papers, inspected for more direct contributions to our research question by either (1) add to the understanding the DS practices and activities (about the *process*) or (2) helping to identify attributes and/or requirements of the IT-solution (about the *artefact*).

Tables 7 and 8 highlight some of the contributions found in this narrowed list of papers, that informed our specific research question, respectively, about the *process* of DS and about the user-perspective over the *artefact* for DS, quoting some relevant papers. Some contributions are new questions targeting design goals we used in subsequent work in practice.

Next, we briefly discuss the findings and the impact on the practice of our work.

4.1   About the DS Process: A Generic Workflow for the Full Lifecycle

Organizing the papers revealed a pattern of emergent research focus on the process itself, with a clear call for methodologies to organize the process of DS, namely, in the areas of activities related to: 'Data Acquisition and Quality' (how to collect and prepare data for confident usage); 'Data Visualization and Data Discovery' (scalability issues to deal with larger datasets and improve people's understanding of results); 'ML Modelling and Training' (emerging as an iterative, creative and collaborative process, urging for improved interaction design accounting for trial and error).

From reviews and evolution studies of the area, such as the DS journey presented by recent Cao's overview of the field [50], we learn that DS lifecycle is an evolving concept in itself, aggregating activities, and a creative process "in need of other methodological research" [46]. The found case studies and literature reports on the application of DS in a specific project or sector, and the problems researchers and practitioners report (or not) having in practice with the process, the toolbox and the needed technical competences are important to our understanding about the DS full lifecycle.

In Fig. 1, we propose a generic workflow for DS lifecycle (DSL) that structures the main activities of a full DS process.

These activities or phases are performed in loop, with possible forward and backward contextual cycles between phases. Current DS projects and available tools usually account for (all or part of) phases from *1. Data Acquisition* to *4. Experi-*

Table 7 Understanding the *PROCESS*: our research question guided the paper analysis for contributions from previous work, to the context of design for DS

	Guiding research questions/main problems identified	Quotes/Examples of contributions from literature
Our Research Questions	**About the Process** *Which are the DS phases and activities to support?* *Is there a framework to structure the practice that can be used to inform the design of a system for DS?*	*"An essential need of the DS state lies in the standardization of its components, methods, tools, data formats, and analytic processes"* [45] Kazakci [46] talks about *"controlled creativity"* and claims to use design methods to structure the DS activities and its innovation dynamics Larson [47] presents a most comprehensive overview of DS process, in particular, in agile development contexts. Phases for the complete process are proposed A *"business Data Science model, focusing on the model and experimental development"* allowing *"different functions, processes and roles"* is proposed by Newman [40] Saltz [44] also provides a framework for DS (not so for designing for DS) and Demchenko [48] states that *"the education and training of DS lacks a commonly accepted, ... design the whole lifecycle of data handling in modern, data driven research and digital economy."*
Main Problems Identified	Albeit some shared phases on the processes, there is *"no consensus on DS definition"* Different DS activities and practices to structure Integration of DS into agile development environments is difficult There is a huge gap between model and deployment phases (targeting a full life-cycle)	

New Questions to Consider when Design for DS

How to deal with data acquisition and data quality?
How to manage the DS process activities?
Which problems to solve when digitalizing each DS phase?
How to account for the complex and creative nature of the DS process?
Can we reduce the technical skills along the phases of the process? Where? How?
How much of the process resorts to memory and recall from user?
What can be re-used among phases, activities or DS projects?

Table 8 Understanding *the user perspective over the ARTEFACT*: contributions from previous work and new questions to the context of design for DS

	Guiding research questions/main problems identified	Quotes/Examples of contributions from literature
Our Research Questions	**About the Artefact:** *Which functionality has to be provided/supported, giving the new technologies available (functionality)?* *How to lower the skills and competences needed to do DS (from the user-side)?*	Chuprina [51] proposes an ontology of DS to improve DS skills for CS, since *"both industry and academia have met a growing gap"*; Dichev proposes a set of DS skills and competences, such as *"ability to visualise and report summary data and formulate productive questions"*, calling for data science literacy [39]; Grainger [37] explore visualization of data to be communicated and shared (to non-scientists) Carbone [45] argues about the *"social dimension of DS"* and the problems associated with data misuse, considering that an essential need for DS lies *"in the standardization of its components, methods, tools, data formats, and analytic processes"*
Main Problems	Skill and competences needed to use the available tools are highly technical Shortage of Data Scientists urges the call for DS to be accessible to diverse professional backgrounds as a needed literacy There is a set of tools (toolbox) instead of an integrated tool Lack of standardization (e.g. data and model formats). Repetitive and 'boring' tasks along with more creative ones	

Contribution/New Questions to Our Work

How to support full lifecycle, with integration of tools and collaborative work support?
Can an IT-solution help with standards and integration? How?
How to have improved usability and user experience, while performing the activities?
How humans can cope with the increasing complexity and scale? How can the tool help?
How to evaluate the data products and data science solutions?
How to support the creativity of user activities? How to avoid the 'boring' tasks?
How to conciliate ethics and the designer's responsibility in designing for DS?

mentation and Model Evaluation in loop. In some projects, phases *5. Deployment* and *6. Feedback and Model Tuning* are often typically left for different teams or just postponed.

We argue that there is an increasing need to account for them as a part of the DS project and to narrow the gap between the design and production phases, and back.

The deployment activities of *5. Deployment* phase are typically reserved for the engineer teams, due to very different runtime environments, usually requiring advanced technical skills in a process tailored for each project and that can be very challenging and time-consuming. On the other hand, entering Production is an iter-

Fig. 1 Generic data science
lifecycle loop (DSL)

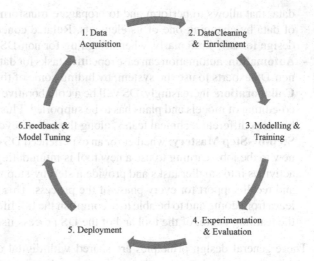

ative process of deploying, evaluating, benchmarking the runtime results against the
expected performance, represented on the *6. Feedback and Model Tuning* phase.

In order to design for DS, we need to consider also the 'data science' work that is
done in these post-design phases, and increasingly bring them into the DS lifecycle
loop, as proposed here. This has great impact on the workflow of the teams and the
respective knowledge management, within each project and among projects.

4.2   *About the* **Artefact** *for DS: Guiding Design Principles*

Overall, there is a growing need to spread the DS competences and literacy among
professionals, by either shortening the time to produce DS professionals with the
needed skills OR to improve the tools they use so that—at least—some activities
could be done by professionals with different technical backgrounds.

From a user-centered perspective, the design of an interactive solution ultimately
intends to empower the end-user. Papers discussing the challenges in educating for
data science or concerned with improving data-related skills and competences of
other professionals reveal potential user insights to account when designing for DS.

We consider a pertinent research effort to develop an integrated approach and a
supportive platform to democratize DS. That could be of interest to research and of
practical relevance in relation to the future data-related challenges of various areas.

For discussion and work, we propose a set of design principles to account for and
guide a design approach for an integrated system for the proposed DS Lifecycle:

– **Abstraction**: abstractions and meta-level concepts let users deal with data and data
   operations on a higher conceptual level. Some examples come from lazy binding

data, that allows to perform and to propagate transformations on a set or cluster of data by changing one of its elements. Related concepts should guide UI/UX design for DS, particularly, when designing for non-DS experts;

- **Automation**: automation can ease repetitive tasks for data scientists and may allow non-DS experts to use the system, by hiding some of the complexity;
- **Collaboration**: increasingly, DS will be a collaborative work and co-creation and co-editing of models and plans has to be supported. Plus, supporting collaboration between different technical teams, along the full lifecycle, is mandatory;
- **Step-by-Step Mastery**: whether for an experienced DS expert or for someone still new to the job, learning to use a new tool is intimidating, so decompose complex activities into smaller tasks and provide a step-by-step workflow, with inline help and recall support for every phase of the process. This allows non-DS experts to learn from doing and to be able to accomplish the full lifecycle process, shortening the learning curve, of the tool and of the DS process itself.

These general design principles are shared with digital design and creative tools, lacking further work to operationalize and translate them into specific requirements for the system. It was claimed by [46] that some design methods can be used in DS, to analyze and make sense of the phenomenology (e.g. studying factors that affect success of a DS project) or to help the data scientist (or other professional, as we are targeting) in structuring the creative exploration process in a controlled way.

We agree and argue that there is potential to use and adapt hybrid design methods to structure other DS activities, with eventual impact to the proposed DSL model. Plus, for future work, fruitful design inspiration can be found in the tested solutions of existing digital collaborative design studios and of digital tools for creativity.

5 Conclusions and Future Work

The work presented results from a DSR project to design and develop an IT-solution for supporting the DS full lifecycle. Work has been done in partnership with a company and the system is targeted to be used by its collaborators and clients.

This paper aims at a scoping review of previous work outlining which consensus is shared across the major fields of IS development and HCI, regarding the emergent theme of "*Data Science*". For a theoretical background, we started with a systematic literature review (over 519 articles retrieved from the databases of Web of Science, Science Direct and ACM Library databases). Then we defined a search strategy and criteria to iteratively refine and narrow this initial list to a selected list of 214 publications regarding '*Data Science*', for a categorization. The papers were classified in three main categories and ten related sub-categories, in order to better understand '*what is data science*' and how to approach the design of a system. The structured review already reveals DS, with ML, AI and sophisticated algorithms to be a fertile area of interdisciplinary inquiry and work, given the multidimensional phenomena.

This list of paper was narrowed to 23 papers, inspected for direct contributions to our understanding about the *process* of DS and about the user-perspective attributes of an *artefact* that supports the iterative activities and lifecycle. Resulting from the findings, we propose a generic DS lifecycle model (DSL) to structure the activities and elicit a set of generic design principles to guide our future work in practice.

With the found application pitches, from researchers and practitioners in different disciplines, a future research agenda should increase research efforts with real life contexts, cross referencing rigor and relevance in research projects to be carried out [7]. Improving the usability of the available tools or—more relevant and challenging—design new tools and integrated solutions for digitally support the DS lifecycle, focusing on a broader set of user's technical profile is a research gap.

A shared framework to structure DS activities, standardizing data formats, for instance, and guidelines to address the design of an IT-solution supporting the innovation and creative dynamics of the process, particularly, when targeting non-expert users in DS, is lacking and worth further research and practice.

As also argued, design methods can provide, to some extent, a framework for the innovation and creative dynamics of data-related processes and DS activities. When designing for DS, design inspiration can be found in the solutions of digital collaborative design studios and of digital tools for creativity.

Finally, evidences were found sustaining the potential of using hybrid design methods and shared research and practice perspectives on interaction, experience and service design, as promising avenues for future work.

Acknowledgements The research work was partially funded by the European Commission, under the PORTUGAL 2020 structural fund (CENTRO2020), for the period of 2014–2020 (Project Ref. 2016/017728).

References

1. Chen, H., Chiang, R.H.L., Storey, V.C.: Business intelligence and analytics: from big data to big impact. MIS Q. **36**, 1165–1188 (2012)
2. Manyika, J., Chui, M., Bughin, J., et al.: Big Data: The Next Frontier for Innovation, Competition, and Productivity, pp. 1–22. McKinsey Company (2011)
3. McAfee, A., Brynjolfsson, E., Davenport, T.H., et al.: Big data: the management revolution. Harv. Bus. Rev. **90**, 61–67 (2012). https://doi.org/00475394
4. Mockus, A.: Operational data are missing, incorrect, and decontextualized. In: Perspectives on Data Science for Software Engineering, pp. 317–322 (2016)
5. Hevner, A.R., March, S.T., Park, J., Ram, S.: Design science in information. Syst. Res. **28**, 75–105 (2004). https://doi.org/10.2307/25148869
6. Peffers, K., Tuunanen, T., Rothenberger, M.A., Chatterjee, S.: A design science research methodology for information systems research. J. Manage. Inf. Syst. **24**, 45–77 (2008). https://doi.org/10.2753/MIS0742-1222240302
7. Nagle, T., Sammon, D.: The development of a design research canvas for data practitioners. J. Decis. Syst. **25**, 369–380 (2016). https://doi.org/10.1080/12460125.2016.1187386
8. Webster, J., Watson, R.T.: Analyzing the past to prepare for the future: writing a literature review. MIS Q. **26**, xii–xxiii (2002). https://doi.org/1210112213

9. Levy, Y., Ellis, T.J.: A systems approach to conduct an effective literature review in support of information systems research. Inf. Sci. J. **9**, 181–212 (2006). https://doi.org/10.1049/cp.2009. 0961

10. Tranfield, D., Denyer, D., Smart, P.: Towards a methodology for developing evidence-informed management knowledge by means of systematic review*. Br. J. Manage. **14**, 207–222 (2003). https://doi.org/10.1111/1467-8551.00375

11. Lee, I.: Big data: dimensions, evolution, impacts, and challenges. Bus. Horiz. **60**, 293–303 (2017). https://doi.org/10.1016/j.bushor.2017.01.004

12. Storey, V.C., Song, I.-Y.: Big data technologies and management: what conceptual modeling can do. Data Knowl. Eng. **108**, 50–67 (2017). https://doi.org/10.1016/j.datak.2017.01.001

13. Cheng, S., Liu, B., Shi, Y., et al.: Evolutionary computation and big data: key challenges and future directions. In: Tan, Y., Shi, Y. (eds.) Data Mining and Big Data 2016, pp. 3–14. Springer International Publishing, AG, GEWERBESTRASSE 11, CHAM, CH-6330, Switzerland (2016)

14. Philip Chen, C.L., Zhang, C.-Y., Chen, C.L.P., Zhang, C.-Y.: Data-intensive applications, challenges, techniques and technologies: a survey on Big Data. Inf. Sci. (Ny) **275**, 314–347 (2014). https://doi.org/10.1016/j.ins.2014.01.015

15. Rabl, T., Sadoghi, M., Jacobsen, H.-A., et al.: Solving big data challenges for enterprise application performance management. Proc. VLDB Endow. **5**, 1724–1735 (2012). https://doi.org/ 10.14778/2367502.2367512

16. Miller, H.G., Mork, P.: From data to decisions: a value chain for big data. IT Prof. **15**, 57–59 (2013). https://doi.org/10.1109/MITP.2013.11

17. Demirkan, H., Delen, D.: Leveraging the capabilities of service-oriented decision support systems: putting analytics and big data in cloud. Decis. Support Syst. **55**, 412–421 (2013). https://doi.org/10.1016/j.dss.2012.05.048

18. Kowalczyk, M., Buxmann, P.: An ambidextrous perspective on business intelligence and analytics support in decision processes: insights from a multiple case study. Decis. Support Syst. **80**, 1–13 (2015). https://doi.org/10.1016/j.dss.2015.08.010

19. Hashem, I.A.T., Yaqoob, I., Anuar, N.B., et al.: The rise of "big data" on cloud computing: review and open research issues. Inf. Syst. **47**, 98–115 (2015). https://doi.org/10.1016/j.is.2014. 07.006

20. Haug, F.S.: Bad big data science. In: Joshi, J., Karypis, G., Liu, L., Hu, X., Ak, R., Xia, Y., Xu, W., Sato, A.H., Rachuri, S., Ungar, L., Yu, P.S., Govindaraju, R., Suzumura, T. (eds.) 2016 IEEE International Conference on Big Data (BIG DATA), pp. 2863–2871. IEEE, New York, USA (2016)

21. Hazen, B.T., Boone, C.A., Ezell, J.D., Jones-Farmer, L.A.: Data quality for data science, predictive analytics, and big data in supply chain management: an introduction to the problem and suggestions for research and applications. Int. J. Prod. Econ. **154**, 72–80 (2014). https://doi. org/10.1016/j.ijpe.2014.04.018

22. Vedula, S.S., Hager, G.D.: Surgical data science: the new knowledge domain. Innov. Surg. Sci. **2**, 109+ (2017). https://doi.org/10.1515/iss-2017-0004

23. Westra, B.L., Sylvia, M., Weinfurter, E.F., et al.: Big data science: a literature review of nursing research exemplars. Nurs. Outlook **65**, 549–561 (2017). https://doi.org/10.1016/j.outlook.2016. 11.021

24. Roy, S., Ray, R., Roy, A., et al.: IoT, big data science & analytics, cloud computing and mobile app based hybrid system for smart agriculture. In: Chakrabarti, S., Saha, H. (eds.) 8th Annual Industrial Automation and Electromechanical Engineering Conference (IEMECON), pp. 303–304. IEEE, New York, USA (2017)

25. Woodard, J.: Big data and Ag-analytics: an open source, open data platform for agricultural & environmental finance, insurance, and risk. Agric. Financ. Rev. **76**, 15–26 (2016). https://doi. org/10.1108/AFR-03-2016-0018

26. Liu, M.-C., Huang, Y.-M.: The use of data science for education: the case of social-emotional learning. Smart Learn. Environ. **4**, 1 (2017). https://doi.org/10.1186/s40561-016-0040-4

27. Conte, R., Giardini, F.: Towards computational and behavioral social science. Eur. Psychol. **21**, 131–140 (2016). https://doi.org/10.1027/1016-9040/a000257

28. Chang, R.M., Kauffman, R.J., Kwon, Y.: Understanding the paradigm shift to computational social science in the presence of big data. Decis. Support Syst. **63**, 67–80 (2014). https://doi.org/10.1016/j.dss.2013.08.008

29. Bibri, S.E., Krogstie, J.: Smart sustainable cities of the future: an extensive interdisciplinary literature review. Sustain. Cities Soc. **31**, 183–212 (2017). https://doi.org/10.1016/j.scs.2017.02.016

30. Fischer, F., Fuchs, J., Mansmann, F., Keim, D.A.: BANKSAFE: visual analytics for big data in large-scale computer networks. Inf. Vis. **14**, 51–61 (2015). https://doi.org/10.1177/1473871613488572

31. Talbot, J., Lee, B., Kapoor, A., Tan, D.S.: EnsembleMatrix: interactive visualization to support machine learning with multiple classifiers. In: Proceedings of the SIGCHI Conference on Human Factors in Computing Systems, pp. 1283–1292 (2009)

32. Bandi, A., Fellah, A.: Crafting a data visualization course for the tech industry. J. Comput. Sci. Coll. **33**, 46–56 (2017)

33. Snyder, J.: Vernacular visualization practices in a citizen science project. In: Proceedings of the 2017 ACM Conference on Computer Supported Cooperative Work and Social Computing, pp. 2097–2111. ACM, New York, NY, USA (2017)

34. Bumblauskas, D., Nold, H., Bumblauskas, P., Igou, A.: Big data analytics: transforming data to action. Bus. Process. Manage. J. **23**, 703–720 (2017). https://doi.org/10.1108/BPMJ-03-2016-0056

35. Horita, F.E.A.A., de Albuquerque, J.P., Marchezini, V., Mendiondo, E.M.: Bridging the gap between decision-making and emerging big data sources: an application of a model-based framework to disaster management in Brazil. Decis. Support Syst. **97**, 12–22 (2017). https://doi.org/10.1016/j.dss.2017.03.001

36. Crotty, A., Galakatos, A., Zgraggen, E., et al.: The case for interactive data exploration accelerators (IDEAs). In: Proceedings of the Workshop on Human-in-the-Loop Data Analytics—HILDA'16, pp. 1–6. ACM Press, New York, New York, USA(2016)

37. Grainger, S., Mao, F., Buytaert, W.: Environmental data visualisation for non-scientific contexts: literature review and design framework. Environ. Model Softw. **85**, 299–318 (2016)

38. Howe, B., Franklin, M., Haas, L., et al.: Data science education: we're missing the boat, again. In: 2017 IEEE 33RD International Conference on Data Engineering, pp. 1473–1474. IEEE, New York, USA (2017)

39. Dichev, C., Dicheva, D., Salem, W., et al.: Towards data science literacy. Procedia Comput. Sci. **108**, 2151–2160 (2017). https://doi.org/10.1016/j.procs.2017.05.240

40. Newman, R., Chang, V., Walters, R.J., Wills, G.B.: Model and experimental development for business data science. Int. J. Inf. Manage. **36**, 607–617 (2016). https://doi.org/10.1016/j.ijinfomgt.2016.04.004

41. Das, M., Cui, R., Campbell, D. R., et al.: Towards methods for systematic research on big data. In 2015 IEEE International Conference on Big Data, pp. 2072–2081. IEEE, New York, USA (2015)

42. Hoffman, S., Podgurski, A.: Big bad data: law, public health, and biomedical databases. J. Law Med. Ethics **41**, 56–60 (2013). https://doi.org/10.1111/jlme.12040

43. Brunswicker, S., Bertino, E., Matei, S.: Big data for open digital innovation—a research roadmap. Big Data Res. **2**, 53–58 (2015). https://doi.org/10.1016/j.bdr.2015.01.008

44. Saltz, J., Shamshurin, I., Connors, C.: Predicting data science sociotechnical execution challenges by categorizing data science projects. J. Assoc. Inf. Sci. Technol. **68**, 2720–2728 (2017). https://doi.org/10.1002/asi.23873

45. Carbone, A., Jensen, M., Sato, A.-H.: Challenges in data science: a complex systems perspective. Chaos Solitons Fractals **90**, 1–7 (2016). https://doi.org/10.1016/j.chaos.2016.04.020

46. Kazakci, A.O.: Data science as a new frontier for design. In: Weber, C., Husung, S., Cantamessa, M., Cascini, G., Marjanovic, D., Venkataraman, S. (eds.) Design Information and Knowledge Management, ICED 15, vol. 10. DESIGN SOC, Glasgow, England (2015)

47. Larson, D., Chang, V.: A review and future direction of agile, business intelligence, analytics and data science. Int. J. Inf. Manage. **36**, 700–710 (2016). https://doi.org/10.1016/j.ijinfomgt.2016.04.013
48. Demchenko, Y., Belloum, A., Los, W., et al.: EDISON data science framework: a foundation for building data science profession for research and industry. In: 2016 8th IEEE International Conference on Cloud Computing Technology and Science (CLOUDCOM 2016), pp. 620–626. IEEE, New York, USA (2016)
49. Anya, O., Moore, B., Kieliszewski, C., et al.: Understanding the practice of discovery in enterprise big data science: an agent-based approach. Procedia Manuf. **3**, 882–889 (2015). https://doi.org/10.1016/j.promfg.2015.07.345
50. Cao, L.: Data science: a comprehensive overview. ACM Comput. Surv. **50**, 1–42 (2017). https://doi.org/10.1145/3076253
51. Chuprina, S., Alexandrov, V., Alexandrov, N.: Using ontology engineering methods to improve computer science and data science skills. Procedia Comput. Sci. **80**:1780–1790 (2016)

On the Influence of Tools on Collaboration in Participative Enterprise Modeling—An Experimental Comparison Between Whiteboard and Multi-touch Table

Anne Gutschmidt

Abstract The paper presents an experiment about the influence of the modeling tool on group work in the context of enterprise modeling. A goal modeling task was set where three groups of three persons worked with a whiteboard, and three groups of three persons worked with a multi-touch table. Comparisons of working styles between the two tools indicate that multi-touch tables promote parallel working and that a team member's position plays a role in taking on certain tasks. Whiteboard users may more easily lose track of what teammates are doing.

Keywords Enterprise modeling · Participative modeling · Multi-touch table · Group work · Experiment

1 Introduction

Enterprise modeling (EM) is a powerful way of capturing important information about a company, such as structures, processes and dependencies. It enables a company to identify problems and their causes as well as potential for change. Finally, it helps to prepare for and implement such changes [1]. EM is, however, not only about mapping processes and structures. In the modeling method 4EM [1], it is suggested that EM should start with basic models comprising general goals and problems a company might have. This resembles a brainstorming task involving collecting and capturing knowledge and ideas.

When creating an enterprise model, usually comprising several intertwined sub-models, it is necessary to involve all stakeholders. Participative EM suggests that the modeling be performed by the stakeholders themselves with the support of facilitators

A prior version of this paper has been published in the ISD2018 Proceedings (http://aisel.aisnet.org/isd2014/proceedings2018).

A. Gutschmidt (✉)
University of Rostock, Rostock, Germany
e-mail: anne.gutschmidt@uni-rostock.de

© Springer Nature Switzerland AG 2019   151
B. Andersson et al. (eds.), *Advances in Information Systems Development*,
Lecture Notes in Information Systems and Organisation 34,
https://doi.org/10.1007/978-3-030-22993-1_9

representing the experts of the modeling method [2]. The stakeholders are domain experts that directly provide the necessary knowledge in the modeling process.

This paper focuses on tools which may support teams of stakeholders particularly in the area of modeling tasks where brainstorming activities are required. Multi-touch tables appear to be a useful tool for such modeling tasks. In contrast to modeling at a whiteboard or with pen and paper, content can be easily changed and deleted, and, what is of greatest advantage, models can be saved digitally, shared and reused at any time. The differences in handling this tool may also cause differences in the way a group works together. In this paper, a study is presented which examines the influence of tool on the way groups work together. We compared a multi-touch table (MTT) with a whiteboard, the latter representing a traditional tool. We focused on the following research questions: (1) How and to what extent do single team members contribute to the modeling task? This should also show how evenly distributed individual contributions are, depending on the tool. (2) Are there different working styles depending on the tool? The latter question concerns aspects such as task division and coordination. (3) Are there any differences in team performance depending on the tool? The goal of this research is to find out whether the MTT already provides advantages that must be taken into consideration when deciding on a modeling tool. Furthermore, we wanted to look for hints on working styles of whiteboard users that might be transferred to the MTT, e.g. by aspects of function and design of modeling software for the MTT.

In the next section, some background on group work will be presented showing relations to participative EM. Moreover, research on MTT will be described briefly. In the third section, the method of the study is presented, followed by results in Sect. 4. The last section concludes the paper with a discussion of the results, including limitations of the study and implications for future research.

2   State of the Art

2.1   *Group Work and Participative Enterprise Modeling*

The main reason why we work in groups is that we hope to perform better by gathering performance and ability of several individuals. However, group work may bring both increase and decrease in performance with regard to motivation, individual skills and coordination (see e.g. [3] for more information). The mere presence of other persons can motivate someone to put more effort in a task. Furthermore, in some teams, persons compensate weaker performances of their teammates [3, 4]. On the other hand, persons might be less motivated because they do not see the concrete value of their contribution in the team effort [5]. With regard to individual skill, performance decrease might occur because teammates interrupt the flow of ideas of a person by keeping on voicing their own ideas. However, being inspired by others' ideas may also lead to new ideas and thus a performance increase [3]. Group work, of course, also requires more effort on coordination the larger a group is, e.g., there has to be an agreement on who is allowed to talk at a certain moment. Lamm and Trommsdorff [6] showed that people produced less ideas in a brainstorming task when working in a group than when working individually.

Participative EM represents classic group work which is just as prone to the above-mentioned effects. It involves a variety of activities which the members of the group must perform. In this paper, we focus particularly on tasks of EM which involve gathering knowledge and ideas in terms of brainstorming. Performed in a team, such activities require a significant effort on coordinating the contributions of all members. Secondly, situations may occur when one of several alternatives has to be chosen by the group. If a person is dominating this decision process because of their knowledge or intelligence, this might lead to good overall performance. However, if such dominance is based on characteristics such as the rank of a group member, this might deteriorate results and lead to a decrease in the motivation of other team members to voice their ideas. Especially when tasks are at hand where there is no complete knowledge and the group has to base decisions on guesses, more extroverted persons may possibly dominate discussions at the expense of the result's quality (see [1] for more information on EM, and [7] for information on task types). This paper will scrutinize EM especially from this perspective of group work and its challenges concerning individual participation, group performance and coordination.

2.2 Studies on Multi-touch Use

There have been several studies dealing with MTTs in general. Especially in educational context, advantages of these devices are underlined. They allow sketching ideas that can be easily changed or erased from screen, thus being less fixed and restricting than notes on paper [8, 9]. On the other hand, studies report that input via touch keyboard is more laborious and time consuming [10]. Several studies compared MTTs with other tools assuming an influence of the tool on collaboration. Setting a brainstorming task, Buisine et al. [11] discovered that users of MTTs contributed less verbally and in gestures than users of a table covered with paper, but more than users of a flip chart. They hypothesize that the novel medium is distracting and thus restrains collaboration. Basheri and Burd [12] observed closer collaboration of teams using a MTT compared to pen and paper. When comparing PC and MTT for UML modeling, Basheri et al. [13] found the team members' contributions in terms of modeling more evenly balanced and the collaboration to be closer at the MTT. Rogers et al. [14] considered laptop and MTT with and without tangible objects where the laptop turned out to cause less evenly distributed verbal contributions. All in all, MTTs seem to be promising for the purpose of participative EM. However, several other factors play a role in this, such as the orientation of the medium [15] and the task at hand [11] which may vary in EM.

3 Method

3.1 Experimental Design

As the influence of the tool on group work was to be explored, the following experimental design was applied. The independent variable was represented by the tool which was either whiteboard or MTT. It was decided to use a between-subjects design. In a within-subjects design, teams would have to work with both tools one after the other. On the one hand, this would have allowed direct comparisons where variables such as personal traits and modeling experience would have been kept constant for both treatments. However, the learning effect was assumed to have a more severe influence; i.e. groups would have developed their team roles and work strategy while using the first tool, and then would have continued with the second tool based on their recent experience. Following a between-subjects design, an EM task was to be solved in teams of three either on the whiteboard or the MTT. The team size of three was chosen due to the limited size of the media and because Nerdinger et al. [16] claims that group effects are to be encountered with only a team size of at least three.

The dependent variables corresponded to the participation of the group members, perceived team coordination and organization. The group members' participation was measured based on their contributions in terms of talking and modeling including activities such as writing, drawing and moving elements on the respective medium, e.g. cards on the whiteboard. Participation was assessed via observation using video recordings of the modeling sessions. Perceived coordination and organization among team members were assessed via individual interviews. The participants were asked whether certain team members were responsible for or often took on certain tasks and how such task divisions arose. Moreover they were asked to describe how their group approached the task, with a special focus on modeling activities. Furthermore, group performance was measured by considering the complexity of the final solution in terms of number of components and relations drawn. As the participants had to solve a very open task comprising brainstorming activities, we did not assess quality aspects related to the content, e.g. semantic quality [17]. The team members were asked to take the perspective of entrepreneurs and collect ideas instead of mapping concrete knowledge. It was up to them on which aspects of the task they wanted to concentrate. To include the aspect of model quality when analyzing the modeling process we, however, examined to what extent the participants used the repertoire of modeling components offered by the notation, adapting the approach of [18] to our issue.

3.2 Procedure

The study took place at a laboratory of the computer science department at the University of Rostock. The participants were recruited by personal request. The assignment of persons to groups was organized taking the participants' personal schedules into consideration. The groups were assigned to the tool randomly. The EM task the participants were expected to perform referred to the modeling of goals and problems of a pizza delivery service, an application field the participants would probably connect with. Moreover, goal and problem models belong to the most basic enterprise models in the 4EM method suggested by Sandkuhl et al. [1]. They should be easy to apply even for less experienced modelers. It was made sure that at least one team member had at least some experience with the 4EM notation of goal models. If the participants' time schedule allowed it, a face-to-face tutorial was provided before the study in a separate meeting.

At the beginning of each trial, the three participants of a group and the investigator met in the laboratory. Beside the investigator, at least one person in charge of the technical equipment was present, but stayed in the background. In some cases the participants had not met before such that they had to be introduced to each other. Refreshments were provided to create a relaxed atmosphere. Each participant received a handout containing the modeling task and a short reference of the 4EM notation for goal models. They were explicitly asked to work together on the task. In case the group had to work with the MTT, an introduction to the user interface of the self-developed modeling software was given (see right-hand screenshot in Fig. 1). The software provides an editor for 4EM goal and problem modeling enabling several users to model at the same time. Menus can be opened at every spot of the canvas to create components such as goals and problems. All components can be moved and rotated at will. If a user wants to add a description to a component, a keyboard will pop up right below the component. Thus, users do not have to share a keyboard; multiple keyboards allow parallel editing. Each keyboard's position depends on the position of the component they are appended to. If the component is moved, the keyboard will follow. Components can be linked by drawing arrows. These component relations can be further described by selecting one of the predefined annotations, e.g. "hinders" for a problem hindering a goal. We did not introduce a facilitator because one purpose of the study was to provide insights into natural working behaviors that may help facilitators in chairing modeling sessions. That is why the teams where required to comprise at least one member experienced in the notation.

After the participants had finished reading and remaining questions were answered by the investigator, they started to work on the task. Three groups used a MTT (size: 1210×680 mm) as can be seen in Fig. 1, the other three groups used a whiteboard (size: 2000×1000 mm). The whiteboard groups were additionally equipped with colored cards, magnets to pin cards to the board, and pens. A time limit of 30 min was set for the task. The modeling sessions were video and audio-recorded using two cameras, one installed at the ceiling and another one standing on a tripod. After the task was finished, interviews were conducted with each participant in parallel in

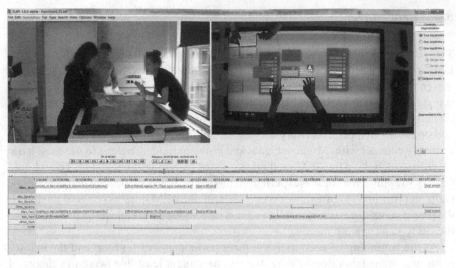

Fig. 1 Marking and annotating activity units in the video recordings with ELAN [19]

separate rooms. The procedure was concluded by letting each participant fill out a questionnaire to capture demographics, experience with modeling notations and use of MTT.

3.3 Sample

Overall, 18 persons took part in the study, i.e. three teams using the whiteboard and three teams using the MTT. They were all students of business information systems or computer science. Three participants were female, two of them joined one team that was assigned to the MTT, the third woman joined a team working with a whiteboard. In the whiteboard group, participants were 24.9 years old on average ($\sigma = 2.2$, max $= 28$, min $= 22$), in the MTT group, participants were 23.6 years old on average ($\sigma = 1.9$, max $= 28$, min $= 22$). The participants came from three different nations. There was one completely Russian team, one completely Indian team and a mixed team of two German students and one Indian student. In two of the teams, the members knew each other already, in one team only two members knew each other before. The whiteboard group comprised two completely German teams whose members all knew each other before, and one mixed team of all three nations whose members had not met before. The level of experience of the 4EM notation, measured with a 5-point scale with 1 representing no experience, was at 2 on average for the MTT group ($\sigma = 1$, max $= 3$, min $= 1$) and at 3.7 on average for the whiteboard group ($\sigma = 0.6$, max $= 4$, min $= 3$). On a 5-point scale, the participants of the MTT group estimated their experience with MTTs at an average value of 1.7 with 1 representing no experience ($\sigma = 1.3$, max $= 5$, min $= 1$).

3.4 Data Evaluation Methods

The data from the questionnaires were statistically evaluated using the software SPSS. The interviews were transcribed, and qualitative content analysis according to Mayring [20] was applied, supported by the Software MaxQDA. First, the interviews were scanned for statements about coordination among team members and the organization of their work. The resulting coding units were inductively ordered into categories.

For the evaluation of the video recordings, the software ELAN was used [19]. To determine all time units of talking and modeling of each single person, the respective sections had to be marked on a timeline in the software as Fig. 2 shows. Furthermore, the time units of modeling were annotated with a detailed description of the according activity. In a subsequent step, the activities were again categorized, leading to major activities such as creating a new component (e.g. goal), moving a modeling component over the screen of the MTT or the whiteboard, respectively, writing or drawing relations between components. Each activity was linked with a time stamp such that talking and modeling behavior of each participant in the course of the whole session could be depicted and analyzed. Special focus was put on particular events in the modeling referring to the creation of content (e.g. create component, write, draw relation, pin component). The team members' contributions were determined by considering individual speaking and modeling time in relation to speaking and modeling time of the whole team. That way we could also evaluate on team level how many components and relations were drawn, and how many component types of the eight offered types had been used.

4 Results

4.1 Participation

Figure 2 shows the time proportions spent on talking and modeling in separate, and on talking and modeling on the whole for each member of each team. For all members in all groups it was captured when they contributed to the modeling work in a creative way in terms of adding content, comprising the creation of components (e.g. goal), writing, drawing relations between components and pinning components to the whiteboard. For the latter, there is no corresponding event on the MTT. Figure 3 shows the occurrence of these events in all teams in the course of the modeling session (30 min).

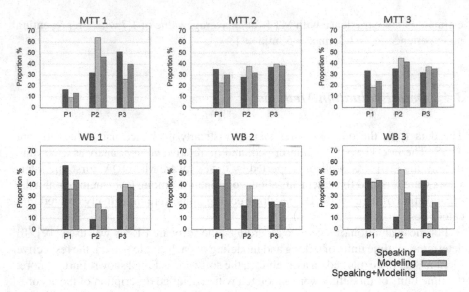

Fig. 2 The time proportions spent by the members (P1–P3) of each team on speaking, modeling as well as speaking and modeling in sum; MTT = multi-touch table, WB = whiteboard

4.2 Coordination and Organization

Based on statements on team coordination and organization occurring in the inter-views, six major categories arose which deal with (I) the subjects the team members explicitly agreed on, (II) statements that collective approval was part of the pro-ceeding, (III) the existence of task divisions and if so, which form they took, (IV) reasons for certain task distributions, (V) parallel working, and (VI) awareness of the teammates' activities during the task.

Subjects of explicit agreement. One participant of a team working with a MTT and one participant of a whiteboard group mentioned that the team explicitly agreed on how to start working. E.g. the latter said, "We soon agreed that we would start with goals and then move to problems and then the rest, like adding constraints and opportunities to the model ..." (6,3,1,39, translated from German).[1] During the task, some teams consulted about how they would further proceed, as was mentioned by four interviewees from two MTT groups and two whiteboard groups. One participant who had worked with a whiteboard stated that the team had to agree on the level of abstraction with which they approached the task. Three participants from two MTT groups and one from a whiteboard group mentioned that they explicitly agreed on how or when to use the tool. E.g., "They directly wanted to do it on the software, but I convinced them, consoled them like it's better list it first and just go there and put it on" (3,1,1,11).

---

[1] Citations from interviews are given with number of trial, number of participant, page and paragraph.

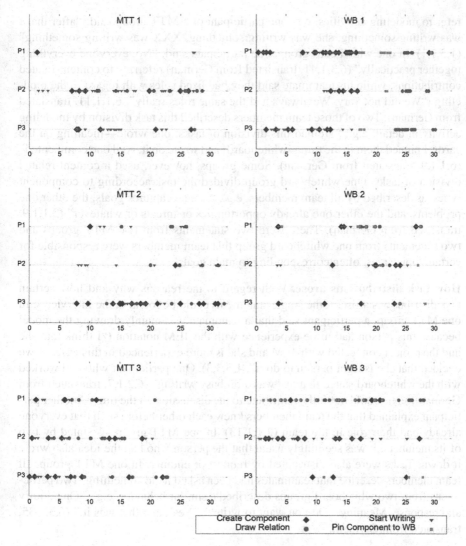

Fig. 3 Modeling events where content was created by the participants in the course of the 30 min modeling session

Getting collective approval. Two participants of a MTT group mentioned that during their work they constantly searched for a common agreement, e.g. "Before we did anything, we always said first: we can do that" (4,3,1,37, translated from German). In each whiteboard group, there was always one person who described a similar behavior.

Division of tasks. In every group, except for one whiteboard group, at least one team member stated that there was no fixed division of tasks. In most cases, the statements refer to modeling activities, e.g. one participant of a MTT group said: "after that I was writing something, she was writing something, XXX was writing something" (1,3,1,1). In one whiteboard group, one participant said, "No, everyone everything together practically" (6,3,1,41, translated from German) referring to content-related contributions, while his teammate said they had fixed roles with regard to the modeling ("We did not vary. We always had the same roles really", 6,1,1,11, translated from German). Two of those team members described this task division by modeling activity in detail, e.g., "We had this division of tasks, one wrote—meaning on the cards. I pinned them to the thing [whiteboard] and wrote on it. And one commented" (6,1,1,9, translated from German). Some groups, however, used a content-related division of tasks. One whiteboard group divided the task according to component types, as described by all team members, e.g., "… one captures goals, the other one problems, and the other one already opportunities or threats or whatever" (2,1,1,9, translated from German). There were two statements from two MTT groups and two statements from one whiteboard group that team members were responsible for certain topic areas, often corresponding to main goals.

How task distributions arose. With regard to the reasons why and how certain task distributions arose, some single statements could be found in the interviews. In one MTT group, a participant said that a teammate was mainly drawing the model because this person had more experience with the 4EM notation ("I think that she had the project connected with 4EM and she is more experienced in this case, so we decided that she is right person to do it", 1,3,3,3). One participant who had worked with the whiteboard stated that he "was a bit busy writing" (6,2,1,7, translated from German), so he could not fully contribute to the discussion all the time. Another participant explained that the team members knew each other before such that everyone already had their role in the team (2,1,1,13). In one MTT group, as stated by two of its members, it was seemingly usual that the person who had the idea also wrote it down. Tasks were also distributed by request or enquiry. In one MTT group, all team members describe that teammates had been asked to do something. Two participants from two whiteboard groups described a similar behavior, e.g., "On enquiry and response. Meaning, 'Do you want to write?', 'Yes', and that was it." (6,3,1,35, translated from German).

In all MTT groups, participants mentioned that the team members' position was a reason why certain persons turned out to be responsible for certain modeling activities. According to one participant, the orientation of the screen played a role ("… we staying the different sides and the first orientation, the right orientation were only for one person, so XXX stayed in the right position and we stayed in the other sides", 1,3,3,3). Two participants said that proximity was another reason ("I was doing, because I was […] right side and the creating menu was the right side. So every time I was doing this thing.", 3,3,1,16). One of these participants also considered space as important ("… because he always had a lot of space up there in his corner …", 4,3,1,65, translated from German). The participant further explained that the keyboards, which were automatically attached to every component as soon as the edit mode was opened, and the menu to create components, of which several instances could be opened everywhere on the screen, restricted the team's space.

Some participants described that the distribution of tasks in their team arose out of its own. One participant from one MTT group and four participants from all three whiteboard groups said that the task distribution emerged without any apparent reason, e.g., "It just happens" (5,2,1,27).

Parallel working. Two participants from two MTT groups mentioned that they worked in parallel. One of them explained further that parallel working concerned modeling activities in particular and that they did not choose to model in parallel at the beginning, but they changed to this mode in the course of the task. This participant and another one from the second aforementioned MTT group also describe that they had been discussing while teammates were modeling at the same time. However, some participants also said that they did not work in parallel. A participant from a whiteboard group even said "when somebody was writing, there was mostly silence during that time" (6,1,1,23, translated from German). One MTT group seemed to have had some trouble with the software such that it appeared to them that parallel working was not supported, as mentioned by one member ("Actually, we've tried in the beginning to do at the same time, but the system was not that cooperative for that. We thought of like, we'll do one by one. When one was completed with the goal, and the second person will start at goaling", 4,1,1,25). The other two team members stated that they changed to non-parallel working particularly later in the process, e.g., "because later at the end when..., there was mostly just one working ..." (4,2,1,17, translated from German).

Awareness. Two participants of one MTT group mentioned that the MTT helped them to keep an overview of what was going on during the task, e.g., "Once again wrote something, then you looked. What did the other one do? Ah yes, okay, then you can still write that ..." (4,2,1,11, translated from German). However, two participants from two whiteboard groups said that there had been a moment where they lost track of what was done by the others, e.g., "where I was concentrated on this and I lost track of what XXX and YYY were doing at the other corner of the whiteboard, what lines they were drawing. And then I confined myself to my right side of the board" (2,3,3,3, translated from German).

4.3 Group Performance

Table 1 describes the complexity of the goal models the groups created including the number of components, among them decomposition elements (and, or), the number of relations in general and relations that have been annotated, e.g., a problem may hinder a goal. The last line represents the percentage of component types that had been used based on a repertoire of eight different components offered in the 4EM notation.

Table 1 Parameters describing the complexity of the respective groups' final model

	MTT 1	MTT 2	MTT 3	WB 1	WB 2	WB 3
#Components	13	14	17	29	17	19
#Decompositions	1	1	1	1	3	0
#Relations	14	15	20	27	16	31
#Annotated rel.	0	13	18	23	0	31
% Used component types	75.0	50.0	62.5	87.5	75.0	50.0

5 Discussion

5.1 Summary and Interpretation

A study was presented that compared the use of MTT and whiteboard in the context of participative EM. First, verbal contributions and modeling contributions of the members within each group were analyzed. Addressing our first research question, Fig. 2 gives hint on more evenly distributed participation as the respective charts appear more compact for group MTT 2 and MTT 3. For MTT 2, the participants' origin, India, might have played a role in their team work. Some team members often repeated what another one had said as a sign of confirmation, possibly reflecting their desire for consensus. However, looking at modeling events triggered by the individual team members in Fig. 3, the distribution of modeling activities appears less balanced. It seems that with regard to really creating content, one team member was particularly dominating. Experience with the modeling notation might also have influenced the distribution of individual contributions. In team MTT 1, there is mainly one person performing the modeling activities as this team member is the only one with sound experience in the modeling notation. A second team member, however, is dominating in the discussion whereas the third team member has a low proportion of verbal and modeling contributions. Although WB 1 and WB 3 comprised experienced modelers, they showed similarly uneven activity distributions. This gives hint that the tool might have been a stronger influencing factor than experience. Nevertheless, it might be the case that these persons had undergone similar collaborative tasks together before as the members of WB 1 and WB 3 knew each other before. This might have caused that these groups skipped the phase of team forming or at least found their roles more quickly than the others had. Taking a look at WB 2 in Fig. 2 though, we again see unevenly distributed contributions although team members did not know each other before. This still leaves the tool as important influencing factor. All in all, however, the differences between the team members' contributions on whiteboard or MTT are not clear enough to lead to definite conclusions. At least in this study, it seems that the MTT promoted more balanced contributions by the team members.

Addressing the second research question on collaboration styles, the most interesting findings concern parallel working, awareness, and reasons for task assignments. The MTT seems to stimulate parallel working in terms of parallel modeling, but even more so in terms of discussing and modeling in parallel. Probably owing to time pressure at the last phase of the session, teams decided for parallel working. Only one team abandoned trying to work in parallel at the MTT. As the software was just a prototypical implementation, its interface might not have responded in the way the users had expected and thus might have made the impression that parallel working was not supported. This shows that parallel working and the challenges connected with it must be especially considered when designing and implementing user interfaces of a MTT modeling editor.

According to the interviews, MTT users might be more easily aware of what their teammates are working on. The horizontal work surface might be a reason for this as claimed by Rogers and Lindley [15]. Two participants from two different whiteboard teams mentioned that there had been a moment during the modeling session when they lost track of what the others were doing. These findings support statements by Muller-Tomfelde et al. [21] and Buisine et al. [11] that vertical work surfaces are less supportive for collaboration than horizontal. One might also assume that the restricted size of the working surface, which seems at first as a disadvantage of the tool, might also turn out to be an advantage as it is easier to keep an overview of the whole model than on the larger whiteboard.

When asked why certain persons took on a certain task, members of all MTT teams named the position at the MTT as one reason. When a person stood in opposite to the orientation of the user interface, rotating the elements meant additional effort. Still, it was observed that such MTT users were nevertheless engaged in modeling. Another participant reported that proximity implied responsibility, e.g. somebody standing near the main menu became responsible for creating new components. This is similar to the findings of Scott and Carpendale [22] and Ryall et al.[23] stating that the farther away a MTT user is from a part of the interface the less responsibility he or she feels for it. Moreover, it is possible that teams developed a certain routine in terms of a mental set, also known as cognitive fixedness [24]. Menus could be opened at every point on the surface, so other users would have also been able to open a menu and create new components. Due to a mental set, the team members might have stuck to a strategy they have found to be successful once. However, the interviews reveal that space also played a role in this, and thus space management is another challenge when designing the user interface. Team members took on a certain task because they had more space on the working surface where they stood. As a consequence, they were reluctant to open more menus that would take more space.

Concerning explicit arrangements, there do not seem to be many differences between MTT und whiteboard users, as far as can be concluded from the interviews, e.g. on how to start, or how to proceed in the middle of the task. The question of how and when to use the modeling tool seemed to be more explicit for MTT users (mentioned by three users in two groups) than for whiteboard users (mentioned by one user only). Due to the MTT's novelty, users might be more aware of the tool and handling it, and consequently they might be more conscious and careful in the way they use the tool.

In addition to the above-mentioned differences between the tools, general ways of working that may arise within teams engaged in participative modeling could be observed which seem worth mentioning here.

According to the interviews, teams MTT 2, MTT 3 and WB 2 divided their work among their members based on topics, which is reflected in Fig. 3 by the occurrence of all kinds of modeling events for all persons, although not always evenly distributed among team members, and during the whole modeling session without any systematic order. Two members of team MTT 3 mentioned that if a team member presented an idea, this person would also model the according content. This led to more even distributions of creative modeling activities than in teams MTT 2 and WB 2.

The depictions of modeling events are especially characteristic for teams WB 1 and WB 3. In team WB 3, a division of modeling activities arose such that one person wrote on the cards representing model components such as goals and problems, a second person pinned these cards to the whiteboard and drew and annotated relations between the components, and the third person contributed mainly by discussion. On rare occasions, the third team member picked a new card from one of the card stacks only to hand it over to the teammate who had become responsible for writing on the cards, or he pinned a card to the whiteboard, but mostly left this job again to the other teammate who had meanwhile turned out to be responsible for that job. This is underlined by one team member's statement in the interview, describing their roles as fixed. The described behavior might have been caused by the team members modeling experience and by knowing each other. Another reason, however, might also be some kind of cognitive fixedness as observed with the MTT.

Team WB 1, the other team that showed a very significant working behavior, decided for a division of work based on component types; i.e. goals, problems, constraints etc. Thus, all kinds of modeling events can be seen for all team members in Fig. 3. The time sequence in which these events occur is, however, most special. According to the interviews, there must have been an agreement to first gather the model components including their descriptions. Then there must have been a moment when the team decided to pin all the cards to the whiteboard and start drawing and annotating relations between the components. Figure 3 clearly reflects this time sequence. A similar procedure was chosen by team MTT 2, but the working behavior looks different in Fig. 3 due to the different tool used. While the members of a whiteboard team could work with and write on the cards independent of the whiteboard, the MTT users must look for other means of sketching ideas. Team MTT 2 decided to take notes on a sheet of paper before they started to model on the MTT. This is reflected by a longer delay of modeling activities for team MTT 2 at the beginning of the session compared to all other teams. The working behavior implies that MTT users should be provided with a possibility of sketching ideas apart from the MTT, whether by means of paper and pen or technologically supported must be discussed and further examined.

When considering team performance (third research question), the final whiteboard models tended to be slightly more complex. However, a reason for this might be that two of the whiteboard teams, WB 1 and WB 3, already knew each other before, as already mentioned above. One participant said they already knew their roles in the team. Moreover, both of these teams had sound experience in the modeling notation they had learned in compulsory courses at the university. Another reason why MTT models were relatively smaller may be the restricted space. This again points us to the challenge of how to accommodate large models on the working surface. When looking at the percentage of component types used, it seems that experience was not most important as WB 3 seemed to exhaust the component repertoire deliberately less than WB 1. Furthermore, it seems that with the MTT, less component types were used. We may speculate that the tool itself was distracting the participants from the possibilities of the notation. In both treatment groups one model was created containing no annotations for the relations between components. So, the tool did not seem to be especially influential with respect to this aspect.

On the whole, the MTT appeared to be equally suited for the task we presented in the study as the whiteboard. This is confirmed by analyses of perceived usefulness, perceived ease of use and perceived enjoyment which did not show significant differences between both tools [25]. These constructs are considered major factors, determining whether a technology will be accepted or not [26]. The analyses presented here give hint on future challenges when dealing with more complex tasks performed in teams with a MTT. These may, for example, concern the shaping of software for the MTT, e.g. with regard to space management and promoting parallel working while keeping team members' awareness.

5.2   Limitations

When interpreting the findings of this study, certain limitations have to be taken into consideration. The study provides a detailed, mainly qualitative analysis of work behavior in modeling teams. Differences in the participants' culture and their experience in the modeling language complicated the comparison of working styles with both tools. However, it was assumed that with a within-subjects design, a learning effect would have been created within the teams which would have distorted the data even more.

It was meant to explore possible differences in collaboration depending on the modeling tool used. That is why a small sample size of 18 persons assigned to six groups was considered as sufficient. For testing hypotheses and drawing generalizable conclusions, further studies with greater sample sizes are needed. Moreover, more representative samples comprising participants, preferably practitioners, from different domains would be desirable. The behavior of the participants may of course be influenced by their feeling of being observed which can never be prevented completely. It was expected that the feeling of being observed, particularly via cameras, would be weakened overtime while concentrating on solving the task. To explore different ways of working that arise naturally, possibly induced by the different tools, roles, such as domain expert and facilitator, had not been predefined. Future studies may further explore especially the role of facilitator and its tasks. In addition, further kinds of models beside goal models must be examined since they might each require a different extent of creative, knowledge-based, problem-solving activities etc.

Finally, when examining the MTT as a tool, the software that runs on the tool is a crucial factor of technology acceptance. In a study like this, we cannot really separate tool and software. A solution would have been to include several software products to distinguish effects caused by tool and software. This would, of course, have led to a need for a significantly greater sample size and an immense effort in data evaluation exceeding the benefit we expected from this exploratory study.

All in all, however, the study fulfilled its purpose of giving valuable insight into the procedure of participative EM. The next paragraph will give hint on next steps, particularly with regard to research in this area.

5.3 Implications

The study has shown that a MTT is a tool well-suited for participative tasks comparable to goal and problem modeling. With MTTs, all stakeholders can potentially participate and even work in parallel. Moreover, awareness of other teammates' activities is higher on the horizontal work surface. For both MTT and whiteboard, we discovered several ways of how teams organize themselves to solve a modeling task. However, which of these work styles is most efficient and convenient for teams? Is it really necessary to strive for most balanced proportions of contributions, e.g. by having every team member talk and model to the same extent? Is it advisable to let everybody model their own ideas to give every team member a chance to equally contribute both to discussion and modeling? Should modeling sessions be organized in phases of collecting ideas and then formalizing these in models? Further research is needed on the influence of working styles on desired outcomes. These would lead to suggestions on how a facilitator should chair a modeling session and when interventions are advisable and when they become counterproductive. Moreover, we intend to improve the modeling software aiming at preventing functional fixedness, better space management and supporting awareness. Although there has been research on the topic of awareness for several years in the area of computer supported work (see e.g. [27, 28]), there is still a need for more knowledge on how to design shared workspaces to promote awareness.

Finally, the desired outcomes are manifold. Complexity and quality of a model represent typical outcome variables. Nevertheless, subjective perceptions such as the team members' satisfaction with the modeling process, their acceptance of and commitment with the models also determine the success of an EM project. Thus, we will focus our future research especially on this area.

Acknowledgements The author wishes to thank the participants of the study, as well as the members of the chair of Business Information Systems of the University of Rostock for their support and providing the technical equipment. Moreover, the author owes thanks to Sarah Freytag, Pavel Chupryna, Jiawei Yan, and Richard Conradi who helped conducting the study.

References

1. Sandkuhl, K., et al.: Enterprise Modeling: Tackling Business Challenges with the 4EM Method. Springer, Berlin, Heidelberg (2014)
2. Stirna, J., Persson, A., Sandkuhl, K.: Participative enterprise modeling: experiences and recommendations. In: Advanced Information Systems Engineering. Springer, Berlin, Heidelberg (2007)
3. Frey, D., Bierhoff, H.W.: Sozialpsychologie - Interaktion und Gruppe. Hogrefe Verlag (2011)
4. von Rosenstiel, L., Nerdinger, F.W.: Grundlagen der Organisationspsychologie: Basiswissen und Anwendungshinweise. Schäffer-Poeschel (2011)
5. Karau, S.J., Williams, K.D.: Social loafing: a meta-analytic review and theoretical integration. J. Pers. Soc. Psychol. **65**(4), 681–706 (1993)
6. Lamm, H., Trommsdorff, G.: Group versus individual performance on tasks requiring ideational proficiency (brainstorming): a review. Eur. J. Soc. Psychol. **3**(4), 361–388 (2006)
7. Steiner Ivan, D.: Models for inferring relationships between group size and potential group productivity. Behav. Sci. **11**(4), 273–283 (2006)
8. Piper, A.M., Hollan, J.D.: Tabletop displays for small group study: affordances of paper and digital materials. In: Proceedings of the SIGCHI Conference on Human Factors in Computing Systems, pp. 1227–1236. ACM, Boston, MA, USA (2009)
9. Mercier, E., Higgins, S.: Creating joint representations of collaborative problem solving with multi-touch technology. J. Comput. Assist. Learn. **30**(6), 497–510 (2014)
10. Basheri, M.: Multi-touch table for enhancing collaboration during software design. Durham University (2013)
11. Buisine, S., et al.: How do interactive tabletop systems influence collaboration? Comput. Hum. Behav. **28**(1), 49–59 (2012)
12. Basheri, M., Burd, L.: Exploring the significance of multi-touch tables in enhancing collaborative software design using UML. In: 2012 Frontiers in Education Conference Proceedings (2012)
13. Basheri, M., Burd, L., Baghaei, N.: A multi-touch interface for enhancing collaborative UML diagramming. In: Proceedings of the 24th Australian Computer-Human Interaction Conference, pp. 30–33. ACM, Melbourne, Australia (2012)
14. Rogers, Y., et al.: Equal opportunities: do shareable interfaces promote more group participation than single user displays? Hum.-Comput. Interact. **24**(1–2), 79–116 (2009)
15. Rogers, Y., Lindley, S.: Collaborating around vertical and horizontal large interactive displays: which way is best? Interact. Comput. **16**(6), 1133–1152 (2004)
16. Nerdinger, F.W., von der Oelsnitz, D., Weibler, J.: Grundlagen des Verhaltens in Organisationen. Kohlhammer (2012)
17. Krogstie, J., Sindre, G., Jørgensen, H.: Process models representing knowledge for action: a revised quality framework. Eur. J. Inf. Syst. **15**(1), 91–102 (2006)
18. Spence, C., Michell, V.: Measuring the quality of enterprise architecture models. J. Enterp. Archit. **12**(3), 64–74 (2016)
19. Wittenburg, P., et al.: ELAN: a professional framework for multimodality research. In: 5th International Conference on Language Resources and Evaluation (LREC 2006). Genoa (2006)
20. Mayring, P.: Qualitative Inhaltsanalyse. Grundlagen und Techniken, 6. Beltz Deutscher Studien Verlag (2008)
21. Muller-Tomfelde, C., Wessels, A., Schremmer, C.: Tilted tabletops: in between horizontal and vertical workspaces. In: 2008 3rd IEEE International Workshop on Horizontal Interactive Human Computer Systems (2008)
22. Scott, S.D., Carpendale, S.: Theory of tabletop territoriality. In: Müller-Tomfelde, C. (ed.) Tabletops—Horizontal Interactive Displays, pp. 357–385. Springer, London (2010)
23. Ryall, K., et al.: Exploring the effects of group size and table size on interactions with tabletop shared-display groupware. In: Proceedings of the 2004 ACM conference on Computer supported cooperative work, pp. 284–293. ACM, Chicago, Illinois, USA (2004)

24. Myers, D.G., et al.: Psychologie. Springer, Berlin, Heidelberg (2015)
25. Gutschmidt, A.: Empirical Insights into the Appraisal of Tool Support for Participative Enterprise Modeling, pp. 70–74 (2018)
26. Venkatesh, V., Bala, H.: Technology Acceptance Model 3 and a Research Agenda on Interventions, vol. 39, pp. 273–315 (2008)
27. Dourish, P., Bellotti, V.: Awareness and coordination in shared workspaces. In: Proceedings of the 1992 ACM conference on Computer-supported cooperative work, pp. 107–114. ACM, Toronto, Ontario, Canada (1992)
28. Isenberg, P., Fisher, D.: Collaborative brushing and linking for co-located visual analytics of document collections. Comput. Graph. Forum **28**(3), 1031–1038 (2009)

Social Position and Gender Perspectives of eLearning Systems: A Study of Social Sustainability

Ahmed D. Alharthi, Tawfeeq Alsanoosy, Maria Spichkova and Margaret Hamilton

Abstract The use of information and communication technologies has an increasing impact on our everyday life. The large impact of software engineering on society also means that sociocultural factors are becoming crucial for software systems. Gender and cultural diversity have a significant effect on software development, the sustainability of the software and on the society where the software is used. Thus, these diversity aspects should be analysed while developing a software system. This chapter presents an empirical study that investigates the social position of learner and instructor, gender and cultural differences in needs and use of system features. Our focus is on eLearning systems used in Australia and Saudi Arabia. The results of the study might also be expanded to other application domains such as eHealth and eGovernment. To explore the differences, we applied a combination of qualitative and quantitative methods to data collected from 174 participants. The results demonstrated that social position, gender and cultural diversity have significant impacts on users' needs and preferences.

Keywords Social sustainability · Requirements engineering · Society · Gender · Culture · eLearning systems

A prior version of this paper has been published in the ISD2018 Proceedings (http://aisel.aisnet.org/isd2014/proceedings2018)

A. D. Alharthi (✉) · T. Alsanoosy · M. Spichkova · M. Hamilton
RMIT University, Melbourne, Australia
e-mail: ahmed.alharthi@rmit.edu.au; adharthi@uqu.edu.sa

T. Alsanoosy
e-mail: tawfeeq.alsanoosy@rmit.edu.au

M. Spichkova
e-mail: maria.spichkova@rmit.edu.au

M. Hamilton
e-mail: margaret.hamilton@rmit.edu.au

1   Introduction

The impact of software on our daily lives has increased, with tasks such as communication, banking and shopping being performed more often on devices such as mobile phones and laptops. Modern societies are relying more and more in their daily routines on software and software systems in the education, transportation, health and entertainment domains [36]. This large impact of software on society and culture also means that the sociocultural factors have to be taken into account while developing software systems, especially when their longevity is required.

Social sustainability aspects refer to the quality of life, human rights and equality including the equal distribution of resources and opportunities and economic conditions, etc. [27]. Software systems provide a means of increasing social sustainability because they make many kinds of resources more accessible. For example, eLearning systems provide a platform for accessible teaching and learning, online access to learning resources and online support for learning and teaching. In developing countries such as Bangladesh, particularly in rural areas, eLearning systems allow educational equity for people who cannot afford to pay for private tutors [25].

From a software engineering perspective, social sustainability is defined as the equitable, diverse, connected, maintained and democratic relationships among people within society [22]. One principle of social sustainability is gender equality. Almost 66% of the world's illiterate adults in 2015 were women who do not have even rudimentary literacy skills [34]. Thus, access to education in developing countries is still an issue. Besides, males dominated particular subjects or areas of education. For example, females rarely have access to civil engineering in higher education in Saudi Arabia. We cannot radically change this situation immediately, however, software engineering solutions might help to overcome inequality by increasing the level of interconnection and access to resources, services and opportunities, which will lead to changes in society over time in an evolutionary rather than revolutionary way.

In previous work, we analysed individual and social sustainability requirements on software systems [4, 5]. In this chapter , we explore the gender and cultural diversity aspects in depth for the use of eLearning systems. For our analysis, we selected two countries with widely different cultures and gender-related laws: Australia and Saudi Arabia. In addition, according to Hofstede's culture theory [20], which has been widely adopted by researchers in many disciplines as well as in software engineering research over the past few decades [12, 24], the index of the cultural value of both studied cultures is different in many dimensions.

In the current study, we investigated the gender and cultural differences in needs and use of system features, focusing on eLearning systems in (1) Australia, having mixed-gender education and left-to-right text direction, and (2) Saudi Arabia, having a single-gender education and right-to-left text direction. We applied a thematic coding method (a mix of qualitative and quantitative methods) to analyse the data collected from 174 female and male participants. The results of our study could be expanded and applied to other application domains.

Outline We organised the chapter as follows. Sections 2 and 3 introduce the related work and the basic ideas of Hofstede's culture theory. In Sect. 4, we discuss the research questions. Section 5 explains the methodology including data collection and analysis. We present the results in Sect. 6 and the discussion and conclusions in Sect. 7.

2 Related Work

Sustainability has become one of the emerging topics in software engineering only over the last decade. In this section, we discuss the related work on sociocultural aspects of sustainability in software engineering as well as on cultural aspects within Requirements Engineering (RE).

Willis et al. [37] analysed how education systems can help to create social sustainability. The authors defined social sustainability as 'a positive and long-term condition within communities and a process within communities that can achieve and maintain that condition' highlighting that this concept focuses attention on the mid-to-long-term future.

Al Hinai and Chitchyan [2] conducted a systematic literature review on social sustainability, and identified over 600 indicators of social sustainability, which they aggregated into 12 groups: employment, health, education, security, services and facilities, equality, human rights, social networks, social acceptance, resilience, cultural and political. Al Hinai [1] also introduced several metrics and an accompanying method for analysing social sustainability requirements of software systems.

Based on a generic model for sustainability introduced by Penzenstadler and Femmer [28], Al Hinai and Chitchyan [3] analysed equality as a social sustainability aspect and studied how it can be engineered through software systems. The authors identified three values to achieve equality requirements: sociocultural equality, fairness and social equality for accessing services and resources. Their study suggests extra-functional requirements for equality, i.e. reporting, tracking and alerts features for citizens' complaints, and quality functions such as accessibility and integration.

Betz et al. [11] introduced a concept of sustainability debt to assist the discovery, documentation and communication of sustainability issues in RE. The authors defined this concept as the hidden impact of past decisions about software-intensive systems that negatively affect economic, technical, environmental, social and individual sustainability on the systems under design. Analysis of the correlation between digital longevity and sustainability was introduced by Becker in [9]. Becker et al. [10] presented a cross-disciplinary initiative to create a common ground and develop a focal point of reference for the global community of research and practice in software and sustainability: The Karlskrona Manifesto on Sustainability Design and Software, cf. also [35].

Chitchyan et al. [13] presented the results of a qualitative study, whose goal was to explore perceptions and attitudes towards sustainability, of RE practitioners.

The authors identified barriers to the engagement with sustainability design in RE practice, as well as proposed possible solutions to overcome these barriers.

Gibson et al. [17] analysed the perception of sustainable software engineering among UK students enrolled in computing degree programs and junior software developers in industries. The authors conducted an interview study with respect to sustainability, sustainability requirements and the relationship of these concepts to software engineering principles and practices. The results of their study were that while sustainability is not a primary focus for the study participants, the concept of sustainability is valued highly by them.

Several works analysed the cultural aspects of RE. However, none of these studies investigated/measured the correlation between culture and sustainability during the RE phase. For example, Tuunanen and Kuo [33] analysed the effect of culture on prioritising and selecting users' requirements during the development of an information systems project. Three different cultures were included in this study, Finland, China and the U.S. The authors argue that the impact of culture on requirement prioritisation, as part of the overall RE process, has been insufficiently investigated. The findings showed that there are no differences between the values of groups of individuals (in the case of the study context). However, the research confirmed that culture does influence the user's requirements. Thanasankit [32] investigated the implication of Thai culture and hierarchical decision-making on the RE process. According to the author, the concept of power contributes towards bureaucratic decision-making, so there is a need to explore the implication of culture and gender differences in software development.

3   Cultural Dimensions

Many attempts have been carried out to define and model culture. Hofstede's model is one of the most accepted and adopted cultural models in software engineering cultural studies [6, 8, 12, 23]. Hofstede's model allows researchers to analyse the impact of national culture on people's practices between cultures. Hofstede et al. [20] defined 'culture' as 'the collective programming of the mind which distinguishes the members of one group or category of people from another'. He introduced the cultural dimensions based on a survey conducted on IBM employees in more than 70 countries. Based on that survey, he introduced the first four listed below. The other two were added years later following extensive additional research:

- **Power distance index (PDI)**: concerns inequalities of the distribution of power among society members. The quality of learning in cultures with high power distance is dependent on instructors' excellence, while in low power distance cultures it is largely determined by learners' excellence [19].
- **Individualism versus collectivism (IDV)**: the extent to which people are attached to the community, society or family. For instance, software that connects individuals is more smoothly and easily integrated into individualist cultures than

collectivist ones [20]. Further, the education process in individualist cultures is dependent on how to learn, rather than what to learn, but in collectivist cultures, it is vice versa.

- **Masculinity versus femininity (MAS)**: the extent to which the social gender roles are distinct (i.e. in a masculine society the gender roles are distinct, in contrast to a feminine society in which social gender roles overlap). Learners in masculine cultures compete with each other in class, while in collectivist countries learners practice mutual solidarity.
- **Uncertainty avoidance index (UAI)**: the extent to which people feel tolerant or intolerant in unstructured situations and an unknown future. Instructors in weak uncertainty avoidance countries are allowed to say 'I don't know', in contrast to strong uncertainty avoidance societies where instructors are expected to have all the answers.
- **Long-term versus short-term orientation (LTO)**: the extent to which the society maintains and links the challenges of the present and the future with its own past. Learners, for instance, in long-term orientation cultures prefer memorisation, accurate and systematic methods, while in short-term orientation cultures learners prefer an approach that incorporates investigative and analytical thinking.
- **Indulgence versus restraint (IVR)**: the extent to which society opts for gratification ranging from enjoyment to restriction. In indulgence societies, people have loosely prescribed gender roles and an open society, in contrast to restraint cultures which have strictly prescribed gender roles and a closed society.

Understanding the cultural background of various stakeholders can assist in understanding their needs and preferences, that is, to elicit the correct requirements. For instance, in countries such as Saudi Arabia, female opinions and needs might be misunderstood during requirements' elicitation due to the lack of face-to-face communication. To resolve this cultural issue, engineers would need to determine which differences in software system requirements are, due to the gender gap, and to consider the cultural background when including special functions or providing extra resources and information. Thus, engineers should be educated about gender and the cultural background of stakeholders as well as understanding software domains. We adopted Hofstede's cultural theory when analysing participants' responses to gender-based differences and cultural background. According to Hofstede's theory, each country has been allocated a numerical score running from 0 to 100 with 50 as an average for each dimension. If a country score is above the average, the culture rates relatively highly in that dimension.

Figure 1 presents the differences between Australia and Saudi Arabia as regards the six cultural dimensions according to Hofstede et al. [20]. The power distance of Australia is lower than that of Saudi Arabia. This indicator in the educational context means that Australian instructors expect learners to take the initiative in the class, whereas in Saudi Arabia, instructors take the initiative. Australia has a higher individualism percentage than Saudi Arabia, which indicates that the latter is higher in collectivism than the former. This finding demonstrates that the goal of the Australian education process is to encourage learners to discover their own abilities.

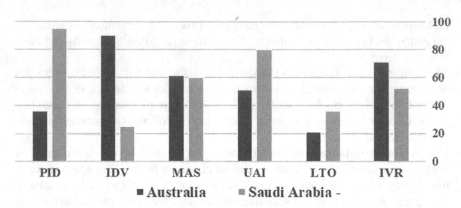

Fig. 1 Comparison of Australia and Saudi Arabia using Hofstede's cultural dimensions and data [20]

In contrast, Saudi education is more about passive learning where learners depend on the instructor. Saudi Arabia, with a score of 80, is a high uncertainty avoidance culture where instructors are supposed to have all the answers. In contrast, Australian instructors, in a low uncertainty avoidance culture, may say 'I do not know'.

Both Australia and Saudi Arabia have a 60% masculinity index value, which determines they both have low femininity value. In education, this indicator means that men and women study different subjects. Both Australia (21) and Saudi Arabia (36) rate lowly on LTO. Although in education, learners associate their academic success with effort and hard work, the Australian culture is more indulgent while Saudi Arabia ranked midway between enjoyment and restriction.

The education systems of these two countries are extremely different. In Australia, as in Europe and the United States, women and men attend the same campuses and classes, that is, women are not excluded from any learning activities and have access to exactly the same tutorials, labs, presentations and resources. In contrast, Saudi Arabia has single-gender education, which means that women and men attend different campuses that are physically disconnected. All classes and learning activities (including eLearning) are separated, which implies the need to duplicate them.

4 The Research Problem

The literature reflects increased interest in determining the social sustainability of software systems, especially for cultural diversity and gender equality. Nevertheless, this issue requires further investigation from psychological experts and software engineers on the cutting edge of social sustainability for the longevity of software systems. The broad research problem that guided this study was 'How can we address cultural diversity and gender equality in sustainability requirements of eLearning systems?' To ensure the social sustainability of software, we have to ensure that:

- There are equal opportunities and access to functionalities provided with high-quality across all cultures and genders;
- All functionalities and information that are tailored to meet the needs and interests are identified and provided;
- A range of functionalities for systematic risk assessment and monitoring processes are implemented and specified for gender-based and sociocultural changes over time.

These points lead to the following research questions:

RQ1 For learner and instructor, what are the social positions, gender and cultural differences in the use of the features provided by the system?

RQ2 How do the functionalities required by users of eLearning systems differ due to social position, gender or culture?

We address both questions in the context of eLearning systems in Australia and Saudi Arabia.

5 Research Methodology

To address the research problem, we applied the thematic coding approach [30], which is a combination of qualitative and quantitative methods. We followed the sequential exploratory model of the mixed approach that was presented in [15]. First, the qualitative method was employed during the data collection stage to conduct an open-ended questionnaire. Then, the results were converted to quantitative data through coding themes to perform statistical analysis. This combined process is a common strategy used in empirical software engineering studies to explore and understand the research problem [30, 31].

5.1 Data Collection

An online questionnaire with open-ended questions was emailed to learners and instructors who use eLearning systems in Australia and Saudi Arabia. The aim was to explore the differences in needs and use of system features of end-users who have different cultural backgrounds, also covering the gender aspects.

The questionnaire consisted of two sections. The first section had demographic questions about the country, university, role and eLearning systems. In the second section, learners and instructors had to answer three open-ended questions:

Q1: What kind of functionality are you using, such as chat, discussion board, etc.?
Q2: Which functionality do you request which is not provided in your system?
Q3: What would you change to improve features in the current system and how important is this?

5.2 Data Analysis

We performed coding themes (predefined themes) to extract the free description of short answers based on gender from those in learner and instructor roles. The themes included five characteristic categories of eLearning systems. Four characteristics *content, communication, assessment* and *explicit learner support* were identified by Goldsworthy and Rankine [18]. We added a new category, *quality functionality*, to cover functional as well as non-functional characteristics of eLearning systems during the analysis. We also believe that quality functionality is a crucial characteristic, and hence define the five categories as follows:

- **Content functionality**: including course content resources such as lecture notes, slides, media recording, reading materials and interactive resources;
- **Communication functionality**: having email, discussion board, social media, announcements, text and video chats;
- **Assessment functionality**: consisting of tests and quizzes, assignment management, grade books, practice activities, past exams, feedback and surveys;
- **Explicit learner support functionality**: involving calendar and schedule, Turnitin for plagiarism reporting, a checklist for tasks, and external supported software; and
- **Quality functionality**: involving all software quality such as availability, performance, integrability, usability and portability.

Each answer to the three open-ended questions was transformed from variables to values against the five categories. For example, one participant responded to

What kind of functionality are you using?

with the statement 'Discussion board and assignments page, as well as coursework page (lectures and tutorials/labs)', so we annotated 1 against *content functionality*, *communication functionality* and *assessment functionality*. Notably, we annotated 1 if a participant's answer included more than one of each category. For instance, if the participant responded with 'Discussion board, email and text chat', we assigned 1 to *communication functionality*. After interpreting the responses, we performed a statistical analysis to examine the data, to determine meaningful relationships and to visualise the representation of results.

6 Results and Discussion

The questionnaire was sent via email to two different universities in Australia and Saudi Arabia. A total of 174 male and female participants, who used eLearning systems either as learners or as instructors, completed and returned their responses. There were 11% female and 40% male participants from Australia. In Saudi Arabia, there were 6% female and 43% male participants (see Table 1). In what follows, we discuss the major findings of the study, in connection with the research questions.

Table 1 Participants:
statistics by social position,
gender and country

Country	Gender	Social position		Total
		Learner	Instructor	
Australia	Male	54	15	69
	Female	15	5	20
Saudi Arabia	Male	55	20	75
	Female	3	7	10
Total		127	47	174

RQ1: For learner and instructor, what are the social positions, gender and cultural differences in the use of the features provided by the system?

Saudi Arabian females, as shown in Fig. 2, provided the highest number of all participants who use the content and assessment functionalities of eLearning systems, at 30 and 40%, respectively. In Australia, more female participants than male participants used the content, communication and explicit learning support features. Males in Saudi Arabia had the lowest percentages for content and communication functionalities of eLearning systems, but they used the assessment feature more than Australian males.

The results presented in Fig. 2 indicate that females' and males' preferences for use of eLearning system features are different in Saudi Arabia, whereas in Australia both genders had no significant differences in the functionalities they used. This finding correlates with results of Pan and Jordan-Marsh [26] as well as of Jones et al. [21], who analysed gender and cultural differences in Internet use. Similarly, Rovai [29] reported culture and gender influence on communication and understanding during the online discussions in eLearning systems. The reason that female learners in Saudi Arabia access and use eLearning systems more than male learners might be the single-gender education system: Female learners communicate with male instructors online, as they might not be allowed face-to-face interaction in classrooms. In contrast, in Australia learners of both genders can meet their instructors face-to-face in classrooms.

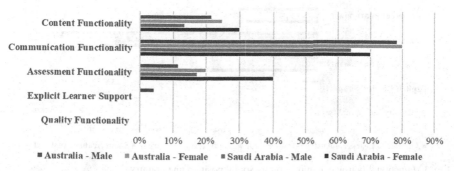

Fig. 2 Functionality usage: comparison by gender and country

Figure 3 shows the social position of learner and instructor perspectives of functionality usage. Australian learners used content and assessment functionalities more than Australian instructors. However, instructors are more likely to use communication functionality than learners. Further, instructors in Saudi Arabia were more likely to use the content, communication and assessment features than Saudi learners. The results in Fig. 3 show that social positions influence the use of eLearning systems. Saudi learners, who have a high PDI and UAI culture, are dependent on instructors' excellence and they were less likely to use the functionalities of eLearning systems. However, Australian learners, who have a low PDI and UAI society, determine their excellence using more the content and assessment functionalities, whereas instructors used communication functionality.

RQ2: How do the functionalities required by users of eLearning systems differ due to social position, gender or culture?

Thus, what types of functionalities of eLearning systems are in demand? What functionalities are not provided and what needs to be improved from social position and gender perspectives in Australia and Saudi Arabia?

Figure 4 illustrates the differences in the requested functionalities of eLearning systems between Australia and Saudi Arabia for both genders. The quality and assessment functionalities were the most demanded by females in Australia and Saudi Arabia. Australian males requested more functionalities than did Saudi Arabian males. Further, the communication functionality in Australian systems, also, was requested mostly by females. However, the results in Figs. 4 and 5 show that there are differences across-culture in the requested functionalities as well as improvements required of features in eLearning systems. These findings agree with these of Tuunanen and Kuo [33] in the point that culture affects user needs.

More than 40% of females and males in Australia requested quality improvements for eLearning systems, which was the highest (see Fig. 5). Almost 25% of female participants in Australia requested that the communication functionality of eLearning systems be improved, while 20% of female participants in Saudi Arabia requested the improvement of the assessment feature. The content functionality of

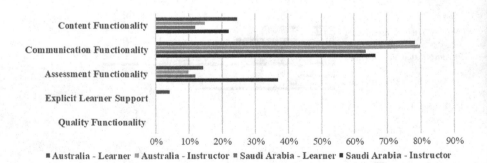

Fig. 3 Functionality usage: comparison by social position and country

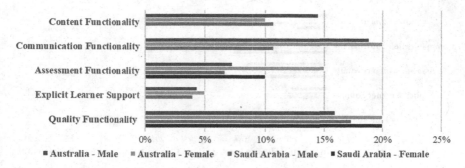

Fig. 4 Functionalities requested: comparison by gender and country

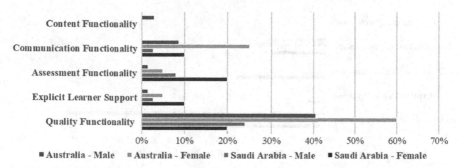

Fig. 5 Comparison of deficient functionalities between female and male responses in Australia and Saudi Arabia

eLearning systems was requested to be improved by only by ~5% of Australian male participants.

Figure 6 shows the Saudi and Australian learner and instructor perspectives of the requested functionalities in eLearning systems. Saudi learners and Australian instructors provided the highest demand of quality functionality at 21 and 30%, respectively. However, more than 10% of instructors in Saudi Arabia requested communication and assessment functionalities of eLearning systems. This low number of responses, compared with Australian instructors with 15%, might be linked to the fact that email, as a communication functionality, is less attractive and less frequently used in collectivist cultures: Saudi Arabia [19].

The results of our survey showed that the content, communication and assessment functionalities of eLearning systems were requested more by Australian learners than instructors. According to Hofstede [19], the purpose of education in individualist cultures is to encourage learner-centred education. This approach demonstrates the need for more lecturing materials by the Australian learners because it supports the idea of a learner-centred education approach.

Figure 7 presents the Saudi and Australian learner and instructor differences in the perception of deficient functionalities in eLearning systems. Australian learners were the highest participants in requesting the improvements of quality functionality,

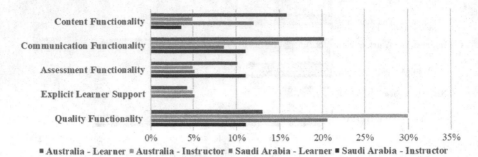

Fig. 6 Functionalities requested: comparison by social position and country

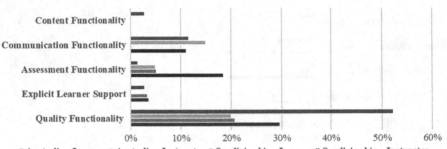

Fig. 7 Comparison of deficient functionalities between learner and instructor responses in Australia and Saudi Arabia

whereas instructors in Australia were more demanding to improve the communication functionality of eLearning systems. In individualist cultures such as Australia, the Internet holds a strong attraction and is frequently used to link individuals [19]. Therefore, Australian learners and instructors requested more improvements of quality and communication functionalities to increase attraction and communication with individuals during the use of the eLearning system. Although eLearning systems support the learner-centred approach, Saudi instructors, who are in high PDI and collectivist cultures, requested the improvements of assessment and quality functionalities to encourage the instructor-centred learning instead of demanding the improvement of the content feature of eLearning systems.

6.1 Practical Implications

The findings from our study have potential implications for social sustainability of eLearning systems. In this research, we focused on the sociocultural (social position of learner and instructor and gender) differences in needs and use of eLearning system features between Saudi Arabia and Australia. The results of gender perspectives indicate that there were differences, so the educational institutions and software developers in Saudi Arabia and Australia should consider the gender and cultural background needs when they develop and maintain eLearning systems. For example, involving more Saudi Arabian and Australian females during the elicitation of an eLearning system would improve the quality of system functionalities. They were from masculinist cultures around 60%, and in both cultures they used more functionalities of eLearning systems than males.

In addition, our findings on the social position of learner and instructor perspectives indicate that learners and instructors in Saudi Arabia and Australia have used eLearning systems based on their cultural background. Instructors in high power distance and collectivistic cultures need to provide more learning materials in content functionality. They also have to encourage learners to use collaborative and communication functionalities for supporting learner-centred education. While instructors in individualist cultures should support and inspire learners from collectivistic cultures to communicate and collaborate with others.

In our previous work, we also found that RE practices are different between Saudi Arabia and Australia [7]. In this study, we indicate that there are social culture differences in needs and use of eLearning system features between Saudi Arabia and Australia. Therefore, researchers should consider the gap of social culture differences between developers and users to improve the social sustainability of eLearning systems.

6.2 Validity and Reliability

To ensure the validity and reliability of this research, we addressed and mitigated potential threats. Creswell [14] and Easterbrook et al. [16] suggested four criteria for validity (*construct*, *internal*, *external* and *reliability*) to provide an inference and valid study.

- **Construct validity**: The questionnaire was translated into the Arabic language, and hence, the received responses, which are in Arabic, were translated into English before extracting the description. The threat of extracting different responses in the languages was addressed by involving two external translators.
- **Internal validity**: To ensure the validity of developing knowledge about eLearning systems in different geographical areas, questionnaires were distributed to targeted participants at the end of the semester.
- **External validity**: The questionnaire was voluntary, and the selection of participants was not controlled. Thus, we sent the invitation three times to mitigate this threat.
- **Reliability**: To validate the transformation, besides including the five characteristic categories of eLearning systems in Sect. 5.2, the first author analysed the responses and inspected responses within assigned codes and categories. The other authors

randomly chose participants and checked their replies to ensure that values were assigned to appropriate categories.

7 Conclusions

This study explored female and male perspectives on using eLearning systems in Australia and Saudi Arabia to analyse the used, requested and deficient functionalities. Participants of both genders were asked about the functionalities of eLearning systems that they use or would like to have, as well as those that had defects and needed to be improved. Participant responses were collected and analysed using a coding approach.

The study demonstrated that social position, gender and cultural background do influence the use and needs of stakeholders for systems and quality functionalities. If a female user deals with a certain function, and at the same time a male user in the same country deals with the same function, both genders will manage it differently. While a user of one gender may think the feature is hard to use, a user of the other gender may believe the functionality is amazing and easy to use. Similarly, if software is developed based on learner and instructor stakeholders in a country with low power distance, the software might not be accepted by those stakeholders who have high power distance cultures. To fill this gap, software systems may provide the following:

- Monitoring and generating of reports providing culture- and gender-disaggregated data and cultural and gender-sensitive indicators over time;
- Involvement of gender and cultural diversity in user acceptance testing, especially to cover usability aspects; and
- Tailored and distinct features and functionalities to allow appropriate customisation to adapt the system to user preferences while also taking into account cultural diversity.

The strengths of this study are that the participants come from different countries, Australia and Saudi Arabia, and all participants are part of either single-gender or mixed-gender educational systems. We have not achieved gender balance in the responses: only 18% of participants were female. Because the participation in the survey was completely voluntary, and the invitations were disseminated among learners and instructors in the same gender-independent way, we may conclude that in both countries most female learners and instructors either prefer to focus on compulsory activities or are not keen to express their opinion. We would encourage researchers to ensure gender equality of the participants by increasing their efforts in recruiting and inspiring females. For example, providing some discussion about the importance of taking part in gender equality studies before distributing the questionnaires may have resulted in involving more females.

This conclusion highlights the fact that social position, gender and cultural background should be considered during requirements engineering activities and for eLearning software system operation to ensure social sustainability. Developing tailored and distinct needs analyses of stakeholders, providing resources and training, and reporting gender-disaggregated data and gender-sensitive indicators are core social sustainability requirements for the longevity of software systems.

Acknowledgements We would like to thank all Saudi Arabia and Australian participants for taking part in our research. Also, we acknowledge that Alharthi and Alsanoosy are supported by scholarships from Umm Al-Qura and Taiba Universities, Saudi Arabia, respectively.

References

1. Al Hinai, M.: Quantification of social sustainability in software. In: 22nd International Requirements Engineering Conference (RE), pp. 456–460. IEEE (2014)
2. Al Hinai, M., Chitchyan, R.: Social sustainability indicators for software: initial review (2014)
3. Al Hinai, M., Chitchyan, R.: Building social sustainability into software: case of equality. In: Fifth International Workshop on Requirements Patterns, pp. 32–38. IEEE (2015)
4. Alharthi, A.D., Spichkova, M.: Individual and social requirement aspects of sustainable elearning systems. In: Proceedings of International Conference on Engineering Education and Research. Western Sydney University, Sydney, Australia (2016)
5. Alharthi, A.D., Spichkova, M., Hamilton, M.: Sustainability requirements for elearning systems: a systematic literature review and analysis. Requirements Eng. 1–21 (2018). https://doi.org/10.1007/s00766-018-0299-9
6. Alsanoosy, T., Spichkova, M., Harland, J.: Cultural influences on requirements engineering process in the context of Saudi Arabia. In: Proceedings of the 13th International Conference on Evaluation of Novel Approaches to Software Engineering ENASE, pp. 159–168 (2018). https://doi.org/10.5220/0006770701590168
7. Alsanoosy, T., Spichkova, M., Harland, J.: Cultural influences on the requirements engineering process: lessons learned from practice. In: 23rd International Conference on Engineering of Complex Computer Systems (ICECCS). IEEE (Dec 2018). https://doi.org/10.1109/iceccs2018.2018.00015
8. Ayed, H., Vanderose, B., Habra, N.: Agile cultural challenges in Europe and Asia: insights from practitioners. In: Proceedings of the 39th International Conference on Software Engineering: Software Engineering in Practice Track, pp. 153–162. IEEE Press (2017)
9. Becker, C.: Sustainability and longevity: two sides of the same quality? In: 3rd International Workshop on Requirements Engineering for Sustainable Systems (RE4SuSy). CEUR-WS (2014)
10. Becker, C., Chitchyan, R., Duboc, L., Easterbrook, S., Penzenstadler, B., Seyff, N., Venters, C.C.: Sustainability design and software: the Karlskrona Manifesto. In: 7th IEEE International Conference on Software Engineering, pp. 467–476. IEEE (2015)
11. Betz, S., Becker, C., Chitchyan, R., Duboc, L., Easterbrook, S.M., Seyff, N., Venters, C.C.: Sustainability debt: a metaphor to support sustainability design decisions (2015)
12. Borchers, G.: The software engineering impacts of cultural factors on multi-cultural software development teams. In: Proceedings of the 25th International Conference on Software Engineering, pp. 540–545. ICSE'03, IEEE Computer Society, Washington, DC, USA (2003)
13. Chitchyan, R., Becker, C., Betz, S., Duboc, L., Penzenstadler, B., Seyff, N., Venters, C.C.: Sustainability design in requirements engineering: state of practice. In: Proceedings of the 38th International Conference on Software Engineering Companion, pp. 533–542. ACM (2016)

14. Creswell, J.W.: Educational Research: Planning, Conducting, and Evaluating Quantitative. Prentice Hall, Upper Saddle River, NJ (2002)
15. Creswell, J.W.: Research Design: Qualitative, Quantitative, and Mixed Methods Approaches, 3rd edn. SAGE Publications, Incorporated (2009)
16. Easterbrook, S., Singer, J., Storey, M.A., Damian, D.: Selecting empirical methods for software engineering research. In: Guide to Advanced Empirical Software Engineering, pp. 285–311. Springer, Berlin (2008)
17. Gibson, M.L., Venters, C., Duboc, L., Betz, S., Chitchyan, R., Palacin Silva, V., Penzenstadler, B., Seyff, N.: Mind the chasm: a UK fisheye lens view of sustainable software engineering (2017)
18. Goldsworthy, K., Rankine, L.: Identifying the characteristics of e-learning environments used to support large units. In: Proceedings Australasian Society for Computers in Learning in Tertiary Education, pp. 338–345. ASCILITE (2009)
19. Hofstede, G.: Cultural differences in teaching and learning. Int. J. Intercult. Relat. **10**(3), 301–320 (1986). https://doi.org/10.1016/0147-1767(86)90015-5
20. Hofstede, G., Hofstede, G.J., Minkov, M.: Cultures and Organizations—Software of the Mind. McGraw-Hill Education Ltd. (2010)
21. Jones, S., Johnson-Yale, C., Millermaier, S., Pérez, F.S.: Us college students' internet use: race, gender and digital divides. J. Comput.-Mediated Commun. **14**(2), 244–264 (2009)
22. Lago, P., Koçak, S.A., Crnkovic, I., Penzenstadler, B.: Framing sustainability as a property of software quality. Commun. ACM **58**(10), 70–78 (2015)
23. Lim, S.L., Bentley, P.J., Kanakam, N., Ishikawa, F., Honiden, S.: Investigating country differences in mobile app user behavior and challenges for software engineering. IEEE Trans. Software Eng. **41**(1), 40–64 (2015)
24. MacGregor, E., Hsieh, Y., Kruchten, P.: Cultural patterns in software process mishaps: incidents in global projects. SIGSOFT Softw. Eng. Notes **30**(4), 1–5 (2005)
25. Mridha, M., Nihlen, G., Erlandsson, B.E., Khan, A.A., Islam, M.S., Sultana, N., Reza, S., Phone, G., Srinivas, M.B.: E-learning for empowering the rural people in Bangladesh opportunities and challenges. In: Second International Conference on E-Learning and E-Technologies in Education (ICEEE), pp. 323–328. IEEE (Sept 2013)
26. Pan, S., Jordan-Marsh, M.: Internet use intention and adoption among chinese older adults: from the expanded technology acceptance model perspective. Comput. Hum. Behav. **26**(5), 1111–1119 (2010)
27. Partridge, E.: Social Sustainability, vol. 12, pp. 6178–6186. Springer, Dordrecht (2014)
28. Penzenstadler, B., Femmer, H.: A generic model for sustainability with process-and product-specific instances. In: Proceedings of the 2013 Workshop on Green in/by Software Engineering, pp. 3–8. ACM (2013)
29. Rovai, A.P.: Facilitating online discussions effectively. Internet High. Educ. **10**(1), 77–88 (2007)
30. Runeson, P., Höst, M.: Guidelines for conducting and reporting case study research in software engineering. Empir. Softw. Eng. **14**(2), 131–164 (2009)
31. Seaman, C.B.: Qualitative methods in empirical studies of software engineering. IEEE Trans. Software Eng. **25**(4), 557–572 (1999)
32. Thanasankit, T.: Requirements engineering—exploring the influence of power and Thai values. Eur. J. Inf. Syst. **11**(2), 128–141 (2002)
33. Tuunanen, T., Kuo, I.T.: The effect of culture on requirements: a value-based view of prioritization. Eur. J. Inf. Syst. **24**(3), 295–313 (2015)
34. UNESCO, E.: Global monitoring report 2015: education for all 2000–2015: achievements and challenges (2015)
35. Venters, C., Becker, C., Betz, S., Chitchyan, R., Duboc, L., Easterbrook, S., Penzenstadler, B., Rodriguez-Navas, G., Seyff, N.: Mind the gap: bridging the sustainable software systems research divide (2015)

36. Venters, C.C., Seyff, N., Becker, C., Betz, S., Chitchyan, R., Duboc, L., McIntyre, D., Penzenstadler, B.: Characterising sustainability requirements: a new species, red herring, or just an odd fish? In: Proceedings of the 39th International Conference on Software Engineering: Software Engineering in Society Track, pp. 3–12. ICSE-SEIS'17, IEEE Press (2017)
37. Willis, P., McKenzie, S., Harris, R.: Introduction: challenges in adult and vocational education for social sustainability. In: Rethinking Work and Learning, pp. 1–9. Springer, Berlin (2009)

The Process of Co-creation in Information Systems Development: A Case Study of a Digital Game Development Project

Karlheinz Kautz, Gro Bjerknes, Julie Fisher and Tomas Jensen

Abstract This paper investigates the development of a digital game on a social media platform which involved primarily youths as co-creators. As we are interested in the unfolding of the development process, we applied a process model for crowdsourced development as a framework to understand information systems development (ISD) as co-creation in a not-for-profit environment. Using innovation theory, we further discuss why co-creation fostered the co-creators to successfully carry out the investigated project. On this background, we provide lessons learned for practical use.

Keywords Co-creation · Information systems development · Process model

1 Introduction and Research Setting

The research presented here is part of a larger project that investigated the concept and the role of co-creation in information systems development (ISD) based on different frameworks . In this article we report on the application of one of these frameworks.

A prior version of this paper has been published in the ISD2018 Proceedings (http://aisel.aisnet.org/isd2014/proceedings2018).

K. Kautz (✉)
RMIT University, Melbourne, Australia
e-mail: karlheinz.kautz@rmit.edu.au

G. Bjerknes
Monash University, Melbourne, Australia
e-mail: gro.bjerknes@monash.edu

J. Fisher
Melbourne, Australia
e-mail: j.fisher@bigpond.net.au

T. Jensen
Communication Knowledge & Change Consulting, Cairns, Australia
e-mail: tjensenconsulting@gmail.com

© Springer Nature Switzerland AG 2019
B. Andersson et al. (eds.), *Advances in Information Systems Development*,
Lecture Notes in Information Systems and Organisation 34,
https://doi.org/10.1007/978-3-030-22993-1_11

187

The overall objective of our research is to contribute to a better understanding of ISD in practice. ISD is traditionally recognized as a technical process and dominated by normative techno-centric and engineering approaches [1]; however, research has recognized that ISD is not just a rational, methodical and controlled process, but more an adaptive, agile, and emergent process [2, 3]. Recently, co-creation in ISD, in particular in open source software and community-based service systems [4] has also gained some wider interest as web technologies enable businesses, governments and people alike to collaborate [5]. Much of the literature on co-creation reports on research conducted in commercial, predominantly e-commerce environments [6, 7]. In such environments co-creation has been used in a variety of ways to develop new products and services, to evaluate ideas and to propose solutions [6].

There is limited research on intergovernmental, not-for-profit, and non-government organisations'—organisations that are neither a part of a government nor conventional for-profit businesses—utilisation of information technology (IT) compared with for-profit organisations [8]; their use of IT generally is less advanced compared to for-profit organisations [8]. The United Nations Children's Fund (UNICEF) of the United Nations (UN) is such an intergovernmental, not-for-profit organisation and program for which it is vital that their information reach as many people as possible. It provides humanitarian and developmental assistance to children and mothers in developing countries.

UNICEF (Pacific),[1] a UNICEF chapter, has recognised social media's value, particularly for distributing important information on matters such as health, emergencies, education and climate change [9]. UNICEF (P) were challenged by Pacific youth to be 'younger and less boring' in using social media. UNICEF (P) thus invited Pacific youth to participate in different roles in the co-creation of an information system, a Facebook-based game [10], which had the objective to inform about climate change.

While the game development project can also be understood as an example of gamification, the application of game-design elements and game principles in non-game contexts [11, 12] to improve stakeholder engagement [13] and learning [11, 14], our focus here is on the process of co-creation as an approach to ISD, especially in not-for-profit environments. In this paper, we therefore present this project as a case study of co-creation as an approach to ISD in a not-for-profit environment with limited resources and with a number of youths on a social media platform. Consequently, our research question is: How is co-creation as an ISD approach performed, in particular in a not-for-profit environment with limited resources and with a number of youths on a social media platform?

For this purpose we use a process model for the management and development of crowdsourced information systems [4] as an analytical framework. The framework emphasizes characteristics, principles, roles and relations of, as well as implications for, the co-creation process. We analyse the project in terms of the process model

---

[1]For the remainder of the article we will refer to UNICEF (Pacific) as UNICEF (P); the Pacific Islands comprise the following 14 countries: Cook Islands, Fiji, Kiribati, Marshall Islands, Federated States of Micronesia, Nauru, Niue, Palau, Samoa, Solomon Islands, Tokelau, Tonga, Tuvalu, and Vanuatu.

and specifically discuss the actual occurrence of its elements and their impact on the course of the project and its outcome. The remainder of the article is structured as follows: Sect. 2 introduces the theoretical background and analytical framework. Our research approach is explained in Sect. 3, and the case narrative is provided in Sect. 4. Section 5 includes the analysis of the co-creation process in the case setting. Section 6 discusses our findings and their implications for research and practice. We conclude with our conclusions and a summary of our contributions in Sect. 7.

2 Theoretical Background

Aligning co-creation with the shift in society and business from a goods to a service-dominant logic [4] and focusing on co-creation in the e-commerce marketplace Zwass [7] provides an extensive literature review of the concept. He credits the original definition of co-creation to Kambil et al. [15] who in the late 1990s defined it as co-creation of value by a firm's customers by engaging customers directly in the production or distribution of value. According to Zwass [7] the subject was further developed by Prahalad and Ramaswamy [16] in the sense of firms creating value with customers to produce a unique customer experience.

Zwass [7] himself defines co-creation as the participation of consumers along with producers in the creation of value in the marketplace in the commercial realm, particularly e-commerce, and argues that co-creation can be read to stand both for consumer creation or collective creation. He further suggests that co-creation is enabled by digital technologies, infrastructures, and ecosystems, in particular Internet and Web technologies. Co-creation takes place in virtual communities with collective intelligence through open innovation with organisations involving unaffiliated individuals and customers which leads to common co-created outcomes that are largely placed for open access.

To conceptualise co-creation Zwass [7] develops an input and outcome-oriented taxonomy with strong focus on entities and structural features and as a foundation for an integrated research perspective and the development of a co-creation theory. The taxonomy comprises elements such as categories of co-creators and their motivations, different modes of creation, characteristics of the development tasks and the forms of governance, as well as types of value, economic beneficiaries and product aggregation.

Compared to other conceptualisations of co-creation beyond and including co-creation as an approach to ISD, the focus on motivation and value can be especially useful in a not-for-profit environment which we studied, as there is no way to force volunteers, in our case youths as the intended beneficiaries, to contribute to the development and use of a co-created information system. Our earlier application of the taxonomy provided an in-depth comprehension of the digital game development project as co-creation in a not-for-profit environment with regard to the co-creators' motivation and the types of value they created [17].

However, as we are here interested in the unfolding of the development and co-creation process, we take our starting point in the work of Kazman and Chen [4] who focus on the co-creation process. They identify two major forms of crowdsourced systems, open source software development and community-based service systems and propose a process model for the management and development of co-created and crowdsourced information systems (Fig. 1).

They call this model the metropolis model as they liken this form of producing systems to constructing a city rather than a single building. Cities are not built by a single organisation, have no or only little centralized control concerning the building process, and are continuously evolving. The characteristics of the co-creation process of crowdsourced systems are [4]: (1) open design and development teams with little or no central control and management, (2) unstable resources where contributors come and go and work is not necessarily assigned but chosen by mostly self-selecting participants, (3) creation by composition, known as mashability, (4) conflicting, a priori unknowable requirements, (5) continuous evolution of the systems under development, (6) a focus on operations, (7) a settlement for sufficient correctness and acceptance of ongoing incompleteness, and (8) complex emergent behaviours of the systems under creation beyond the vision of their co-creators. Different stakeholders have different roles within such co-creation processes and the authors distinguish three realms of roles within their model, kernel, periphery, and masses. Examples for roles involved in the kernel include designer, architect, business owner, or policy maker. Roles at the periphery include developer and prosumer,

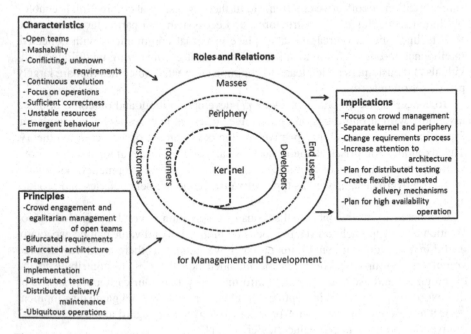

Fig. 1 A process model for the co-creation of crowdsourced information systems

someone who both produces and consumes the outcome of the co-creation process. Roles for the masses include customer and end user.

These characteristics are underpinned by seven principles of development:

1. Crowd engagement and egalitarian management of open teams—which typically consist of volunteers—through an infrastructure and rules to create the social and technical mechanisms to engage in long-term participation, encourage community custodianship, recognize merits of individuals, and to protect the community from malicious participants. Crowd management supersedes conventional project management and is hardly top down.

2. A bifurcated architecture divided into a kernel infrastructure and a set of peripheral services created by different groups through different processes. Kernel services are designed and implemented by a select set of highly experienced and motivated developers who are themselves users of the resulting system. These services provide a platform on which subsequent development is based. The architecture of periphery components is enabled and constrained by the kernel, it is otherwise unspecified.

3. Bifurcated requirements are split into kernel service requirements that deliver little or no end user value and periphery requirements contributed by the peer network of prosumers that deliver the majority of end user value. The nature of the requirements is different, kernel service requirements concern technical quality attributes and their trade-offs, while periphery requirements mostly concern end user functions.

4. Fragmented implementation where a distinct group, not a crowd, implements the kernel, while the periphery develops at its own pace, to its own standards, using its own tools, releasing outcomes as it pleases, and co-creators contribute their own resources and adhere hardly to any deadlines but their own. There is no overarching implementation plan and schedule and no coordination of the activities of the periphery.

5. Distributed testing through a dispersed network of testers where verification differs. The kernel must be highly reliable, highly controlled, and slow to change whereas the reliability of the periphery is indeterminate with sufficient correctness acceptable.

6. Distributed delivery and maintenance where these activities differ for kernel and periphery. The kernel must be stable and backwards compatible. At the periphery there is no stable system state, gradual and fragmented change is typical with a constant stream of independent, uncoordinated releases.

7. Ubiquitous operations to allow for continuous access to the outcomes of the co-creation process.

The implications of these principles are according to Kazman and Chen [4]: (1) focus on crowd management, (2) separate kernel from periphery, (3) increase attention to architecture, (4) change the requirements process, (5) plan for distributed testing, (6) create flexible automated delivery mechanisms, and (7) plan for high availability operation.

3 Research Approach and Method

Our research follows the interpretive paradigm. Given the limited literature concerning the role of co-creation in ISD and how it unfolds in our particular context, our investigation is based on an exploratory, qualitative, single case study [18]. While it is often stated that it is not possible to generalise and certainly not to theorise from a single case study, Walsham [19] suggests that it is possible to generalise case study findings among others in the form of a contribution to rich insight. On this background we used the features of the process model for our data analysis. The roles and length of stay in the field varied for the four authors of this paper. The fourth author has been involved in the project as a reflective practitioner [20] throughout the whole period. As the UNICEF (P) communications specialist and project sponsor, he was involved as the overall project co-coordinator at all stages of the project. He shared correspondence and provided reflections on the process. As an employee and insider, he enhanced the depth and breadth of understanding the case setting that may not be accessible to a non-native researcher [21]. The third author also participated during the whole project, as an involved, accompanying [19] researcher impacting the design and development of the game.

Given the background of these authors the purpose of the research presented here was to investigate in a less biased manner how co-creation takes place in practice. Thus, the first and the second author acted as outside observers [19] and were included in the reflective process. They conducted interviews with the involved researchers and independently analysed all available empirical material. The combination of intervention, interpretation, and collaboration between the three academic researchers and the fourth author was chosen to bring interpretive rigor to our analysis.

In line with the research topic and the interpretive approach, our understanding of co-creation in the digital game development project has come about through an iterative process of interpretation, comparison and connecting of prior research and empirical data. Our data collection and analysis were guided by the framework which allows studying the co-creators, their roles and relationships, their interactions, and the process by which co-creation unfolds.

Due to the distributed location of the co-creators the extensive email trail between the different co-creators was the main data source. These emails contained status information, reflections before, during and after the development and implementation of the game, conceptual feedback, reflections and recollections concerning input into the design of the game, the elements of climate change which it was addressing, test results as well as technical feedback. The empirical data also comprised social media postings by the four Fiji adolescents who served as facilitators between the technical development team and the juvenile Pacific crowd and their responses to the request for input. Project documentation such as the UNICEF (P) strategic plan for digital engagement, its project description, brief and evaluation as well as a terms of reference document were included as valuable data sources as were the field notes by the sponsor and the accompanying researcher.

Further empirical data for the study was collected through semi-structured, open-ended interviews conducted by the accompanying researcher with the three members of the technical development team and by the outside researchers with the accompanying researcher concerning her role and experience during the co-creation project. The developers were interviewed for about 45 min in length with the interviews focusing on the issues around the co-creation process and their reflections as co-creators on the project. The issues included how they undertook the development process, how they managed the interactions with the other co-creators, the mechanisms for communication and how they incorporated new ideas and change requests. The interviews also explored how the developers generated and refined their ideas particularly in relation to the sponsor's brief and explored their motivations for becoming involved apart from the modest amount they were paid.

We wished to achieve an interaction between the existing literature and our observations from the case setting to explain interrelationships and contribute to theory with new insight from practice that might be useful for scholars and practitioners. Our analysis takes its starting point in September 2010 when the project was conceived and ends in August 2011. As a first step in the analysis, we produced a timeline spanning that period and a case narrative which is included here in a condensed form.

We then returned to the literature and identified the metropolis model as one of two suitable conceptual frameworks.[2] It provides a perspective which views co-creation as a dynamic process where the co-creators and the organisational setting in which they operate impact on each other and cannot be separated from each other to make sense and provide an understanding of the nature of co-creation. The next stage involved revisiting the narrative and the empirical data. By mapping the co-creator concept on the roles and relationship concept, we identified the co-creators and their relationships. Then we mapped the data onto the management and development process model's characteristics and principles and categorised our findings accordingly. Using the metropolis model as a framework helped us to increase our understanding of ISD practice and to identify and characterise co-creation as significant in the context of the development process in the case setting. Before providing a more detailed analysis, we next present a narrative account of the investigated project.

4 A Narrative of the Co-creation Process

We identified five phases of the project: 1 Initiation of the idea and funding; 2 Establishment of the team; 3 Conceptual design of the game; 4 Development of the consolidated game; 5 Launch of the consolidated game.

Phase 1—Initiation of the Idea and Funding
Mid 2010 the Communication Expert at UNICEF (P) proposed a project to the organisation. He was concerned that although UNICEF (P) had a strong social media pres-

---

[2]The other framework was Zwass' taxonomy for an integrated research perspective on co-creation [7].

ence and was regularly communicating with their audience via social media, two-way interaction was very limited. His vision was to engage youth through encouraging them to participate in a co-creation project via social media. Given the threats posed to small Pacific Islands from climate change the proposal was to develop a co-created game which would help Pacific youth to learn more about how to respond to climate change. He put this proposal to Commonwealth of Learning (COL), a Commonwealth of Nations organisation, in November 2010 which provided modest funding early January 2011. The Communication Expert who was located on the Pacific Islands immediately approached the third author of the paper in Melbourne, Australia who was known to him from previous collaboration with a request to join the project to help establish and manage if necessary, a development team. This led to the second phase.

Phase 2—Establishment of the Team
In January 2011 the third author approached three research students in her network who fulfilled the position requirements. These accepted the invitation and were in the same month appointed as the developers for a period of 30 working days with an original project runtime from February 1 to April 15, 2011. Two of them were Chinese by birth and one was from Bangladesh. One developer was living in Hong Kong, another lived in regional Victoria, Australia and the third member was living in Melbourne. The latter two knew each other, but they did not know the third developer on beforehand, nor did they meet this developer in person during the project. The Communication Expert took on the role as project Sponsor. The Sponsor's first email to the development team described his vision and what he wanted to achieve: the game was not to be about climate change, but about how people could respond to its impact. In January 2011, the Sponsor identified and contacted four adolescents from Fiji to be social media facilitators for soliciting and gathering ideas from Pacific youth about the game. The Social Media Facilitators posted a photo with a message inviting input on the game and launched this as a Facebook album with text encouraging UNICEF (P) Facebook fans to participate and to contribute to the design of the game. Input and comments came from 16 fans, as well as 15 fans hitting the 'like' button. During the same period the accompanying academic facilitated a process among the members of the core development team and the Sponsor who also acted as project co-ordinator where protocols for how the development team would operate were agreed on. The Sponsor was happy for the developers to manage the project themselves in terms of ideas for the game and how the work was undertaken. The developers' first meeting was a telephone conversation about how they would manage the process given they were geographically dispersed. They agreed that they would email each other every couple of days to cater for the quite short timeline for finalising the game. They also planned to use Skype to talk regularly and instant messaging and chat to communicate. Although there was no formal team leader, the student from Bangladesh quickly became the person who took charge. She kept minutes of the meetings including the decisions that were taken, the next discussion topics and who would be responsible for the determined tasks. The tasks were reviewed at each meeting confirming what had been done and establishing the next tasks and

responsibilities. At the end of each meeting an email summarising progress was sent to the Sponsor by the informal leader. He reviewed the progress, and if he thought there was something that needed to be changed or wanted to provide feedback, he would email the informal leader or alternatively he called her using Skype. Brief notes were taken from the Skype meetings focusing on any requested changes.

Phase 3—Conceptual Design of the Game
The first stage of development was to reach agreement on what the game would be and its look and feel. One developer researched relevant aspects of climate change, another looked at different approaches to and types of Facebook games and the third investigated appropriate technologies, tools and development approaches. As the development of ideas for the game progressed, the Sponsor was sharing these ideas with experts from the funding organisation, climate change experts and UNICEF staff. Input from these groups was sought on the direction of the game. Further information on climate change was also provided on a regular basis by relevant experts to the Sponsor. The Sponsor provided the feedback including the ideas of the involved Pacific youth provided through the Facebook page and facilitated by the four adolescents from Fiji to the developers. The requirements of the Sponsor and ideas of the key stakeholders, Pacific youth, and UNICEF (P) staff, guided the developers. The team used the following process to decide on their final game: At the beginning the Sponsor asked the developers to think about some ideas. They gave themselves a week to open their minds to brainstorm and think about every idea without technology constraints, and then collected their ideas to see which of these ideas could be combined together. This led to three major ideas; each with a particular focus from one of the developers which reflected what they individually thought that the youths and UNICEF (P) should concentrate on. This resulted in the game which consisted of three sub-games. Each sub-game was quite different in the way that the players would interact; the CO_2 Reducer Challenge requires players to identify potential CO_2 emitters; the Evacuate Life Challenge requires players to understand the climate change threats and initiate action; the Flood Tales Challenge highlights the causes of floods and the need for flood mitigation. An important design principle was to ensure that each game was not too complicated. The developers found the fan page postings very helpful. The responses from the Pacific youth had suggested that the game needed to be very interactive, interesting and colourful; it should have graphics, be fun and focused on action, something which promoted to be positive and to make change.

Phase 4—Development of the Consolidated Games
After the developers and the Sponsor had agreed on the consolidated game's design, development proper, including detailed design, coding, testing and evaluation could begin. The development team took an active role in ensuring input in the form of further information. Feedback was managed effectively and encouraged further participation by the Sponsor and UNICEF staff. As there was no opportunity to discuss, elaborate and clarify ideas and concerns face to face with anyone except the Sponsor every piece of information and communication had to be very concise. As the team members were working independently and each component of the game was

developed separately, several issues concerning the different build and layout of the consolidated game arose during this phase. The Sponsor and UNICEF staff reviewed the first version of the consolidated game and provided feedback; this included the colours, fonts and graphics, the text and help provided with the game. He highlighted that further work was needed on standardisation and how the three components linked together to be one game. The Sponsor also reinforced the need for the links to further information be embedded in each game. Technical testing and evaluation were iterative. The developers each first conducted technical unit and system testing to uncover programming errors. Each developer tested the work of the other two and provided feedback. The game was functionally tested by UNICEF (P) staff that played the game and provided feedback to the Sponsor. A technical person within UNICEF also tested the consolidated game and provided technical feedback once the team had incorporated the earlier feedback. The developers were asked by the Sponsor to find a platform to run the game on, and they decided on Google which had a free service. Further user evaluation similar to user acceptance testing was undertaken by three friends of the developers in China who were young and used Facebook. They played the game and provided advice, suggesting that the graphics and artwork needed to be still more attractive. They thought players would be encouraged to play longer if the game was even more interesting. The Social Media Facilitators also provided feedback along these lines, suggesting the game be more colourful and easier to play. All feedback was considered, further changes made, and the final version of the game was ultimately accepted by the Sponsor.

Phase 5—Launch of the Consolidated Game
An email to various international UNICEF groups announced the launch of the game in July 2011. The game had a favourable reception as many positive comments on what had been achieved were made by UNICEF worldwide, Pacific youth and Facebook fans. A press release [9] showed UNICEF's positive assessment of the initiative. Postings on the UNICEF (P) fan page highlighted how successful the game was with requests for the game to be translated into Pacific languages and to include it on the Madagascar UNICEF page. Voices of Youth, a UNICEF organisation designed to support young people requested that they embed the game on their website. Lastly, the launch event marked the end of the project for the development team and sparked the developers' pride about their achievement. The consolidated game is now in use and distributed through three other Facebook sites.

5   Analysis

We now apply the chosen process model [4] as a framework when appreciating the game development project as a co-creation process.

5.1 Co-creators Roles and Relationships

The Fiji-based UNICEF (P) Sponsor held a central role as a co-creator in the kernel of the co-creation process. Not only was he the initiator of the process, he also interacted with all other co-creators with varying intensity except for the Testers and the Pacific Islanders Youth Requirements Contributors. In the kernel he was the ultimate decision maker and approver of the intermediate and final result, and he filtered requirements and feedback from the UNICEF Headquarter, the Fiji-based UNICEF (P) staff, and the international Climate Change Experts. His interaction with the COL resulted in the monetary support for the co-creation process.

The Developers can also be considered as part of the kernel. They provided the functional and technical design of the consolidated game, its components as well as the programming and technical testing. They interacted intensively with each other, with the Sponsor, as well as with the Social Media Facilitators. They were the only co-creators to interact with the Chinese Testers whom they had attracted, and who can be considered on the project periphery.

The Australia-based Facilitator recruited the Developers and provided them both with project management and information systems development knowledge and advice, but after an initial phase did not interact intensively with them until research data after the project were collected. In the initial phase she belonged to the kernel as she interacted regularly with the Sponsor advising him on the project's feasibility and providing competent developers on short notice and within the available budget. Later she became more of an observer with occasional interactions, having little influence on the process and the product. She thus moved into the periphery of the game development endeavour.

The Social Media Facilitators are difficult to place. They definitely played a crucial role in providing requirements as individuals and as gatekeepers and interactors with the Youth Requirements Contributors who were fans of the UNICEF Facebook page established by these facilitators. Their intensive interaction with the Sponsor as well as directly with the Developers with regard to requirement provision and with feedback on the game's intermediate and test versions, might qualify them as kernel members. However, beyond filtering the youth requirements despite their valuable contributions, they had limited decision power and thus confined influence on the ultimate outcome of the process. Therefore, they might be considered as being in the periphery.

Equally difficult to position is the role of the Pacific Islanders Youth who provided ideas and requirements for the game but were only to a limited extent actively involved in the evaluation of the intermediate game versions. They might thus be placed in the periphery of the process. However, as they were self-selected, they might also be considered as part of the masses, putting them on the border between the periphery and the masses. Thus, although not developers, the Pacific Islanders Youth represented prosumers, consumers and end users.

The other co-creators are easier to categorise. The COL's only contact with the project was the Sponsor to whom they provided modest monetary resources for the development work. They had a limited, but important influence on the process and thus can be viewed as members of the periphery. The same is true for the UNICEF Headquarter which provided general advice concerning the game development.

Equally involved, and important in the periphery, were several international Climate Change Experts who interacted both with the Sponsor and the other Fiji-based UNICEF staff to provide knowledge that is accessible and interesting for youth about climate change in general and in particular in the Pacific region.

Last, the other Fiji-based UNICEF staff interacted with the Climate Change Experts and with the Sponsor. They provided requirements but were also actively involved in the design and evaluation of the game. Though influential, their involvement was more informal and casual, thus we see them in the periphery of the process. The analysis of the co-creators, their roles and relationships reveals a complex network of geographically dispersed actors which Fig. 2 depicts.

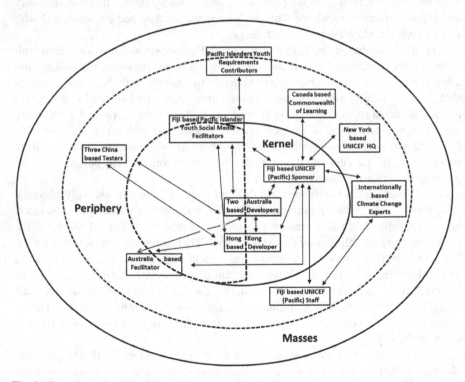

Fig. 2 The roles and relationships of the geographically dispersed co-creators

5.2 Co-creation Process Characteristics, Management Principles, and Implications

The game development exhibits some similarities and attributes of an open team. The UNICEF Sponsor initiated the project, but it was not solely organised around him. Although he was the ultimate decision maker, he was supported by different facilitators and the developers who had been preselected, and who were regularly consulted and took certain decisions independently of him. This might hint at a closed team of dedicated members. This resembles a kernel of a small group of tightly co-ordinated, cooperating and at times controlled collaborators who focus on core tasks and functions which allowed for uncoordinated activities at the periphery as is customary in crowdsourced systems development. The project was open for other co-creators as evidenced by the Requirements Contributors, the UNICEF Headquarter and Fiji-based staff who were not selected or formally appointed. Upon a general call for participation they all voluntarily joined the process to provide requirements, feedback and content. Accordingly, the principle of crowd engagement applied.

Facebook was used as a technical infrastructure and mechanism with both the Social Media Facilitators and the Sponsor representing the social mechanism implementing the rules of engagement with the crowd and the links to the Developers. In this respect the project was not managed primarily top-down, but rather egalitarian with regard to the different groups of youth involved. The same applied for the Sponsor's relationship to the Developers. Although he had the decision mandate, he spent his time more co-ordinating the Developers' work than strongly directing them.

The Developers had a flat, egalitarian management structure where one of them, self-appointed and accepted by the other two, co-ordinated the work internally in their team. This implied that though dealing with a small crowd and what could be characterised as a semi-open team, the process had considerable focus on crowd management. The crowd management was executed by the Social Media Facilitators, to some extent by the Developers, and mostly by the Sponsor through communication, negotiation, leadership and guidance. It handled the input from unknown people at disparate locations and the work of the partly self-governing Developers over whom little or no control could be exerted to co-create the game.

The project separated kernel and periphery in the project's organisation with different groups of participants being involved in different development tasks. It did not technically distinguish between kernel and peripheral software and thus did not apply the principles of bifurcated architecture and requirements as described in the original model. However, the project organisation with a kernel of, among others, three loosely collaborating, independent Developers resulted in a modified form of bifurcated architecture. This consisted of three, modular-structured, independent sub-games and bifurcated requirements, in the shape of three sets of varying demands.

For the requirements however, the principle of bifurcated requirements with a common kernel for a standardised user interface and diverse, specific requests for the formation of each sub-game was ensured. The principles of bifurcated architecture and requirements were implemented through the described form of separation of kernel and periphery, and separation within the core and implied, if not an increased, as outlined, a focussed attention to architecture.

Although the Sponsor had a very clear vision and overall requirements which he expressed at the start of the project, the project had to deal with the unknowable and unknown requirements of the Pacific Islanders Youth Fans when they independently provided requirements for, and evaluations of, the game under development. The same is to some extent true for the input from the Testers and the contributing staff. Handling such requirements lead to a change in the requirements gathering and analysis process, in which the Social Media Facilitators and the Sponsor largely acted as two layers of brokers who filtered requirements. The Sponsor only handed those requirements which he deemed appropriate over to the Developers. Sometimes this structure however was broken and direct communication between the Social Media Facilitators and the Developers took place to clarify certain requests.

Although to a lesser extent than in widely open systems development, with crowdsourced contributions from thousands of participants, unknowable requirements as a characteristic of crowdsourced systems are related to the characteristics continuous evolution and emergent behaviours. Continuous evolution took place in the confines of the project where the game was under constant, iterative agile development which took new requests and changes into account. Eventually it reached a state where it was declared stable and finished and ready to launch with no further immediate development occurring.

With regard to emergent behaviours, a particular instance demonstrates this characteristic: Neither the Sponsor nor the Academic Facilitator considered involving other young people such as the Testers or the Requirements Contributors in further feedback cycles on the design and early versions of the game, the idea emerged during the Developers' interactions and was put forward to the Facilitator and the Sponsor. When subsequently applied, feedback such as avoiding finger pointing to what should have been done instead of pointing to future solutions and depicting people in the game to look like Pacific islanders was provided and changed the game and its behaviour accordingly.

Unknowable requirements as well as continuous evolution and emergent behaviours are related to the principles of fragmented implementation, distributed testing and evaluation, and distributed delivery and subsequent maintenance. The game development project did not follow the principle of fragmented implementation in its original sense which usually takes place in the periphery of crowdsourced systems development. The periphery did not perform any technical development work, but rather contributed unknowable, fragmented requirements. Distributed testing, or more precisely evaluation was executed for functional and acceptance testing, while technical testing was performed by the core development group with a few UNICEF staff also performing this type of test. Thus, no extensive plan for distributed testing needed to be developed. The game, once approved, was launched on the Facebook platform, the same platform was used to distribute early versions of the game for evaluation, thus again, no further flexible or sophisticated automated delivery mechanism for the game as necessary for large scale crowdsourced systems was needed. From the outset, the project emphasised reliability and public accessibility, thus it had a focus on operations. That was the reason why Facebook which was popular with the target audience, was chosen as a platform. Facebook guaranteed high availability based on the numerous tests and evaluations which also ensured that the game could be played with sufficient correctness. This approach implemented the principle of ubiquitous operations although beyond these measures no extensive plan for high availability was needed or developed.

To some extent the co-creation process had to deal with unstable and rather limited resources. The instability of resources mostly played out at the periphery where the Requirements Contributors and the various UNICEF staff joined and left the project as they wanted. In contrast, the resources in the kernel were stable, but scarce given the small amount of monetary remuneration and available time. Here the management principles of crowd engagement and management, bifurcation and distributed testing and evaluation with their accompanying earlier described implications and effects contributed to the positive outcome of the co-creation process.

Finally, mashability, though may be not to the same extent than in large-number co-creation projects, can also be traced in the process. The Developers included links to other information resources and used accessible code from other games. They integrated it into the game and related to the issue at hand from other sources. They also shared code between them.

6 Discussion

Our analysis provides an in-depth understanding of the digital game development project as a co-creation process in a not-for-profit environment. Ours is a case of genuine co-creation through NGOs and mainly youths in an ISD project of a digital game with which we empirically confirm the usefulness of the metropolis model by Kazman and Chen's [4] as a framework. The analysis of the co-creators reveals a complex network of geographically dispersed actors in a transient project organisation. Placing the co-creators was demanding as some co-creators could not simply be placed in one category; they could be placed in several categories and held ambiguous roles.

The principle of ubiquitous operations was followed as proposed. Others such as crowd engagement and management of open teams were adjusted to the project context of a small crowd and semi-open teams. Some principles such as bifurcated architecture and bifurcated requirements were applied in a modified form as the project did not distinguish between kernel and peripheral software but consisted of three modular sub-games based on three sets of varying demands. As the game was not further developed after its launch the principles of fragmented implementation and distributed maintenance were not relevant.

In an environment characterised by web-technologies and social media, crowd-sourced development is an effective complement to more conventional forms of co-creation in ISD such as selected user representatives when the users are known, or personas [22] as substitutes for representatives of a more general unknown user population. As our case shows for ISD projects that want to engage the crowd, it can be beneficial to consciously consider the principles and implications stated in the metropolis model for keeping in mind that a principle such as ubiquitous operations paired with distributed delivery of a constant stream of releases of systems which are continuously evolving is a challenge for ISD.

The project was considered successful by all stakeholders. To accomplish a more exhaustive explanation and to answer why co-creation in ISD played out the way it did and was successful in the presented case as well as to draw more general lessons learnt, we move beyond mere description. Madsen et al. [23] emphasise the significance of organisational structure, individual participants' characteristics as well as the interplay between social context and social process for the successful enactment of ISD methods as organisational innovation. Considering the described network of organisations and individuals as an organisation and drawing on innovation theory we find that the co-creation process as an approach to ISD bears the characteristics of such an organisational innovation.

From this perspective co-creation worked because of the distinctly identifiable categories of co-creators and their role distribution. Especially the UNICEF Communication Expert and the three Developers in the core of the project acted as individual leaders, champions and mediators in terms of the chosen development and design approach and as contact to the other groups of co-creators, a responsibility, which has been identified as decisive for the successful utilization of innovations. The Social Media Facilitators were intermediaries for the Youth Requirements Contributors; the Social Media Facilitators comprehended their assignment as true representatives of the Youth Requirements Contributors. Backed up by the Communication Expert and the Developers their understanding as facilitators and communicators strongly supported the other youths' pronouncing of opinion and gave them an influential voice.

This had an impact on and lead to an effective social process, another facet of thriving innovation, which focuses on the interaction of the engaged stakeholders. The interaction between the different stakeholder groups went well: The Communication Expert had contact with most other co-creator groups especially other UNICEF staff and Climate Experts as additional resources, the Developers included a group of Testers in the project, and the Social Media Facilitators extended the project to other youths and interacted intensively with the Communication Expert and the Developers.

The distribution of power, the second characteristic of a well-functioning social process, provides further explanation: The Communication Expert held a clear mandate and authority to ultimately decide on all design matters and used these based on the valued input and work of the Developers and the Social Media Facilitators who themselves exercised a great amount of individual autonomy when performing their individual tasks to the satisfaction of all other co-creators. This lead to genuine co-creation and controlled a possible dominance of the development team.

In this setting, good social relations and a social infrastructure consisting of a broad range of different, highly motivated co-creators made up the social context in which co-creation could strive. This was ultimately supported by a structural context in which a sophisticated governance and project structure had been set up where co-creators could be distinguished as members of a kernel, a periphery, and the masses and which partnered up different co-creator groups. In addition, a communication structure with weekly and further regular virtual meetings had been implemented. In this setting the development approach had been clearly communicated and shared with the principal sponsoring organisation, the Communication Expert, the Developers, and the Facilitators.

This environment helped to overcome project challenges such as the distribution of the co-creators over different geographical and time zones, limited time resources, high change rate, and evolving Developer competences. The Communication Expert's and the Developer's close interaction with each other and the other co-creators compensated for minimal documentation and for the limited number of tests and helped resolving any issues concerning the Developers' growing competences. Together with the communication structure it also managed the high change rate.

Co-creation has also been related to the concept of participatory design [24] where people are directly involved in the collaborative design of IS and IT they are supposed to use [25, 26]. Much of the activity in participatory design understood as a practice of collective creation is now labelled co-creation [27] and by some regarded as an extension of participatory design [28].

Holmquist [29] highlights how some methods used for co-creating information systems are related to participatory design, but argues that they are somehow different, because they have to deal with contributors and co-creators that may largely be unknown to those who manage the process with the challenges of managing volunteer co-creators in mainly virtual teams with different roles and varying time and effort contributions. While these issues are largely covered by the process model, it is important to recognise that the concepts have different roots and therefore should be treated differently.

Participatory design has its roots in the ISD and design community in the 1970s in Scandinavia and from its very beginnings had a strong emphasis on the political aspects of technology design with the objective to develop and co-create digital technologies in an equal partnership to upskill and empower people [30]. The concept of co-creation with its roots in the economic and marketing literature of the business studies community [7] has a lesser emphasis on the political, but more on the commercial aspects of information technology design and use and is not about an equal relationship and empowerment, but emphasizes the need to listen to the customers to survive in a market where the customers become a necessary resource [31] and co-creation a strategy for capturing and keeping customers.

A further discussion of this aspect of co-creation goes beyond the scope of this research, but a separate interpretation of the digital game development project as an instance of distributed participatory design can be found in [32].

Finally, it has also been argued that research on the design and co-design process is part of design science research in the information systems discipline where a part of design science and design theory concerns the effectiveness and suitability of development and design approaches and methods [33, 34]. In this respect, our work adds to the studies and theory of the co-creation and design process in ISD.

Wastell et al. [34] further contend that design science generates knowledge of direct practical relevance. Our work shows how actual co-creation in ISD can be organized in a project to result in a process and outcome that all stakeholder groups appreciate. In practice, the process model can be used as a framework for: (1) preparing for the organisation of co-creation processes in intergovernmental, non-government organisation and other contexts, (2) coping with co-creation during the development process by providing an understanding of co-creation as an approach to ISD, and (3) for after-the-fact reflection and collection of lessons learnt.

7 Conclusion

In this paper, we investigated how co-creation as an ISD approach is performed and how it unfolds in the case of a not-for-profit environment. Our analysis shows that the chosen process model can be fruitfully applied as a framework in a new context to understand what co-creation is and how, when and where it can be performed as an instance of ISD practice. By drawing on innovation theory, we provide an additional argument of how and why co-creation contributes to the success of the digital game development project. The presented framework can be used to prepare for co-creation, while recognizing that the actual course of an ISD project will evolve with the situation.

We recognize that our study is exploratory and that the digital game development project belongs to a special class of development project, which may limit the generality of our findings. We also acknowledge that knowledge gained through case studies may not be formally generalizable but, like others [19], we contend that this does not mean that it does not contribute to the collective body of knowledge, both academic and practical, of a discipline. Further research, which applies and refines the framework, is necessary to allow for more theorizing about co-creation in ISD. As the process model refers to concepts such as continuous evolution and emergence, complex adaptive systems theory [35] might provide further explanations for how and why co-creation is a viable approach to ISD.

References

1. Kautz, K.: Improvisation in information systems development practice. J. Inf. Tech. Case App. Res. 11(4), 30–59 (2009)
2. Highsmith, J.: Adaptive Software Development: A Collaborative Approach to Managing Complex Systems. Dorset House, New York (2000)
3. Truex, D., Baskerville, R., Travis, J.: Amethodical systems development: the deferred meaning of systems development methods. Acc. Mgt. IT. 10(1), 53–79 (2000)

4. Kazman, R., Chen, H.: The metropolis model a new logic for development of crowdsourced systems. Comm. ACM **52**(7), 76–84 (2009)
5. Baltzan, P., Lynch, T., Fisher, J.: Business Driven Information Systems, 3rd edn. McGraw Hill, North Ryde (2015)
6. Füller, J., Mühlbacher, H., Matzler, K., Jawecki, K.: Consumer empowerment through internet-based co-creation. J. Mgt Inf. Sys. **26**(3), 71–102 (2009)
7. Zwass, V.: Co-creation: toward a taxonomy and an integrated research perspective. Int. J. of E. Com. **15**(1), 11–48 (2010)
8. Chang, Y.-J., Chang, Y.-S.: Investigation of organizational interaction and support in an NGO through computer-mediated discussions. J. Edu. Tech. Soc. **14**(3), 130–140 (2011)
9. UNICEF: Pacific Island Countries: Behind the Bytes. Press releases. http://www.unicef.org/pacificislands/media_15625.html. Accessed 18 Jan 2018 (2011)
10. Fisher, J.: Engaging Pacific youth through a Facebook game. ACM Inroads **4**(3), 79–85 (2012)
11. Deterding, S., Dixon, D., Khaled, R., Nacke, L: From Game Design Elements to Gamefulness: Defining Gamification. In: Mindtrek. ACM, New York, 9–15 (2011)
12. Hamari, J., Koivisto, J., Sarsa, H.: Does gamification work?—A literature review of empirical studies on gamification. In: 47th Annual HICSS (2014)
13. Hamari, J.: Transforming homo economicus into homo ludens: a field experiment on gamification in a utilitarian peer-to-peer trading service. E-Comm. Res. Appl. **12**(4), 236–245 (2013)
14. Scott, M., Ghinea, G.: Integrating fantasy role-play into the programming lab: exploring the 'projective identity' hypothesis. In: ACM Technical Symposium on Computer Science Education, pp. 119–122 (2013)
15. Kambil, A., Friesen, B., Sundaram, A.: Co-creation: a new source of value. Outlook **2**, 38–43 (1999)
16. Prahalad, C., Ramaswamy, V.: The Future of Competition: Co-Creating Unique Value with Customers. Harvard Business School Press, Boston (2004)
17. Kautz, K., Bjerknes G., Fisher, J., Jensen, T.: Applying a taxonomy as a framework to understand co-creation as an approach to information systems development. In: Proceedings 27th ISD2018, Lund, Sweden (2018)
18. Creswell, J.: Research Design—Qualitative, Quantitative and Mixed Methods Approaches. Sage, Thousand Oak, CA (2003)
19. Walsham, G.: Interpretive case studies in IS research: nature and method. Euro. J. Inf. Sys. **4**(2), 74–81 (1995)
20. Schön, D.A.: The Reflective Practitioner. How Professionals Think in Action. Basic Books, New York (1983)
21. Kanuha, V.K.: "Being native" versus "going native": conducting social work research as an insider. Soc. Work Health Care **45**(5), 439–447 (2000)
22. Billestrup J., Stage J., Bruun A., Nielsen L., Nielsen K.S.: Creating and using personas in software development: experiences from practice. In: Sauer, S., Bogdan, C., Forbrig, P., Bernhaupt, R., Winckler, M. (eds). Human-Centered Software Engineering. HCSE 2014, Lecture Notes in Computer Science, vol. 8742. Springer, Berlin, Heidelberg (2014)
23. Madsen, S., Kautz, K., Vidgen, R.: A framework for understanding how a unique and local IS development method emerges in practice. EJIS **15**(2), 225–238 (2006)
24. Iversen, O.S.: What is the difference between co-creation and participatory design? Same or Not? https://www.researchgate.net/post/What_is_the_difference_between_co-creation_and_participatory_design. Accessed 5 July 2018 (2014)
25. Bjerknes, G.: Some PD Advice. Com. ACM **36**(4), 39 (1993)
26. Kensing, F., Blomberg, J.: Participatory design: issues and concerns. Comp. Sup. Coop. Work. **7**(3), 167–185 (1998)
27. Sanders, E., Stappers, P.: Co-creation and the new landscapes of design. Co-Des. **4**(1), 5–18 (2008)
28. Näkki, P., Koskela-Huotari, K.: User participation in software design via social media: experiences from a case study with consumers. Trans. Hum-Comp. Inter. **4**(2), 129–152 (2012)

29. Holmquist, L.: User-driven innovation in the future applications lab. In: CHI'04, pp. 1091–1092. Vienna, Austria (2004)
30. Bjerknes, G., Bratteteig, T.: User participation and democracy: a discussion of scandinavian research on system development. SJIS **7**(1), 73–98 (1995)
31. Vargo, S.L., Lusch, R.F.: Evolving a new dominant Logic for marketing. J. Mar. **68**(1), 1–17 (2004)
32. Kautz, K., Bjerknes G., Fisher, J., Jensen, T.: Distributed participatory design in crowdsourced information systems development. In: ACIS 2018, Sydney (2018)
33. Kautz, K.: Investigating the design process: participatory design in agile software development. Inf. Tech. Peop. **24**(3), 17–235 (2011)
34. Wastell, D., Sauer, J., Schmeink, C.: Time for a "design turn" in IS innovation research? A practice report from the home front. Inf. Tech. Peop. **22**(4), 335–350 (2009)
35. Kautz, K.: Beyond simple classifications: contemporary information systems development projects as complex adaptive systems. In: Proceedings of the 33rd ICIS (2012)

Towards Model-Driven Infrastructure Provisioning for Multiple Clouds

J. Sandobalin, E. Insfran and S. Abrahao

Abstract Companies currently use cloud services to obtain access to computing resources located in virtualized environments. Practitioners and researchers are adopting the Infrastructure as Code approach to cloud infrastructure automation, in addition to attaining the infrastructure for a particular cloud provider in a short amount of time. However, the traditional method of using a single cloud provider has several limitations concerning privacy, security, performance, geographical reach, and vendor lock-in. In order to mitigate these issues, industry and academia are implementing multiple clouds (i.e., multi-cloud). In a previous work, we introduced ARGON, which is an infrastructure modeling tool for cloud provisioning that leverages Model-Driven Engineering to provide a uniform, cohesive, and seamless process with which to support the DevOps approach. In this paper, we present an extension of ARGON that can be employed to support multi-cloud infrastructure provisioning modeling and propose a model-driven approach that allows migration among cloud providers.

Keywords Infrastructure provisioning · Infrastructure as code · Cloud computing · Multi-Cloud · DevOps · Model-Driven engineering

A prior version of this paper has been published in the ISD2018 Proceedings (http://aisel.aisnet. org/isd2014/proceedings2018).

J. Sandobalin (✉)
Escuela Politécnica Nacional, Quito, Ecuador
e-mail: julio.sandobalin@epn.edu.ec

E. Insfran · S. Abrahao
Universitat Politècnica de València, Valencia, Spain
e-mail: einsfran@dsic.upv.es

S. Abrahao
e-mail: sabrahao@dsic.upv.es

1 Introduction

One of the most important challenges in many of today's enterprises is how to deliver a new idea or software artifact to customers as fast as possible. In order to confront this issue, practitioners and researchers are beginning to adopt a new trend, called DevOps (Development and Operations) [1], which promotes continuous collaborations between developers and operation staff through a set of principles, practices and tools with which to improve the software delivery time. The cornerstone of DevOps is the Infrastructure as Code [2], which is an approach for infrastructure automation based on software development practices that emphasizes the use of consistent and repeatable routines for infrastructure provisioning.

Furthermore, cloud computing has become the primary pay-per-use model employed by practitioners and researchers to obtain an infrastructure in a short amount of time. According to Brikman [3], the use of DevOps in cloud-based processes is causing some shifts, such as:

- Rather than managing data centers, many companies are moving to the Cloud, taking advantage of services such as Amazon Web Services, Microsoft Azure, and Google Computing Engine.
- Rather than investing heavily in hardware, many operation teams are spending all their time working on software, using DevOps community tools such as Chef, Puppet, Terraform, and Docker.
- Rather than racking servers and plugging in network cables, many sysadmins are writing code.

Cloud-based processes that use DevOps apply the Infrastructure as Code approach and leverage DevOps community tools to carry out cloud infrastructure provisioning tasks. In this scenario, developers and operation staff focus their efforts on working on software, i.e., writing code to define the cloud infrastructure using scripts. As a result, it is possible to write and execute code (i.e., script) in order to define, deploy, and update the cloud infrastructure.

Every team, department, or software application of a company has its own requirements concerning privacy, security, performance, or geographical reach. Similarly, different cloud providers offer different characteristics. Companies are consequently starting to use multiple clouds to satisfy their needs to attain the flexibility and agility required by the market. In this context, industry, and academia have begun to use the term multi-cloud to refers to the use of multiple clouds without relying on any of the interoperability functionalities implemented by the providers [4].

Despite the enormous contribution that the DevOps community has made towards bridging the gap regarding the orchestration of infrastructure provisioning for multi-cloud approaches, several issues must still be dealt with, such as:

- Managing script languages of different DevOps community tools for infrastructure provisioning is a time-consuming and error-prone activity.

- Cloud providers do not offer the same type of infrastructure. It is, therefore, necessary to define a custom script for infrastructure provisioning for each cloud provider.
- The lack of portability between cloud providers and vendor-lock-in are issues that should be avoided. DevOps community tools still do not support a flexible migration process among cloud providers.

In order to mitigate all the issues mentioned above, in a previous work we presented ARGON [5], which is an infrastructure modeling tool for cloud provisioning. ARGON abstracts the complexity to work with different cloud providers through the use of a domain-specific modeling language. ARGON allows the modeling of an infrastructure model and the generation of the corresponding scripts with which to manage different DevOps community tools for cloud infrastructure provisioning (henceforth, DevOps provisioning tools). In this paper, we present an extension of ARGON that leverages Model-Driven Engineering (MDE) in order to support multi-cloud infrastructure provisioning. The contributions of this work are the following: (1) a multi-cloud infrastructure modeling approach, and (2) a flexible model-driven approach that allows migration among cloud providers. We demonstrate the feasibility of our proposal using cloud providers such as Amazon Web Services and Microsoft Azure.

The remainder of this paper is structured as follows. Section 2 discusses related works and identifies the needs for model-driven multi-cloud infrastructure provisioning. Section 3 provides a brief introduction to ARGON, and Sect. 4 presents our new approaches for model-driven multi-cloud infrastructure provisioning, along with a flexible model-driven approach that allows migration among cloud providers. Section 5 shows the description of a case study carried out to demonstrate the feasibility of our proposal, while Sect. 6 provides a discussion of the pros and cons of our proposal. Finally, Sect. 7 presents our conclusions and future work.

2 Related Work

In recent years, there has been much interest in cloud infrastructure provisioning, and many approaches and strategies have emerged to support it. For instance, Amazon Web Services provides infrastructure modeling tools such as CloudFormation [6] and OpsWorks [7]. The former promotes a common language with which to describe and provision all infrastructure resources, while the latter is a configuration management service that provides managed instances of DevOps provisioning tools, such as Chef and Puppet.

CloudMF [8] is a Cloud Modeling Framework that proposes a Domain-Specific Language (DSL) with which to specify the provisioning and deployment of multi-cloud applications. The Cloud Provider-Independent Model (CPIM), meanwhile, defines the provisioning and deployment in an agnostic manner. Furthermore, the Cloud Provider-Specific Model (CPSM) employs a model@run-time engine to request a list of available resources from cloud providers and uses them to refine the CPIM into a CPSM.

MUSA [9] is a framework that provides a DevOps approach with which to develop multi-cloud applications with the desired security Service Level Agreements (SLAs). The MUSA Modeler Tool relies on a specific modeling language based on CAMEL [10] to describe the application architecture and deployment requirements. The MUSA Risk Assessment Tool carries out a risk assessment process in order to identify the security Service Level Objectives (SLOs) required by the multi-cloud application components. Finally, MUSA generates security Service Level Agreement (SLA) templates using the MUSA SLA Generator tool.

MODAClouds [11] is a European project that delivers an advanced software engineering model-driven approach and an integrated development environment in order to support systems developers when building and deploying applications for multi-clouds. MODAClouds allows the definition of Quality of Service (QoS) requirements at the Cloud Independent Model level (CIM). Cloud-specific aspects are then introduced at the Cloud-Provider Independent Model level (CPIM). Finally, the Cloud-Provider Specific Model level (CPSM) specifies a particular provider and service for the application, runs precise QoS analyses and generates proper deployment, monitoring, and self-adaptation scripts so as to support the runtime phases.

MORE [12] is a Model-Driven Operation Service that focuses on automating the initial deployment and the dynamic configuration of a system. MORE provides a modeling environment in which to model a Service-based Topology Model that specifies the desired deployment topology in the Cloud. MORE also automatically transforms the topology model into executable code.

The research works [8, 9, 11, 12] focus their efforts on providing support for the modeling and deployment of multi-cloud applications, along with managing both the Provider-Independent Model (PIM) and the Provider-Specific Model (PSM). In contrast, ARGON provides a Domain-Specific Modeling Language (DSML) with which to model cloud infrastructure provisioning. The DSML abstracts the complexity of handling the PIM and the PSM. Moreover, ARGON generates infrastructure provisioning scripts for different DevOps provisioning tools.

3 Argon

ARGON [5] is an infrastructure modeling tool for cloud provisioning that leverages Model-Driven Engineering and supports DevOps concepts.

3.1 Cloud Infrastructure Modeling

Several cloud providers, such as Amazon Web Services and Microsoft Azure, provide different types of infrastructures. In order to mitigate the complexity of working with

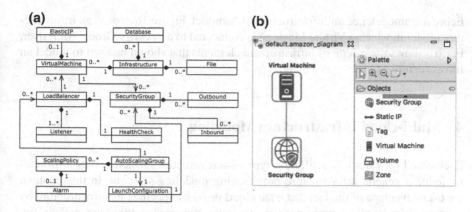

Fig. 1 **a** Infrastructure metamodel. **b** ARGON's graphical notation

different cloud providers, we have developed a Domain-Specific Modeling Language (DSML) with which to model a generic infrastructure model. The main elements of the DSML are abstract syntax and concrete syntax.

Abstract Syntax

ARGON defines a generic Infrastructure Metamodel that abstracts cloud capacities, such as computing, storage, networking, and elasticity. Figure 1a shows an excerpt of the Infrastructure Metamodel. Each metaclass is explained according to its cloud capacities as follows.

- The computing capacity allows Virtual Machines to be modeled with their Security Groups. A Security Group acts like a firewall. Each Security Group enables connections from/to Virtual Machines through the use of Inbound and Outbound rules. A Static IP address can be assigned to a Virtual Machine. A Load Balancer allows distributing workloads among Virtual Machines. A Listener checks connection requests to a Load Balancer, and a Health Check validates that all Virtual Machines attached to a Load Balancer are available.
- The storage capacity allows the modeling of Databases and File Servers.
- The elasticity capacity allows the modeling of a Launch Configuration in which the characteristics of a Virtual Machine are specified, while an Auto Scaling Group determines the minimum and the maximum number of Virtual Machines to be created. Virtual Machines are created or eliminated on the basis of a Scaling Policy in which an Alarm that monitors a metric in a time frame is executed.
- The networking capacity allows the modeling of associations among metaclasses.

Concrete Syntax

We use Eugenia [13] to obtain a graphical notation from the Infrastructure Metamodel. Eugenia facilitates the generation of the models required to implement ARGON in the Graphical Modeling Framework [14] editor from a single annotated

Ecore metamodel, i.e., an Infrastructure Metamodel. Figure 1b depicts an Infrastructure model in which a Virtual Machine is connected to a Security Group. Moreover, Fig. 1b shows the palette of infrastructure elements that should be used to model an Infrastructure Model.

4 Multi-cloud Infrastructure Modeling

Each cloud provider has a different type of infrastructure, which makes it difficult to define a generic infrastructure provisioning modeling solution. In this context, we take advantage of the fact that each cloud provider specifies its infrastructure by following similar cloud capacities (i.e., computing, storage, networking, and elasticity). We, therefore, abstract these capacities at a higher level of abstraction so as to define a generic infrastructure model. Furthermore, in order to support a multi-cloud approach, it is necessary to specify all the features of each cloud provider. We have consequently defined a platform-specific metamodel for each of the cloud providers, such as Amazon Web Servers and Microsoft Azure.

4.1 Multi-cloud Architecture

ARGON follows the Model-Driven Engineering (MDE) principles. We, therefore, define several layers, as is required by MDE, in order to abstract the complexity of working with different cloud providers and different DevOps provisioning tools. Figure 2 shows the ARGON architecture for multi-cloud at different abstraction layers. Each layer is described in greater detail below.

Requirements

This is the most abstract layer, which represents the context, requirements, and purpose of the solution without any binding to a cloud provider. Figure 2a shows the layer in which the criteria required to obtain a (multi-)cloud infrastructure provisioning approach is captured. As a result, we have defined the structure and behavior of the platform-independent model (which is unique and generic) and platform-specific models (one for each cloud platform) by defining their metamodels.

Platform-Independent Model (PIM)

In this layer, we define the behavior and structure of a generic solution so as to model the cloud infrastructure using the Infrastructure Metamodel (see Fig. 1a), regardless of the cloud providers. Figure 2b represents a generic Infrastructure model, which abstracts cloud capacities (i.e., computing, storage, networking, and elasticity). The Infrastructure Metamodel was defined using the Ecore metamodeling language [15].

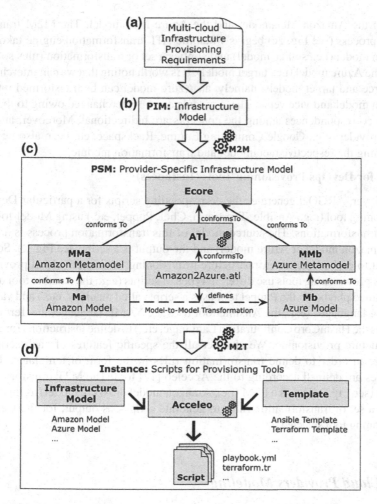

Fig. 2 Multi-cloud architecture

Platform-Specific Model (PSM)

In this layer, we have two cases: (1) PIM to PSM, in which an Infrastructure model is transformed into an Amazon model (based on an Amazon Metamodel) or into an Azure model (based on an Azure Metamodel), and (2) PSM to PSM, in which an Amazon model is transformed into an Azure model (see Fig. 2c). Both the Amazon Metamodel and the Azure Metamodel are modeled using the Ecore metamodeling language. The transformation language employed to perform Model-to-Model (M2M) transformations is ATL [16]. In order to perform the transformation from an Amazon model to an Azure model, we have defined a transformation module (e.g., Amazon2Azure.atl) that contains all the necessary mapping rules. The transformation module uses mapping rules to describe correspondences among concepts between the Amazon Metamodel and the Azure Metamodel. The M2M transformation process (see Fig. 2c) begins when the ATL transformation engine takes the Amazon model (i.e., source model) and applies a set of transformation rules so as to obtain the Azure model (i.e., target model). It is worth noting that we can interchange the source and target models, namely, an Azure model can be transformed into an Amazon model and vice versa. These models can be interchanged owing to the fact that the correspondences among the concepts are bidirectional. Moreover, another cloud provider (e.g., Google Computing Engine, Rackspace, etc.) can also be used by defining the respective metamodel and transformation module.

Scripts for DevOps Provisioning Tools (Instances)

In this layer, ARGON generates the corresponding scripts for a particular DevOps provisioning tool (e.g., Ansible, Terraform, Chef, Puppet, etc.) using Model-to-Text (M2T) transformations. The source model of this transformation process is a PSM (e.g., Amazon model or Azure model) and the output is a script (see Fig. 2). Scripts are used to orchestrate the infrastructure provisioning in different cloud providers. DevOps provisioning tools use different types of scripts (e.g., the Ansible tool uses a script called playbook, the Puppet tool uses a script called manifest, etc.) and various scripting languages (e.g., the Ansible tool uses the YAML language, the Terraform tool uses the HashiCorp Configuration Language, etc.) to define instructions for cloud infrastructure provisioning. We abstract all the specific features of each scripting language in order to define transformation rules in the form of templates. These templates are defined according to the Acceleo [17] tool. The M2T transformation process (see Fig. 2d) takes a PSM (i.e., Amazon model or Azure model) as input and applies a set of transformation rules to generate scripts, as output, for the DevOps provisioning tool selected.

4.2   Cloud Providers Modeling

In order to achieve cloud infrastructure modeling, it is necessary to abstract the cloud capacities (i.e., computing, storage, networking, and elasticity) of each cloud provider. We have abstracted the cloud capacities of cloud providers such as Amazon Web Services and Microsoft Azure so as to show the feasibility of our proposal.

Amazon Web Services Metamodel
Figure 3 shows the Amazon Web Services Metamodel, which has a central metaclass called Service. The Service metaclass plays the role of a container for all the infrastructure elements, and makes it possible to set the region in which the infrastructure will be deployed in Amazon Web Services. The Element metaclass is an abstract metaclass that has fundamental attributes (e.g., name) which will be inherited by the other infrastructure elements. The Tag metaclass allows data to be placed in the key-value style. The remaining infrastructure elements are explained according to the cloud capacities.

Fig. 3 Amazon web
services metamodel

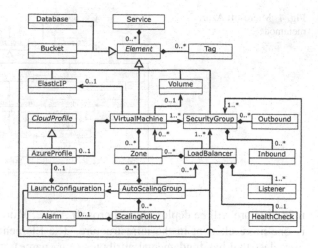

- In terms of the computing capacity, we can model Virtual Machines with their Security Groups. A Security Group acts like a firewall. Each Security Group allows connections from/to Virtual Machines through Inbound and Outbound rules. An Elastic IP address can be assigned to a Virtual Machine. A Volume, which is like an external disk, can be attached to a Virtual Machine. A Load Balancer allows the distribution of workloads among Virtual Machines. A Listener checks connection requests to a Load Balancer, and a Heath Check validates that all the Virtual Machines attached to a Load Balancer are available. A Zone allows the distribution of Virtual Machines across multiple availability zones. Cloud Profile is an abstract metaclass that provides general attributes corresponding to others cloud providers' Virtual Machines. However, an Azure Profile metaclass provides specific attributes corresponding to the Virtual Machines of Microsoft Azure. In order to provide support for another cloud provider, a new metaclass that inherits from the Cloud Profile metaclass should be added.
- In terms of the storage capacity, we can model Databases and Buckets.
- In terms of the elasticity capacity, we can model a Launch Configuration in which the characteristics of a Virtual Machine are specified. An Auto Scaling Group determines the minimum and the maximum number of Virtual Machines to be created. Virtual Machines are created or eliminated on the basis of a Scaling Policy, and a Scaling Policy executes an Alarm with which to monitor a metric in a time frame.
- Finally, the networking capacity makes it possible to model associations among metaclasses.

Microsoft Azure Metamodel

Figure 4 shows the Microsoft Azure Metamodel, which has a central metaclass called the Resource Group. The Resource Group metaclass plays the role of a container for all the infrastructure elements, and makes it possible to set the location in which the

Fig. 4 Microsoft Azure
metamodel

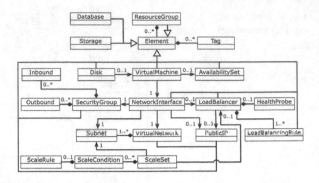

infrastructure will be deployed in Microsoft Azure. Moreover, the Resource Group is one more element in the infrastructure. The Element metaclass is an abstract metaclass that has fundamental attributes (e.g., name), which will be inherited by the other infrastructure elements. The Tag metaclass allows data to be set in the key-value style. The remaining infrastructure elements are explained according to the cloud capacities.

- With regard to the computing capacity, we can model Virtual Machines with their Security Groups. A Security Group acts like a firewall. Each Security Group allows connections from/to Virtual Machines through the use of Inbound and Outbound rules. A Public IP address can be assigned to a Virtual Machine. A Disk that is like an external disk can be attached to a Virtual Machine. A Load Balancer allows the distribution of workloads among Virtual Machines. A Load Balancing Rule checks connection requests to a Load Balancer, and a Heath Probe validates that all the Virtual Machines attached to a Load Balancer are available. An Availability Set ensures that all Virtual Machines are distributed across multiple isolate hardware nodes in a cluster.
- In the case of storage capacity, we can model Databases and Storages.
- With regard to the elasticity capacity, we can model a Scale Set in which the characteristics of a Virtual Machine are specified and the minimum and the maximum number of Virtual Machines to be created should be set up. Virtual Machines are created or eliminated on the basis of a Scale Condition in which a Scale Rule that monitors a metric in a time frame is executed.
- In the case of the networking capacity, we should model a Virtual Network that enables Azure resources (i.e., infrastructure elements) to communicate with each other in a secure network. A Virtual Network can be segmented into multiple Subnets. Finally, a Network Interface allows a Virtual Machine to interact with others resources in a Virtual Network.

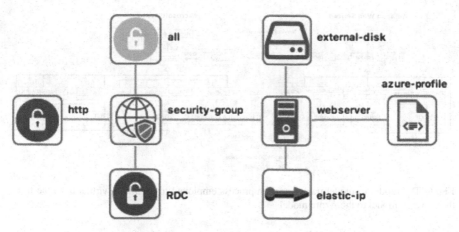

Fig. 5 Amazon model of a virtual machine

4.3 Multi-cloud Infrastructure Modeling

In order to illustrate the viability of our multi-cloud infrastructure modeling approach, we first model an Amazon model as a Platform-Specific Model (PSM). The Amazon model will then be migrated toward an Azure model by means of a Model-to-Model (M2M) transformation process.

Figure 5 shows an Amazon model of a virtual machine modeled by ARGON. The Amazon model has a virtual machine (webserver) connected to a security group. The security group (security-group) has an outbound rule (all) which enables all outgoing connections from the virtual machine. Moreover, the security group has two inbound rules that enable incoming connections through the use of the HTTP protocol (http) and the Remote Desktop Connection (RDC). Finally, the virtual machine is connected to a Volume (external-disk) and an Elastic IP (elastic-ip).

The virtual machine, which is called a webserver (see Fig. 5), has the virtual machine configuration of Amazon Web Services. However, in order to add features for a Microsoft Azure virtual machine (such as a publisher, an offer or a SKU), it is necessary to use an Azure Profile (azure-profile).

Figure 6 shows the M2M transformation process employed to migrate a virtual machine from Amazon Web Services to Microsoft Azure. The changes are explained changes as follows:

- The Service2ResourceGroup and Service2Network transformations specify that, for each Service element of the Amazon model, it is necessary to create a Resource Group element and a Virtual Network with its Subnet in the Azure model.
- The Tag2Tag transformation specifies that, for each Tag element in an infrastructure element of the Amazon model, it is necessary to create the same Tag element in the corresponding infrastructure element in the Azure model.

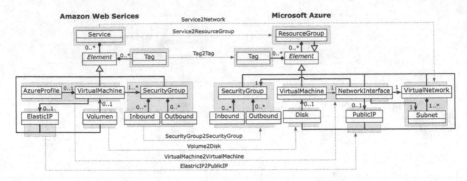

Fig. 6 The model-to-model transformation process employed to migrate a virtual machine from the Amazon model to the Azure model

- The SecurityGroup2SecurityGroup transformation specifies that, for each Security Group with its Inbound and Outbound rules of the Amazon model, it is necessary to create the corresponding Security Group with its Inbound and Outbound rules in the Azure model.
- The VirtualMachine2VirtualMachine transformation specifies that, for each Virtual Machine of the Amazon model, it is necessary to create the corresponding Virtual Machine with its Network Interface in the Azure model.
- The Volume2Disk transformation specifies that, for each Volume attached to a virtual machine of the Amazon model, it is necessary to create the Disk connected to the corresponding virtual machine in the Azure model.
- The ElasticIP2PublicIP transformation specifies that, for each Elastic IP assigned to a virtual machine in the Amazon Model, it is necessary to create a Public IP assigned to the corresponding virtual machine in the Azure Model.

In Fig. 7, a hierarchical tree view is used to show the mapping between the infrastructure elements in the Amazon model (see Fig. 7a) and the Azure model (see Fig. 7b). In this context, the Infrastructure element (virtual-machine) is the container of infrastructure elements in the Amazon model (group A), which is matched to a Resource Group element (virtual-machine) that contains the infrastructure elements from the Azure model (group A'). Moreover, a Virtual Network with its Subnet should be created in the Azure model (group A'). The Virtual Machine and its Azure Profile in the Amazon Model (group B) are matched to the Virtual Machine and its Network Interface in the Azure Model (group B'). The remaining infrastructure elements are matched, one by one, between the Amazon model and the Azure model.

5 Case Study Description

We illustrate our approach by referring to the case of a small company called MODAFIN (adapted and extended from [2]). MODAFIN specializes in IT applications for financial services. Its main product line is a proprietary solution for stock

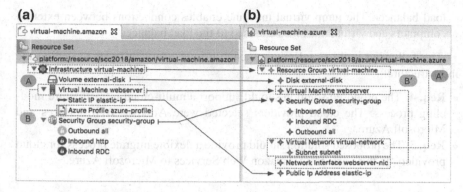

Fig. 7 The mapping of infrastructure elements in order to migrate a virtual machine from the Amazon model to the Azure model

market operations, cash administration, and lending management. MODAFIN's most profitable activities are software customization and life-cycle management for this product line. Customization involves the development of custom modules with which to accommodate new functional requirements.

The consultancy team has spent a considerable amount of time working on a software application, which will be deployed in Linux Servers in Amazon Web Services. However, the consultancy team is worried about issues such as vendor lock-in, security, and application performance and has, therefore, decided to use multiple clouds (i.e., multi-cloud) to deploy the software application. Microsoft Azure has consequently been selected as an alternative platform on which to deploy the application.

5.1 Infrastructure Requirements

The following infrastructure requirements are necessary in order to deploy the software application:

- **Req. 1**: A load balancer, which should distribute workloads between two virtual machines. The load balancer should check connection requests to the port 80 and validate that all the virtual machines attached are available.
- **Req. 2**: A security group, which should enable incoming connections for the SSH protocol (port 22) and the HTTP protocol (port 80) only. The SSH protocol makes it possible to establish connections among virtual machines, while the HTTP protocol provides connections to a software application. Moreover, all outgoing connections should be enabled.
- **Req. 3**: For security reasons, connections from external computers (not belonging to the cloud provider) to virtual machines connected to the load balancer should not be enabled. In this case, a jump virtual machine (jumpbox) should be created to secure the access to and management of virtual machines connected to the

load balancer. The jump virtual machine enables connections between external computers and virtual machines attached to the load balancer.

The following multi-cloud requirements are necessary in order to deploy the infrastructure:

- **Req. 4**: The proposed solution should support a multi-cloud infrastructure modeling process. The cloud providers selected were Amazon Web Services and Microsoft Azure.
- **Req. 5**: The proposed solution should provide a flexible migrate process for cloud providers, in this case, from Amazon Web Services to Microsoft Azure.

5.2 Solution

An explanation of how to provide a solution for the infrastructure requirements is shown as follows:

- **Solution to Req. 1**: Fig. 8 shows an Amazon model in which a Load Balancer element (load-balancer) distributes workloads between two virtual machines that are configured in a Virtual Machine element (webserver). Figure 9a shows the properties of the Virtual Machine element (webserver), in which the count property has the value 2; this means that two virtual machines will be deployed and attached to the Load Balancer element (load-balancer). Moreover, a Listener element (rule) checks connection requests to the Load Balancer element (load-balancer) by means of the port 80. Finally, the Health Check element (health-probe) validates that all the virtual machines attached to the Load Balancer element (load-balancer) are available.
- **Solution to Req. 2**: Fig. 8 shows a Security Group element (security-group), which acts like a firewall. The Security Group element (security-group) has an Outbound

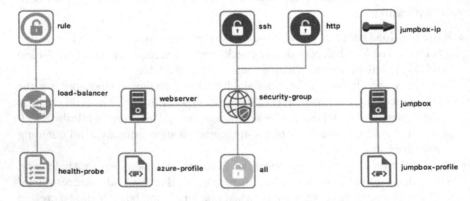

Fig. 8 Amazon model used to support the multi-cloud requirements

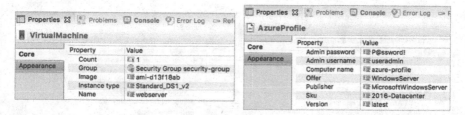

Fig. 9 The virtual machine and Azure profile properties

element (all) to enable all outgoing connections from virtual machines. Moreover, the Security Group element (security-group) has an Inbound element (http) to allows connections to the software application, and another Inbound element (ssh) to establish connections among virtual machines.

- **Solution to Req. 3**: Fig. 8 shows a jump virtual machine (jumpbox) that is connected to a Static IP element (jumpbox-ip) in order to enable connections to external computers that do not belong to the cloud provider. As a result, the jump virtual machine (jumpbox) performs like a bridge, allowing connections between virtual machines attached to the Load Balancer element (load-balancer) and external computers that do not belong to the cloud provider.

An explanation of how to provide a solution for the multi-cloud requirements is shown below:

- **Solution to Req. 4**: On the one hand, the jump virtual machine (jumpbox) provides information about the Amazon Web Services. For instance, the image property (see Fig. 9a) has the value ami-dc2d10a6, which means that it is an image of a Linux Ubuntu Server 16.04-LTS. On the other hand, the Azure Profile element (jumpbox-profile) provides information about the Azure platform, such as the fact that the offer, publisher, and SKU properties (see Fig. 9b) have the values Ubuntu Server, Canonical and 16.04-LTS, respectively. As a result, the Amazon model (see Fig. 8) can be deployed in both Amazon Web Services and Microsoft Azure.

- **Solution to Req. 5**: ARGON supports a migration process among cloud providers based on model-driven techniques. Figure 10 presents, in a hierarchical tree view, the matching among the infrastructure elements of the Amazon model (see Fig. 10a) and the Azure model (see Fig. 10b). We shall now explain the Model-to-Model (M2M) transformation process according to Fig. 10: (1) The Infrastructure element (load-balancer) contains the infrastructure elements of the Amazon model (group A). It is matched to the Resource Group element, which contains infrastructure elements in the Azure model (group A'). Moreover, a Virtual Network with its Subnet should be created in the Azure model (group A'). (2) The Load Balancer, Listener, and Health Check elements of the Amazon model (group B) are matched with the Load Balancer, Load Balancing Rule, and Heath Probe elements, respectively, in the Azure model (group B'). Additionally, a Public IP element (load-balancer-ip) is assigned to the Load Balancer element (load-balancer) to enable connection requests outside the Azure platform. (3) The Virtual Machine element

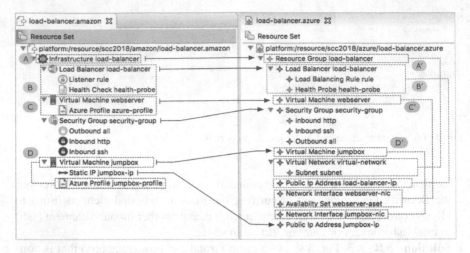

Fig. 10 The mapping of infrastructure elements in order to migrate a load balancer from the Amazon model to the Azure model

(webserver) and its Azure Profile element (azure-profile) from the Amazon model (group C) are matched with the Virtual Machine element and its Network Interfaces element from the Azure model (group C′). It is also necessary to create an Availability Zone element for the virtual machines in the Azure model in order to isolate them in a cluster (group C′). (4) The Virtual Machine element (jumpbox) and its Azure Profile element from the Amazon Model (group D) are matched with a Virtual Machine element and its Network Interface element in the Azure Model (group D′). (5) The remaining infrastructure elements are matched, one by one, between the Amazon model and the Azure model.

6 Discussion

In this work, we have presented two contributions (1) a multi-cloud infrastructure provisioning modeling and (2) a flexible model-driven approach that allows migration among cloud providers.

With regard to the first contribution, it is worth mentioning that ARGON [5] allows the modeling of a generic Infrastructure model and the generation of scripts for DevOps provisioning tools so as to orchestrate cloud infrastructure provisioning. However, in order to provide multi-cloud infrastructure provisioning modeling, it is necessary to specify the infrastructure elements of each cloud provider in detail. We have, therefore, defined the Amazon Metamodel (see Fig. 4) and the Azure Metamodel (see Fig. 5) as platform-specific metamodels (see Fig. 2). Since we are following the requirements of Model-Driven Engineering, the Infrastructure model is a Platform-Independent Model (PIM), and both the Amazon model and the Azure model are Platform-Specific Models (PSM). As a result, in order to provide support for multi-cloud infrastructure provisioning modeling, ARGON works at the PSM layer according to the model-driven architecture (see Fig. 2). This signifies that if we need to add another cloud provider, we must define the corresponding metamodel and specify the model-to-model transformation module.

Both the Amazon Metamodel and the Azure Metamodel were obtained by abstracting each cloud platform; we have consequently used and configured each infrastructure element described in each metamodel. As a result, the metamodels were obtained on the basis of our knowledge and experience. The advantage is that we can follow a similar procedure to obtain a metamodel for another cloud provider. The disadvantage is that a lot of time is required to obtain the knowledge and experience necessary to define a new metamodel.

With regard to the second contribution, a platform-specific model (e.g., Amazon model) should be changed/migrated to another platform-specific model (e.g., Azure model). In order to perform the model-driven migration process, it is necessary to make model-to-model transformations. In this case, we demonstrate the feasibility of our approach by explaining the migration from an Amazon model to an Azure model. However, it is also possible to migrate from an Azure model to an Amazon model, or even, to another cloud provider model. We should meet two conditions: (1) specify the cloud provider metamodel, and (2) define the model-to-model transformation module. As a result, we provide support for a new model-driven approach that allow migration among cloud providers. The advantage is that the migration process is based on two well-known model-driven principles: abstraction and automation. The former helps us to abstract the complexity so as to manage infrastructure elements and complex configuration through the use of (meta)models. The latter helps us to automate the migration process by means of model-to-model transformations and automatically generate scripts for DevOps provisioning tools using model-to-text transformations. The disadvantage is that cloud providers might change their infrastructure elements and, as a consequence, both the platform-independent metamodel (i.e., the Infrastructure Metamodel) and platform-specific metamodels (i.e., the Amazon Metamodel and the Azure Metamodel) would have to be updated. This update means carrying out the maintenance of small changes that do not affect the metamodel core structure, along with large changes that have a significant and substantial effect on the metamodel. This maintenance may be difficult and expensive to carry out depending on the quantity and complexity of the changes that must be made in all the metamodels.

It is worth mentioning that, by default, the infrastructure in Amazon Web Services allows connections from external computers (not belonging to the Amazon platform) to virtual machines on the Amazon platform. However, in the case of Microsoft Azure, the Azure platform forces the definition of a virtual network for the isolation of virtual machines. In order to achieve the isolation of virtual machines in Amazon Web Services, it is necessary to set up a Virtual Private Cloud (VPC). However, in order to model the VPC a further management of the networking is required, which might be considered as future work.

7 Conclusions and Future Work

In this paper, we have presented an extension of ARGON in order to demonstrate the feasibility of multi-cloud infrastructure provisioning modeling, along with a flexible model-driven approach that allows migration among cloud providers. The aim is to provide a new approach with which to manage multiple clouds based on Model-Driven Engineering (MDE). Finally, we believe that our work is aligned with current trends in cloud development, and in particular with DevOps, as a means to abstract and automate the provisioning of cloud resources.

As future work, we plan to run experiments with practitioners and students with experience in cloud infrastructure provisioning so as to identify new needs and improve the user experience when dealing with multi-cloud infrastructure provisioning.

Acknowledgements This research is supported by Adapt@Cloud (TIN2017-84550-R) project, in addition to the SENESCYT and the Escuela Politécnica Nacional (Ecuador).

References

1. Humble, J., Farley, D.: Continuous Delivery: Reliable Software Releases through Build, Test, and Deployment Automation. Addison-Wesley Professional (2010)
2. Morris, K.: Infrastructure as Code: Managing Servers in the Cloud. O'Reilly Media (2016)
3. Brikman, Y.: Terraform: Up and Running. O'Reilly Media (2017)
4. Grozev, N., Buyya, R.: Multi-Cloud Provisioning and Load Distribution for Three-Tier Applications. ACM Trans. Auton. Adapt, Syst (2014)
5. Sandobalin, J., Insfran, E., Abrahao, S.: An Infrastructure modelling tool for cloud provisioning. In: Proceedings—IEEE 14th International Conference on Services Computing, SCC. pp. 354–361. Hawai (2017)
6. AWS CloudFormation, https://aws.amazon.com/cloudformation/. Accessed 25 July 2018
7. AWS OpsWorks, https://aws.amazon.com/opsworks/. Accessed 25 July 2018
8. Ferry, N., Rossini, A.: CloudMF: model-driven management of multi-cloud applications. ACM Trans. Internet Technol. **18**(2), 16–24 (2018)
9. Casola, V., De Benedictis, A., Rak, M., Villano, U., Rios, E., Rego, A., Capone, G.: MUSA deployer: Deployment of multi-cloud applications. In: Proceedings—IEEE 26th International Conference on Enabling Technologies: Infrastructure for Collaborative Enterprises, WETICE. pp. 107–112. IEEE (2017)
10. Rossini, A.: Cloud application modelling and execution language (CAMEL) and the PaaSage workflow. In: Proceedings—European Conference on Service-Oriented and Cloud Computing, ESOCC. pp. 437–439. Springer Verlag, Italy (2016)
11. Nitto, E.Di, Matthews, P., Petcu, D., Solberg, A.: Model-Driven Development and Operation of Multi-Cloud Applications. Springer International Publishing, Cham (2017)
12. Chen, W., Liang, C., Wan, Y., Gao, C., Wu, G., Wei, J., Huang, T.: MORE: A model-driven operation service for cloud-based IT systems. In: Proceedings—IEEE 13th International Conference on Services Computing, SCC. pp. 633–640. IEEE (2016)
13. Kolovos, D.S., García-Domínguez, A., Rose, L.M., Paige, R.F.: Eugenia: towards disciplined and automated development of GMF-based graphical model editors. Softw. Syst. Model. **16**(1), 229–255 (2015)

14. Graphical Modeling Framework (GMF) Tooling, https://www.eclipse.org/gmf-tooling/. Accessed 22 April 2018
15. Steinberg, D., Budinsky, F., Merks, E., Paternostro, M.: EMF: eclipse modeling framework (2008)
16. Jouault, F., Allilaire, F., Bézivin, J., Kurtev, I.: ATL: A model transformation tool. Sci. Comput. Program. **72**(1–2), 31–39 (2008)
17. Acceleo, https://www.eclipse.org/acceleo/. Accessed 25 July 2018

Understanding Individual Differences in Users' Preferences and Responses to an Intelligent Virtual Advisor for Reducing Study Stress

H. Ranjbartabar and D. Richards

Abstract A good teacher knows each student as an individual and encourages them accordingly. An Intelligent Virtual Agent (IVA) designed to provide tailored educational and emotional support also needs to reason and respond according to individual student differences. To collect data to develop models of individual differences in students' preferences and responses to IVAs based on gender, personality and emotional state, we conducted a study with 376 participants using two different virtual advisors (one empathic, one neutral) to "Reduce Study Stress". The experiment consisted of a control group who received tips via pdf documents and two experimental groups designed with one within-subjects factor (virtual advisors with empathic or neutral dialogue) and one between-subjects factor (different order of receiving empathic and neutral advisors). We also collected students perception of the advisors' helpfulness and the students' study stress levels at three time points. Groups using the IVAs reported significantly lower levels of study stress at the end of the study. Some differences were found in preferences for and responses to IVA behaviour based on participants' gender, personality and levels of depression, anxiety and stress.

Keywords Intelligent virtual agents · User/student modelling · Gender · Personality · DASS21

A prior version of this paper has been published in the ISD2018 Proceedings (http://aisel.aisnet.org/isd2014/proceedings2018).

H. Ranjbartabar (✉) · D. Richards
Macquarie University, Sydney, Australia
e-mail: hedieh.ranjbartabar@mq.edu.au

D. Richards
e-mail: deborah.richards@mq.edu.aau

1 Introduction

Intelligent Virtual Agents (IVA) are embodied, usually representing humans, virtual characters designed to interact with humans. IVA researchers have sought to demonstrate believability and social capability through IVAs having situation awareness [1], verbal and non-verbal communication skills and their own memories [2], personality [2], cultural norms [3] and emotion appraisal systems [4]. With the technology having achieved this level of sophistication, the purpose and function of IVAs to improve human life can become the main focus of attention. This requires turning our attention from the ability of the IVA to represent a human to the IVA understanding the human it is interacting with and responding appropriately.

In classroom contexts, a successful human teacher knows each student well and uses strategies to get the best from each one to assist their learning and development. IVAs used in the classroom are typically known as animated pedagogical agents (APA) [5] or simply pedagogical agents. APAs have delivered learning gains and been shown to elicit emotional responses from learners [6, 7]. Given the importance of the learner's emotional state in achieving learning outcomes [8], empathic IVAs (i.e. agents that respond in emotionally sensitive ways) may play important roles in educational contexts. Unlike a human teacher, as software, IVAs should be better able to adapt their appearance, memories and background to be what is most appropriate in a certain context and for a certain individual to enhance student learning.

This research was motivated by earlier studies on adaptive agents. Our novel contribution extends that work by investigating learner preferences for an IVA, the benefit of the IVA to the learner and how learners respond to the use of empathy by an IVA based on their individual differences. Towards understanding these issues, this paper seeks to answer the research questions:

1. Do the users' gender, age, ethnicity, personality or psychological state influence their preferences for an IVA?
2. Do the users' gender, age, ethnicity, personality or psychological state influence the users' derived benefit (i.e. reduced study stress) from interacting with either an empathic or neutral IVA?
3. Do the users' gender, age, ethnicity, personality or psychological state influence the users' responses to either an empathic or neutral IVA?
4. Do these differences suggest variations in IVAs and how IVAs should adapt to their user?

In the next section, we provide an overview of related background on adaptive agents. In Sect. 3 we describe our methodology followed by the results in Sect. 4. We end with discussion of our findings and limitations (Sect. 5) and conclusion and future work (Sect. 6).

2 Adaptive and Customisable Agents

Although there are number of studies on adaptive virtual environments (e.g. [9, 10]), in this paper we focus on the literature on adaptive virtual agents without considering the virtual environments. A number of different types of adaptive agents have been created. A key way of distinguishing these agents is according to the number of modalities they support. A mimicking agent [11] may just copy or mirror the non-verbal behaviours of the human, a listening agent [1, 12], may respond according to the inputs (verbal and non-verbal) of the human in an emotionally congruent way. A laughing agent [13] may tell a joke and laugh with the human, with limited understanding of whether or why the human is laughing and a culturally adaptive agent [14] may copy gestures and postures of the user. While existing research does model factors for agents such as personality [2] and culture [3] and allow the agent to respond in emotionally congruent ways [4], tailoring behaviours in real-time based on individual differences, such as personality or culture, is largely an open question.

IVA adaptation to the user could relate to the appearance of the character, which can represent a particular gender, age or ethnic background. Research has found that the appearance of a character can influence user perception (e.g. [15, 16]) and other work has explored the use of IVAs in helping contexts including fitness and healthier eating [17], reducing alcohol consumption [18] and stress management [19]. However, studies that combine the manipulation of appearance and its effect on the usefulness of the IVA are still lacking.

One approach to provide an IVA model that matches the user's preferences is to allow them to create their own avatar. This can results in participants focusing on their character and also creating characters of their idealized self Ducheneaut et al. [20], Being assigned an avatar, however, has been found to influence how the player/user behaves based on features of the avatar such as players disclosing more when they perceive the avatar as more friendly due to a more attractive appearance. There have also been difference in perceptions of avatars by different age groups. For example, in a system to teach children how to handle bullying situations, Hall et al. [21] children's scores were more positive than the teachers and male children in particular found the storyline more believable. In another study, virtual doctors were perceived to be more knowledgeable by females if the virtual human's body mass index (BMI) was discordant while males deemed the virtual human to be more knowledge if BMIs were similar [22] Bailenson et al. [15] found that the self-reported sense of co-presence increased when the character better resembles a human in looks and behaviour.

The main current virtual agent architectures (i.e. FAtiMA [23], GRETA [24], Listening Agent [12], ODVIC [18] and SimSensei [1]) have been developed and used for different purposes. There is still no unified user model in the current agent architectures to interpret the inputs from the user and respond adaptively. As an example, FAtiMA integrates emotional appraisal theories (i.e. OCC [9]) to have emotion and personality influence the behaviour of the character. Modelling of emotions relies on appraisal theories based on evaluations of events in the environment. Although in FAtiMA the agent has its own personality, beliefs and emotions, the agent is not capable of assessing the personality of the user or adapting according to individual differences in users. Our work towards developing a user model, specifically a student model in the context of educational applications, is motivated by prior work showing that individual features of the user, such as gender or background, influence their preferences and responses towards different agents and addressing the current gap in agents' ability to detect and adapt accordingly.

3   Methodology

In this study, we explored the influence of the users' personality, gender, age and psychological emotional state on preferences for an IVA to help them and their responses to two IVAs, one with neutral and the other with empathic dialogue. We wanted to see if certain individuals preferred one type of dialogue over the other. We designed an experiment consisting of one within-subjects factor (empathic and neutral virtual advisor) and one between-subjects factor (different order of the experimental sequence), forming two experimental groups and one control group (Fig. 1) who received a pdf document to assist them.

Participants were invited via the online recruitment program of the Psychology Department. All participants were volunteers and could choose our study half an hour course credit for their participation. The experiment was approved by the Macquarie University's Human Research Ethics Committee.

3.1   Materials and Methods

We created a meaningful scenario for our population concerning "Reducing Study Stress" involving two versions (empathic/neutral) of Sarah, a virtual advisor who provided tips to students for reducing their study stress. After informed consent and

Fig. 1 Experimental/control groups design

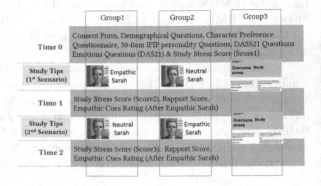

Fig. 2 Sarah, the virtual
advisor

logging into the system, Sarah (Fig. 2) introduced herself and provided study tips
in two rounds. We created two dialogues for the three study groups (scenario 1 and
scenario 2), with two versions (empathic and neutral). The content of the dialogues
was derived from the campus wellbeing and support service of our university, which
included tips about work, study and life balance; exercise and healthy eating; over-
coming exam stress and socializing. For consistency and comparison, these tips were
structured into two documents and presented to the control group in the same order
as the dialogues. Sarah was developed based on the FAtiMA agent architecture and
the Unity3D game engine. We chose FAtiMA [23] because it is a cognitive agent
architecture for creating autonomous, engaging and believable characters. We plan
to extend FAtiMA to include an explicit user model and rules and/or modules that
will allow the IVA to make decisions regarding its behaviour that are tailored to that
user.

To design Sarah's empathic dialogue we used the empathic cues identified from
the literature [25]. Sarah's verbal behaviours seek to establish rapport with the user.
The empathic cues used in her dialogue with related dialogue samples are shown in
Table 1. Both versions of Sarah conveyed a pleasant smiling face and included lip-
synching. No other non-verbal behaviours were used. Dialogue was spoken by Sarah
using TextToSpeech generation of an Australian synthesized voice. Users responded
through selection of answer options.

3.2 Procedure and Data Collection

The Qualtrics research software (Qualtrics.com) provided participants with online
access to all the intervention materials and surveys. It was our goal to understand the
human and how individual differences might influence preference for features and
behaviours of the IVA. Thus, first we collected demographic data including gender,
age, cultural background, degree being studied, computer game activity and attitude
towards study (using 5pt Likert scale from strongly dislike to strongly like) followed by a preference questionnaire (see results). To ascertain cultural background,
participants were asked "What cultural group does your family most strongly identify with?" And the possible answers were: Oceania, Northern-Western European,

Table 1 Empathic cues used in the dialogues

Empathic cues	Example
Social dialogue	I hope you have something nice planned for your weekend
Meta-relational dialogue	I'm hoping to give you some ideas that might help you with your study and life in general
Empathic feedback	Oh dear, sounds like you have some stuff happening. I am here for you
Humor	Life can box you in—look at me, I'm stuck inside this machine—just kidding
Continuity behaviors	It's nice to see you again. I'm hoping I can get to know you better
Self-disclosure	I also get really stressed when I have lots of study
Meta-relational dialogue and sharing knowledge	We're doing some great work together
Mirroring	I do the same
Politeness	Please make yourself comfortable
Inclusive pronoun	Sometimes it's nice to have our own time

Southern-Eastern European, North African and Middle Eastern, South-East Asian, North-East Asian, Southern and Central Asian, People of the Americas, Sub-Saharan African, I don't identify with any cultural group". These categories are based on the Australian Bureau of Statistics that is used in the National Census to identify the ethnic background of Australians. Australia is a highly multicultural country. We did not ask about the country they were born or language/s spoken at home as it does not necessarily indicate their identification with a particular culture.

We also wanted to identify if the humans' personality influenced their preferences and responses to the IVAs. Therefore we made use of International Personality Item Pool (IPIP) which is a personality inventory to model personality of the users [26]. The version used in this experiment contains 50 items, 10 items measuring each of the five personality scales. The scales are known as the Big-Five personality factors and include Openness to experience (Intellect/Imagination) (O), Conscientiousness (C), Extraversion (E), Agreeableness (A) and Neuroticism (conversely, Emotional Stability) (N). To interpret individuals' personality scores and categorise them in low, medium and high levels, we calculated mean and standard deviation (SD) of all participants in each category. Then we interpreted scores within one-half SD of the mean as "average" and outside of that range as "low" or "high".[1]

We also chose to use Depression-Anxiety and Stress (DASS21) questionnaire to capture the psychological emotional state of the user [27]. To interpret participants' scores, we used the guidance to the Depression, Anxiety and Stress Scale in [28].

---

[1] https://ipip.ori.org/InterpretingIndividualIPIPScaleScores.htm.

Next, participants were randomly allocated to one of the three designed groups using the Qualtrics Randomizer feature and they downloaded and ran the corresponding executable Unity3D file (groups 1 and 2) or downloaded the pdf files for the control group. For groups 1 and 2, the users' keyboard and mouse interaction data with the IVA were captured into a separate MySQL database.

To identify if the study tips were useful and whether the IVA was "fit for purpose", we also asked the students' "Study Stress Score" at three time points (before and after each scenario) by asking: think about your emotional feeling towards your study on a scale of 0–10. Zero means "extremely good and relaxed" and 10 means "extremely bad and stressed". To evaluate the empathic dialogue provided by Sarah, we chose one statement for each of the empathic cues that the participant experienced and asked them to indicate if they found it empathic, helpful and/or stupid.

4 Results

To find if there were differences in participants' responses to the IVA according to different user profiles, our results include detailed user profiling including demographics (Sect. 4.1), study stress score result, the changes in participants' study stress levels following conversations with Sarah (Sect. 4.2) and the results of comparisons of individual differences with responses (Sect. 4.3).

4.1 Participants

In total our study involved collecting data from 389 university students from Australia over the period of 14 months. However, 13 participants only completed the consent form but did not start the study and another 66 only completed the IPIP test, DASS21 and preferences questionnaires but did not interact with the virtual character. Moreover, 68 participants interacted with the virtual character but their study scores at time 0, 1 and 2 were missing. The main reason for missing data was an unexpected server issue during running the study, resulting in corruption of around 50 participants' records. Further attrition in numbers occurred due to some participants completing the preferences survey and downloading the application but not interacting with the character.

The final number of 242 students aged between 17-57 (mean age $= 20.27$, SD $= 4.24$) participated in all parts of the study. Only eleven participants were over 30 years old. Due to the homogeneity of the age of the population, we do not present any age specific results and did not conduct any analysis by age. Table 2 shows the gender distribution across each group for the 376 participants who partially completed the study up to the character preferences survey (which we analysed and present later) and the 242 participants who completed the whole study.

Table 2 Gender distribution across experimental groups

	Complete study				Partial study			
Groups	Female	Male	Other	Total	Female	Male	Other	Total
Group 1	92	34	1	127	55	26	1	82
Group 2	83	41	0	124	46	28	0	74
Group 3	81	43	1	125	55	31	0	86
Total	256	118	2	376	156	85	1	242

Table 3 Personality dimension distribution

Personality factors	Low		Medium		High	
Openness	129	34.31%	145	38.56%	102	27.13%
Conscientious	130	34.57%	138	36.70%	108	28.72%
Extravert	122	32.45%	152	40.43%	102	27.13%
Agreeable	122	32.45%	151	40.16%	103	27.39%
Neuroticism	120	31.91%	157	41.76%	99	26.33%

Many cultural groups were involved in the study. The largest group is South-East Asian (21.53%) and the next largest groups are Northern-Western European and Oceania (15.93 and 14.16% respectively). Most of the participants were enrolled in a Psychology degree (78.19%) and less than half of the participants regularly played computer games (42.82%). The majority of participants' were neutral about study (45.48%) while 28.99 and 3.99% of students' chose like and love, and 18.09% and 3.46% of students' chose dislike and hate, respectively. Table 3 shows categorised personality results.

DASS21 results by gender are shown in Table 4. Table 5 shows frequency and percentages by gender for participants' character preferences before interaction.

4.2 Study Stress Score Result

At baseline before our intervention, the mean study stress scores in the three groups are number 5 out of 10 (Group 1 mean = 4.86, s.d = 2.44; Group 2 mean = 5.24, s.d = 2.43; Group 3 mean = 5.52, s.d = 1.91). Categorised scores (low, medium, high), see Table 6, reveal that most students are moderately to highly stressed about their studies.

Table 6 and the corresponding Fig. 3 show the changes in the user's study stress state (score) in each group over time: baseline (score 1), after scenario 1 (score 2), after scenario 2 (score 3). Comparing the three conditions shows that the control group (Group 3) has the least score changes after the second scenario. Only 19.77% of the control group (Group 3) had low emotional feeling towards their study at the end of the experiment. However, 52.44% of Group 1 and 62.16% of participants in Group 2 reported low study stress by the end of the experiment.

Considering group 1 in Table 6, 35.37% of students had high stress score before interaction with Sarah (score 1) and this amount dropped down to 10.98 and 7.32% after first and second interactions respectively. In group 2 we can see the same pattern, where 33.78% of students had high stress score at score 1, then it went down to 16.22% in score 2 and 6.76% in score 3. The high stress score 2 and score 3 in group 3 are far more than score 2 and score 3 in group 1 and group 2. High stress score in group 3 had the least reduction among all groups.

As can be seen in Fig. 3, the change in stress levels is significantly larger for the agent treatments compared to the control. But since we used a crossover for the first two groups, we then separated the analysis into the two treatments (Empathic and Neutral). To compare the score mean differences between the groups we performed mixed Anova test. Figure 3 indicates that the variable group is an important factor. The within subject test indicates that each interaction has a significant effect on the study stress score, $F(4478) = 82.06, p < 0.005$, partial $\eta 2 = 0.256$; in other words, the scores do change over time after experiencing scenario 1 and scenario 2. Moreover, the interaction of score and group is statistically significant $F(4478) = 12, p < 0.005$, partial $\eta 2 = 0.091$) which means that the scores are changing over time depending on the group.

Table 4 DASS 21 Results

		Female		Male		Other		Total	
		N	%	N	%	N	%	N	%
Depression	Normal	97	37.89	57	48.31	1	50	155	41.22
	Mild	33	12.89	22	18.64	0	0	55	14.63
	Moderate	70	27.34	26	22.03	0	0	96	25.53
	Severe	33	12.89	7	5.93	1	50	41	10.90
	Extremely severe	23	8.98	6	5.08	0	0	29	7.71
Anxiety	Normal	74	28.91	33	27.97	0	0	107	28.46
	Mild	47	18.36	26	22.03	0	0	73	19.41
	Moderate	38	14.84	17	14.41	1	50	56	14.89
	Severe	28	10.94	14	11.86	0	0	42	11.17
	Extremely severe	69	26.95	28	23.73	1	50	98	26.06
Stress	Normal	174	67.97	85	72.03	1	50	260	69.15
	Mild	31	12.11	14	11.86	0	0	45	11.97
	Moderate	25	9.77	10	8.47	1	50	36	9.57
	Severe	20	7.81	8	6.78	0	0	28	7.45
	Extremely severe	6	2.34	1	0.85	0	0	7	1.86

Table 5 The preference questionnaire result

Virtual Character Preference		Female		Male		Other		Total	
		N	%	N	%	N	%	N	%
Would you prefer a virtual character to be?	Younger than you	4	1.56	24	20.34	0	0	28	7.45
	Older than you	77	30.08	23	19.49	0	0	100	26.60
	Same age as you	175	68.36	71	60.17	2	100	248	65.96
	Male	43	16.80	55	46.61	0	0	98	26.06
	Female	101	39.45	17	14.41	0	0	118	31.38
	Doesn't matter	112	43.75	46	38.98	2	100	160	42.55
	Same ethnicity	78	30.47	27	22.88	1	50	106	28.19
	Different ethnicity	12	4.69	12	10.17	0	0	24	6.38
	Doesn't matter	166	64.84	79	66.95	1	50	246	65.43
Do you prefer the character to look like you?	Yes	67	26.17	26	22.03	0	0	93	24.73
	No	49	19.14	25	21.19	0	0	74	19.68
	Doesn't matter	140	54.69	67	56.78	2	100	209	55.59

Table 6 Study stress score result by group

		Group 1		Group 2		Group 3		Total	
		N	%	N	%	N	%	N	%
Score 1	Low	25	30.49	17	22.97	12	13.95	54	22.31
	Mid	28	34.15	32	43.24	46	53.49	106	43.80
	High	29	35.37	25	33.78	28	32.56	82	33.88
Score 2	Low	33	40.24	31	41.89	12	13.95	76	31.40
	Mid	40	48.78	31	41.89	50	58.14	121	50
	High	9	10.98	12	16.22	24	27.91	45	18.60
Score 3	Low	43	52.44	46	62.16	17	19.77	106	43.80
	Mid	33	40.24	23	31.08	47	54.65	103	42.56
	High	6	7.32	5	6.76	22	25.58	33	13.64

Fig. 3 Study stress score mean changes over the time

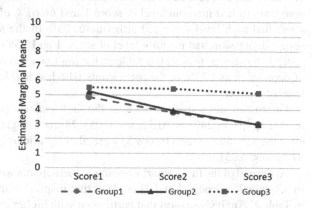

4.3 Relationship Between Individual Factors

Cross tabs/contingency tables were used to analyse categorical data. A chi-square test revealed a significant relationship between the user's gender and the preference for the character's gender ($\chi^2(N = 376) = 46.84, p < 0.05$). We examined the relationships between personality (IPIP) and DASS21 factors. We found significant relationships between extraversion and depression ($\chi^2(N = 376) = 24.31, p < 0.05$), extraversion and anxiety ($\chi^2(N = 376) = 22.93, p < 0.05$), agreeableness and depression (($\chi^2(N = 376) = 17.46, p = 0.03$), agreeableness and anxiety ($\chi^2(N = 376) = 17.18, p = 0.03$), agreeableness and stress ($\chi^2(N = 376) = 23.41, p < 0.05$), emotional stability and depression ($\chi^2(N = 376) = 55.71, p < 0.05$), emotional stability and anxiety ($\chi^2(N = 376) = 41.77, p < 0.05$), emotional stability-stress ($\chi^2(N = 376) = 40.14, p < 0.05$) were identified using chi-square tests.

Regarding personality and study stress score, Chi-Square tests confirmed significant association between extraversion and baseline study stress (score 1), $\chi^2(N = 242) = 11.69, p = 0.02$. We also found significant relationship between score 1 and depression ($\chi^2(N = 242) = 19.63, p = 0.01$) and score 1 and anxiety ($\chi^2(N = 242)$ $= 20.99, p = 0.01$).

Participants with high level of emotional stability reported medium level of study stress at time 2 (55.56%) and participants who had medium level of extraversion reported medium level of study stress at time 1 (50%) and at time 2 (59.18). Students who had medium and high level of agreeableness reported medium level of study stress at time 2 (52.04 and 51.52% respectively). Moreover, participants who had medium level of conscientiousness reported medium level of study stress at time 1 (50.60%) and at time 2 (59.18).

Significant gender and personality differences were found for agreeableness ($\chi^2(N = 376) = 32.78, p < 0.05$) and for emotional stability ($\chi^2(N = 376) = 11.99, p < 0.05$), the two of the personality dimensions.

Cross tabulations between their stress score from the DASS21 and their initial level of study (score 1) related stress show that 33.33% of the students having extremely severe stress had medium level of score 1 and 66.67% of the ones who had severe stress had high level score 1. Furthermore, 25% of the students having extremely severe depression had medium level of score 1 and 75% of them had high level of score 1. Moreover, 60% of the students having low level of score 1 had normal level of depression and 52% of the participants who had low level of score 1 had normal level of anxiety.

Group and study stress score after the first scenario (score 2) were significantly related ($\chi^2(N = 242) = 20.37, p < 0.05$). Moreover, group and study stress score after the second scenario (score 3) were also significantly related ($\chi^2(N = 242) = 37.75, p < 0.05$).

At the end of the first scenario/session 1, participants were asked "Have I been able to help you?" (Groups 1 and 2) or "Was that helpful" (Group 3). Results are shown in Table 7. Analysis suggest that participant with higher openness and agreeableness were more likely to say they felt better. The numbers are too small in many categories for meaningful chi-square test results.

In Group 1 and 2 at the end of the session, Sarah asked "Did you find our discussion useful?" and in the control group there was a question in the survey that asked "Did you find the document useful?" As shown in Table 8, in total 85% of the participants found the session useful. More participants found the conversation useful in group 1 and 2 than group 3 (87.5% and 87% vs. 80%). Note that the question was asked at the conclusion of the experiment, after neutral interaction in group 1 and after empathic interaction in group 2. Analysis with individual factors, show that 80% of

Table 7 Have I been able to help you/was that helpful?

	Yeah I feel better (%)	I feel about the same	No, I feel worse now (%)
1. Empathic-neutral	51	48%	1
2. Neutral-empathic	88	N/A	12
3. Control	42	55%	2

Table 8 Did you find our discussion/the document useful?

Group	Yeah it helped (%)	Not much (%)
1. Empathic-neutral	68	32
2. Neutral-empathic	84	16
3. Control	80	20
Total	78	22

participants who did not find the document helpful had normal or moderate stress compared to 66% in these categories who found the document helpful, suggesting lower stress reduces the value of the study tips.

5 Discussion

In general, our participants can be described as being medium (38.56%) to high (27.13%) open to new experiences/ideas, medium (36.70%) conscientiousness, spread on the extraversion dimension (ranging from introvert (32.45%) to extrovert (27.13), mostly moderate (31.91%)); low (26.33%) to moderate (41.76%) for emotional stability (or conversely high to moderate neuroticism). The sample population was more diverse concerning agreeableness and gender differences in levels of agreeableness were found. Analysis of the data shows that 38.14 and 12.71% of males said they were moderately and highly agreeable, respectively, compared to 41.02 and 34.38% of females, respectively, no gender differences were found for other personality dimensions. This adds validity to our data, as personality is considered a fundamental individual trait, not restricted or connected to a particular gender or other individual factor. Gender differences for agreeableness may be due to genders perceiving themselves differently, possibly due to cultural gender biases regarding the social acceptability of being disagreeable varying for the genders. The literature supports our self-reported findings that females tend to be more cooperative and agreeable than males [29]. Chi-square tests show that participants with low emotional stability (high neuroticism) are more likely to have normal and mild depression, anxiety and stress. Moreover, participants with high extraversion are more likely to have low depression, anxiety and stress. Finally, participants with high agreeableness are more likely to have low depression, anxiety and stress. Our finding is inconsistent with the literature [30] where personality traits have been examined as predictors of depression, anxiety and stress.

Relating to our first three research questions we did find some differences in preferences for and responses to the IVAs and the users' derived benefits based on the participants' gender, ethnicity, personality or psychological state. Our age distribution was too narrow to draw any conclusions regarding age-related preferences or responses.

In answer to the first research question, in general, our results indicate that there is no preference for the character's ethnicity or similarity to the participants. Most of the participants (65.96%) preferred a peer-aged character. Almost half of both genders, preferred an IVA of the same gender and the other half did not care about gender. There is a relationship between the users' culture and the users' preferences for the characters' gender. 71% of participants identifying with "people of the Americas" preferred to interact with a male character while for 70% of southern and Asian participants the gender of the character did not matter. Differences were found in preferences for characters according to the individual's personality and emotional psychological state. For example, high levels of stress (reported via DASS21) showed significant differences regarding ethnicity preferences, for example, in the extremely severe stress category (0.41% of the total sample) 0% did not care about the ethnicity and 85.71 and 14.29% preferred a same and a different ethnicity respectively. In contrast, 69.23, 26.92, 3.85% with normal stress, 71.11, 20, 8.89% with mild stress, 50, 30.56, 19.44% with moderate stress and 53.57, 35.71, 10.71% with severe stress, did not care about ethnicity, preferred the same ethnicity or preferred a different ethnicity, respectively. Moreover, in the extremely severe stress category, there are also differences for character preferences. 80% preferred the character to be looked like them whereas 20% did not care about this matter. There were no differences in participants' result of DASS21 and their cultural group. Moreover, we couldn't find any relation between participants' ethnicity and their ethnicity preferences for IVA.

In answer to the second research question, we found differences concerning initial study stress level (score 1) relating to personality. For example, significantly more individuals who were medium and high on extraversion scale reported feeling medium stress (50 and 40%) and participants with medium on the extraversion experienced medium stress. Some personal factors did not reveal any significant relationships. A Chi-square test reported no significant relationship between the participant playing computer games and the study stress score. We did not find any significant differences between participants' age, gender and study stress score. Finally, a Chi-square test reported no significant relationship between the ethnicity of the agent and study stress score.

We found a relationship between the psychological state of the user (DASS21) and the study stress score reported by the user. The individuals with extremely severe scale of depression reported high level of study stress (75%) at the beginning of the experiment while the participants with normal scale of depression reported medium level of study stress (47%). Regarding anxiety dimension (reported via DASS21), most participants with extremely severe scale of the anxiety reported medium and high levels of study stress score at the beginning of the experiment (43 and 47%) while participants with normal scale of stress reported low and medium study stress (35 and 43%).

The key goal of our agent in this experiment was to "Reduce Study Stress" and the IVAs were shown to achieve that more successfully than reading a pdf file with the same tips. Interacting with the virtual characters resulted in more study stress relief. Specifically, group 2 have received slightly more benefit from the study than group 1 and the control group (group 3) had the least deduction in study stress at the end of the study.

In answer to our third research question, our results (Table 8) also show that participants found the two experimental groups and the control group useful but group 1 was scored slightly less useful. The results for both agent groups are similar and since this question is asked after having received both the empathic and neutral dialogues, our results are inconclusive regarding whether participants found the empathic dialogue more useful than the neutral dialogue. The question regarding if they felt better after the first round (Table 7) indicates that almost all participants who received the empathic agent felt the same or better, whereas 12% with the neutral agent felt worse, compared to 2% who received the document.

The individual differences identified in answer to our first three research questions validate the need for adapting the IVA according to these differences. For example, we found differences in preferences for the gender of the IVA. However, in the literature we most commonly find the use of female IVA models because the literature reports that in line with findings that female physicians are associated with empathic communication and relationship building [31–33]. The implication of our results relating to our last research question is that tailoring of models according to needs and preferences, including gender matched models if desired, should be provided in deployed applications.

In answer to our last research question relating to possible IVA adaptations to individual differences, these findings suggest that IVAs dealing with emotionally unstable, or more neurotic individuals, may need to take into account possibly higher levels of stress and exhibit more empathic or other stress reducing behaviours. An adaptive IVA may need to show more empathic behaviours for depressed and stressed individuals to minimise their stress level. In the current study we randomly assigned individuals to groups. We intend to use data mining methods on the dataset from this study (and another dataset) to discover IVA preference rules based on participant features and whether the document, neutral or empathic delivery of study tips was most useful for certain combination of individual features. For instance, preference rules could be like the following rules:

Rule1: If culture = {c1, c2, c5} and personality = Introvet then character = Empathic
        Else if culture = {c3, c4} and study stress = medium then
            If anxiety = low then character_type = Neutral
            Else character_type = Empathic;

In our next study, we intend to use these rules to allocate participants to treatment groups (i.e. alternative IVAs). For example, we may assign people to an agent with different types of dialogue (neutral, empathic, highly empathic) according to their personality, the intensity of their emotions and stress levels and, if they have a preference, also provide participants with a male or female character according to their preference.

Clearly, there are many factors that come into play when evaluating the relation between an IVA and the human user. According to Moreno and Flowerday [9] students prefer to interact with an APA with more social cues (i.e. facial expression, vocal tone and body language) rather than an APA with only auditory capability. In this study, although our virtual character did not display many facial expressions but she expressed emotions and built rapport with her human-like representation. The FAtiMA model allows researchers to develop rules of user interaction in relation to the agent's emotional state (which can be empathetic or otherwise), the state of the environment they are in and various social norms, values and rituals that can be designed to mimic various cultural protocols and human-human interaction styles [3, 34]. The aim is for agents to create trust; put the user at ease; and convince them of the agent's ability to guide. The research reported here is a part of initiatives to advance and evaluate agent-human interaction. The use of agent models will improve the agent's ability to change to fit the demands of the situation they are in. However, it will require more work to develop the rules that are suitable for different user scenarios.

While we have found some significant results and suggested some tailoring, our study has a number of limitations requiring further future investigation and studies. The majority of our participants are psychology students (294/376) and female (256/376), related to the first limitation, they are predominantly female (206 female, 87 male). Furthermore, we need more participants to represent more age groups, cultures and more equal distributions of experimental groups.

6   Conclusions and Future Work

This study, together with other studies reported in the literature, strongly suggest that IVAs need to adapt in appearance and behaviour according to their purpose. In some cases as in our study where we seek to act as a mentor, friend or coach, the IVA needs to match the user's preferences (i.e. gender, age, culture, similarity to the user). However, in other cases where the purpose is to create empathy and challenge and change biases, attitudes and/or behaviours to certain types, the IVA should behave (e.g. empathic, neutral, tough, neurotic, extrovert, etc.) and represent (through language, voice and visual appearance) whatever is most beneficial in achieving that goal. For example, to educate and change stigmatised attitudes to mental health and Anorexia Nervosa (AN) in particular, participants interacted with a survivor of AN [35]. An IVA can represent a virtual patient to help healthcare students learn patient empathy [34], and feel what it is like to be an elderly person [36]. To reduce racial bias, Peck et al. [37] allowed participants' avatars to take on the skin of a black person and Shi et al. [38] created a feminist (FEMINIST) and non-feminist (MEDICAL) version of an IVA to educate participants about breastfeeding and challenge culture-based gender stereotypes.

To design IVAs that become what the human needs them to be, we require much more sophisticated models of the human as part of our agent architectures. The human should not be seen as a component of the environment and source of input, but be modeled within the architecture and have reasoning modules and rules that enable the IVA to behave accordingly. With increasing access to user data and the growth in the Internet of Things and ambient computing, capturing data about our user's preferences, beliefs, emotional state, exercise regime and diet, etc. should become possible. Now is the time to conduct studies to understand what data is important and how it can best to used. This study seeks to make such a contribution.

References

1. DeVault, D., Artstein, R., Benn, G., Dey, T., Fast, E., Gainer, A., Georgila, K., Gratch, J., Hartholt, A., Lhommet, M., Lucas, G., Marsella, S., Morbini, F., Nazarian, A., Scherer, S., Stratou, G., Suri, A., Traum, D., Wood, R., Xu, Y., Rizzo, A., Morency, L.-P.: SimSensei kiosk: a virtual human interviewer for healthcare decision support. Paper presented at the Proceedings of the 2014 international conference on Autonomous agents and multi-agent systems, Paris, France (2014)
2. Cerekovic, A., Aran, O., Gatica-Perez, D.: Rapport with virtual agents: what do human social cues and personality explain? IEEE Trans. Affect. Comput. 8(3), 382–395 (2016)
3. Lim, M.Y., Dias, J., Aylett, R., Paiva, A.: Improving adaptiveness in autonomous characters. In: International Workshop on Intelligent Virtual Agents, pp. 348–355. Springer (2008)
4. Kutay, C., Mascarenhas, S., Paiva, A., Prada, R.: Intercultural-role Plays for e-Learning using Emotive Agents. In: ICAART (2), pp. 395–400 (2013)
5. Johnson, W.L., Rickel, J.W., Lester, J.C.: Animated pedagogical agents: face-to-face interaction in interactive learning environments. Int. J. Artif. Intell. Educ. 11(1), 47–78 (2000)
6. Lester, J.C., Converse, S.A., Kahler, S.E., Barlow, S.T., Stone, B.A., Bhogal, R.S.: The persona effect: affective impact of animated pedagogical agents. In: Proceedings of the ACM SIGCHI Conference on Human Factors in Computing Systems, pp. 359–366. ACM (1997)
7. Veletsianos, G.: Cognitive and affective benefits of an animated pedagogical agent: considering contextual relevance and aesthetics. J. Educ. Comput. Res. 36(4), 373–377 (2007)
8. Shen, L., Wang, M., Shen, R.: Affective e-learning: using "emotional" data to improve learning in pervasive learning environment. J. Educ. Technol. Soc. 12(2), 176 (2009)
9. Moreno, R., Flowerday, T.: Students' choice of animated pedagogical agents in science learning: a test of the similarity-attraction hypothesis on gender and ethnicity. Contemp. Educ. Psychol. 31(2), 186–207 (2006)
10. dos Santos, C.T., Osório, F.S.: An intelligent and adaptive virtual environment and its application in distance learning. In: Proceedings of the Working Conference on Advanced Visual Interfaces, pp. 362–365. ACM (2004)
11. Caridakis, G., Raouzaiou, A., Bevacqua, E., Mancini, M., Karpouzis, K., Malatesta, L., Pelachaud, C.: Virtual agent multimodal mimicry of humans. Lang. Resour. Eval. 41(3–4), 367–388 (2007)
12. Bevacqua, E., Mancini, M., Pelachaud, C.: A listening agent exhibiting variable behaviour. In: Intelligent Virtual Agents, pp. 262–269. Springer (2008)
13. Pecune, F., Mancini, M., Biancardi, B., Varni, G., Ding, Y., Pelachaud, C., Volpe, G., Camurri, A.: Laughing with a virtual agent. In: Proceedings of the 2015 International Conference on Autonomous Agents and Multiagent Systems, pp. 1817–1818. International Foundation for Autonomous Agents and Multiagent Systems (2015)
14. Kistler, F., Endrass, B., Damian, I., Dang, C.T., André, E.: Natural interaction with culturally adaptive virtual characters. J. Multimodal User Interfaces 6(1–2), 39–47 (2012)

15. Bailenson, J.N., Swinth, K., Hoyt, C., Persky, S., Dimov, A., Blascovich, J.: The independent and interactive effects of embodied-agent appearance and behavior on self-report, cognitive, and behavioral markers of copresence in immersive virtual environments. Presence: Teleoper. Virtual Environ. 14(4), 379–393 (2005)
16. Vugt, H.C.V., Bailenson, J.N., Hoorn, J.F., Konijn, E.A.: Effects of facial similarity on user responses to embodied agents. ACM Trans. Comput.-Hum. Interact. (TOCHI) 17(2), 7 (2010)
17. Bickmore, T.W., Schulman, D., Sidner, C.: Automated interventions for multiple health behaviors using conversational agents. Patient Educ. Couns. 92(2), 142–148 (2013)
18. Lisetti, C., Amini, R., Yasavur, U., Rishe, N.: I can help you change! An empathic virtual agent delivers behavior change health interventions. ACM Trans. Manag. Inf. Syst. (TMIS) 4(4), 19 (2013)
19. Jin, S.-A.A.: The effects of incorporating a virtual agent in a computer-aided test designed for stress management education: the mediating role of enjoyment. Comput. Hum. Behav. 26(3), 443–451 (2010)
20. Ducheneaut, N., Wen, M.-H., Yee, N., Wadley, G.: Body and mind: a study of avatar personalization in three virtual worlds. In: Proceedings of the SIGCHI Conference on Human Factors in Computing Systems, pp. 1151–1160. ACM (2009)
21. Hall, L., Woods, S., Dautenhahn, K., Sobral, D., Paiva, A., Wolke, D., Newall, L.: Designing empathic agents: adults versus kids. In: Intelligent Tutoring Systems, pp. 604–613 (2004)
22. Rivera-Gutierrez, D., Ferdig, R., Li, J., Lok, B.: Getting the point across: exploring the effects of dynamic virtual humans in an interactive museum exhibit on user perceptions. IEEE Trans. Vis. Comput. Graph. 20(4), 636–643 (2014)
23. Dias, J., Mascarenhas, S., Paiva, A.: Fatima modular: towards an agent architecture with a generic appraisal framework. In: Emotion Modeling, pp. 44–56. Springer (2014)
24. Mancini, M., Niewiadomski, R., Bevacqua, E., Pelachaud, C.: Greta: a SAIBA compliant ECA system. In: Troisiéme Workshop sur les Agents Conversationnels Animés (2008)
25. Bickmore, T., Gruber, A., Picard, R.: Establishing the computer–patient working alliance in automated health behavior change interventions. Patient Educ. Couns. 59(1), 21–30 (2005)
26. Goldberg, L.R.: A broad-bandwidth, public domain, personality inventory measuring the lower-level facets of several five-factor models. Pers. Psychol. Eur. 7(1), 7–28 (1999)
27. Henry, J.D., Crawford, J.R.: The short-form version of the Depression Anxiety Stress Scales (DASS-21): construct validity and normative data in a large non-clinical sample. Br. J. Clin. Psychol. 44(2), 227–239 (2005)
28. Gomez, F.: A Guide to the Depression, Anxiety and Stress Scale (DASS 21). Central and Eastern Sydney Primary Health Networks (2016)
29. Weisberg, Y.J., DeYoung, C.G., Hirsh, J.B.: Gender differences in personality across the ten aspects of the Big Five. Front. Psychol. 2, 178 (2011)
30. Vujičić, M.M., Ranđelović, D.J.: Personality traits as predictors of depression, anxiety, and stress with secondary school students of final years. Zbornik radova Filozofskog fakulteta u Prištini 47–3, 217–237 (2017)
31. Baker, S., Richards, D., Caldwell, P.: Relational agents to promote eHealth advice adherence. In: PRICAI 2014: Trends in Artificial Intelligence, pp. 1010–1015. Springer (2014)
32. Baker, S., Richards, D., Caldwell, P.: Putting a new intelligent virtual face on a medical treatment advice system to improve adherence. In: Proceedings of the 2014 Conference on Interactive Entertainment, pp. 1–9 (2014)
33. Schmid Mast, M., Hall, J.A., Roter, D.L.: Disentangling physician sex and physician communication style: their effects on patient satisfaction in a virtual medical visit. Patient Educ. Couns. 68(1), 16–22 (2007). https://doi.org/10.1016/j.pec.2007.03.020
34. Halan, S., Sia, I., Crary, M., Lok, B.: Exploring the effects of healthcare students creating virtual patients for empathy training. In: Intelligent Virtual Agents, pp. 239–249 (2015)
35. Sebastian, J., Richards, D.: Changing stigmatizing attitudes to mental health via education and contact with embodied conversational agents. Comput. Hum. Behav. 73, 479–488 (2017)

36. Yee, N., Bailenson, J.N.: Walk a mile in digital shoes: the impact of embodied perspective-taking on the reduction of negative stereotyping in immersive virtual environments. In: Proceedings of PRESENCE, pp. 24–26 (2006)
37. Peck, T.C., Seinfeld, S., Aglioti, S.M., Slater, M.: Putting yourself in the skin of a black avatar reduces implicit racial bias. Conscious. Cogn. **22**(3), 779–787 (2013)
38. Shi, L., Bickmore, T., Edwards, R.: A feminist virtual agent for breastfeeding promotion. In: Intelligent Virtual Agents, pp. 461–470 (2015)

User-Centered Design for Biomedical Literature Search User Interfaces

Carlos Iñiguez-Jarrín, José Ignacio Panach and Oscar Pastor

Abstract Biomedical literature search tools are crucial resources for the work of physicians, biologists, and bioinformatics. Many of the genetic-medical diagnoses depend on the findings in these literature resources. Despite the importance and value of the information stored in these resources, the user interface (UI) implemented by such tools present several usability problems converting the query and interpretation of the information into complex and time-consuming tasks. In this sense, an user-centered design (UCD) approach can improve the usability of these UIs facilitating the interaction, analysis, and comparison of biomedical information, and, consequently, improving the productivity of practitioners in this domain. This paper presents a user-centered design (UCD) approach for designing UIs for the search of biomedical literature considering the usability problems and proposing design solutions to such problems. How to apply the UCD approach and the design solutions proposed for the usability problems become the main contribution of this work.

Keywords User interface design · Bioinformatics · Usability

A prior version of this paper has been published in the ISD2018 Proceedings (http://aisel.aisnet.org/isd2014/proceedings2018).

C. Iñiguez-Jarrín (✉)
Escuela Politécnica Nacional, Quito, Ecuador
e-mail: carlos.iniguez@epn.edu.ec

J. I. Panach
Universitat de València, Valencia, Spain
e-mail: joigpana@uv.es

O. Pastor
Universitat Politècnica de València, Valencia, Spain
e-mail: opastor@pros.upv.es

1 Introduction

The search of biomedical literature is a task transversal to other tasks carried out by researchers (e.g., physicians, bioinformatics, biologists). The diagnosis and treatment of certain diseases is a clear example of that, where researchers look in the digital repositories of biomedical literature for potential diseases related to the mutations of the genes of a patient. In this way, literature search tools are crucial for the work of biomedical researchers. Among the biomedical literature search tools most frequently used by researchers is PubMed [1] which is one of the databases administered by the National Center for Biotechnology Information (NCBI[1]) containing to date (April 2018) more than 20 million citations of complete scientific-medical articles stored in the MEDLINE database, one of the most important bases of the National Library of Medicine of the United States.

Behind these web search tools are not only machine learning algorithms, but also a user interface (UI) that support the user to interact with the biomedical literature sources. Unfortunately, such interaction faces several problems related to the *querying* and *results interpretation* tasks. These problems have a negative impact on the researchers' work productivity and, even worse, the problems reduce the possibility of finding accurate and adequate results.

For this reason, the scientific community has expressed its growing need to improve the usability of the UIs of these tools [2–4]. A log-based study [5] of PubMed website provides relevant information about the user search behaviour as a foundation to know the user in this domain and motivate the improvement of the biomedical information recovery. NCBI Insights,[2] an NCBI blog dedicated to facilitating the use of its NCBI search resources for users, specifically invites readers through a post titled *"Try Our New, Experimental PubMed Search and User Interface in PubMed Labs"*[3] to experience the improvements and new functionalities at UI level and search algorithms added to a PubMed prototype. The NCBI goal is to test the functionalities and eventually incorporate them into the PubMed real site. Among the characteristics to be experienced are "Best match" (i.e., a search algorithm to rank the search results with respect to the degree of concordance of the content of the article with the search terms), "Responsive design" (i.e., a new look and feel of the site that follows the "mobile-first" design principle to adapt the UI to other deployment devices), "Snippets" (i.e., highlighting the searched terms and their synonyms). Seen in another way, searching for findings in the biomedical literature involves tracing the relationships immersed in the content of literature sources. A complex task due to usability problems at the UI level.

Our research group is focused on studying the human genome from the perspective of the information systems. One of our main concerns is the design of usable UIs for

---

[1]https://www.ncbi.nlm.nih.gov/.

[2]https://ncbiinsights.ncbi.nlm.nih.gov/.

[3]https://ncbiinsights.ncbi.nlm.nih.gov/2017/10/17/try-our-new-experimental-pubmed-search-and-user-interface-in-pubmed-labs.

facilitating the exploitation tasks of genomic information and the literature search is one of these tasks that also is a main and frequent task performed by the bioinformatics [6].

This work is motivated for improving the practitioners' experience when interacting with the UI in search of relevant biomedical literature that fulfills their knowledge interest. In this paper, we describe a UCD approach applied to improve the usability of Biomedical Literature Searching UIs. The process we follow covers from the user research to the materialization of the UI design. To do that, we (a) characterize the users in this domain by defining their search behaviour, (b) analyze, identify, collect, and categorize usability problems involved in the biomedical literature search, and (c) propose the UI design that incorporates the solutions to the usability problems.

The contributions of this work are:

(a) A process to guide the developers, designers, and bioinformatics when designing user interfaces in this domain.
(b) The characterization of the users of this domain based on their search behaviour that can be used for further user research.
(c) Provide design solutions for solving the existing usability problems in this domain.

To explain the solutions, we have incorporated them into a design of a simple and generic UI which focuses on improving the user experience in the search and exploration of large collections of documents. The benefit of such solutions is that they can be re-used by UI designers when designing UIs not only for biological literature search systems but also for designing UIs of general-purpose literature search systems in different domains. Therefore, the proposed UI design becomes a usability heuristic that can be used as a reference to solve interaction design problems in further UI developments.

This work is structured as follows. Section 2 presents some works related to UIs of scientific and biomedical literature search applications. Section 3 presents an overview of the user-centered design process for designing usable user interfaces and the steps are described in detail in the next sections: Sect. 4 specifies the context of use, the first step of the process, where we characterize the users in this domain. Section 5 describes the second step of the process where we identify the user requirements based on usability problems. Section 6 presents the design solutions to the usability problems, the third step of the process, and illustrate them through the design of UIs that incorporate such solutions. Section 7 describes future work, especially those related to the feasibility of the UI's technological implementation. Section 8 presents the conclusions.

2 Related Works

The list of web search tools for biomedical literature sources is varied [7]. However, PubMed is the tool most often used by researchers in this domain. The type of search and exploration that the UIs of these tools support is "query-focused" search, that is, the researcher defines a query as a starting point to start the exploration. In PubMed, for example, the user enters the name of a disease as a search term and the records of biomedical literature obtained from the consultation become the starting point to navigate and explore the issues related to the disease.

From a general perspective, the UIs of search and analysis of scientific literature has made a great leap from text UIs to UIs that allow the exploration and visual analysis of the global properties of the literature collection (e.g., authors, locations, publication dates) [8], as well as, the properties of each of the items in the collection (e.g., co-citation relationships, co-authorship). Tools such as VOSviewer [9] or PubNet [10], for example, show powerful visualizations about bibliometric networks allowing visualizing publications, authors or journals from the point of view of citation relationships, co-citations or bibliographic coupling.

There are also applications that aim to integrate the various bibliographical sources to avoid the researcher visiting each of the sources of literature in search of useful information. The UIs of these systems incorporate global and detailed visualizations of the literature collection.

Mastermind [11] is a specialized search engine to find the relationships between documented diseases and genetic aspects (genetic variations and genes). To achieve this, the application integrates the content of several biomedical repositories from which the researcher interacts mainly through two UIs: search parameters and data exploration. The first one allows the researcher to enter any of the three search parameters supported by the application such as the name of a disease, the identifier of a genetic variation or the name of a gene. The query results are presented in the second UI that includes textual and statistical graph information about the medical-scientific articles found, as well as the genetic information (genetic variants and genes) referenced in the articles. The graphic representation of the articles is well achieved through a zoomable scatter plot where each point becomes a circle of a variable area that represents each of the items in the set. This graphic representation allows visualizing the set of articles from 3 dimensions. The 2 scatter plot axes (XY) represent the date of publication and number of citations dimensions. The third dimension, % match search term in the article, is represented by the variable area of each circle in the graph. The objective of the authors to include functionalities and improvements in the UI is to obtain faster, clinically relevant search results and achieve comprehensive diagnoses. Unlike databases such as PubMed, Mastermind provides full indexing of articles, which makes it possible to match full-text statements in the content of biomedical articles.

Dimensions [12] is a discovery platform with nearly 90 million publications, full-text search, and contextualization of information through links to publications, patents, clinical trials, authors, appointments, among others. Its UI is distributed in four sectors (i.e., search term, list of publications found, fixed area of filters and the view of analytics) fairly similar to other search engines of scientific-academic literature such as Scopus except that the Dimensions' UI facilitates the segregation of results through filters related to the fields of research (e.g., genetics, clinical sciences, immunology), relevant authors, sources of titles (e.g., Plos One) and makes possible, through a 2D chart, the interactive analysis of publication metrics over the years.

Other systems set their UI with visual components that retrieve information from different bibliographic sources. BioGPS [13] is a portal for querying and reporting genes where the UI is built from the combination of plugins which present data retrieved from data sources focused on genes external to BioGP. For example, among the plugins available in the portal that support the literature search about genes include plugins to search on Google Scholar, PubMed full-text search, Gene Wiki,[4] NextBio,[5] among others. The plugins mechanism makes this application configurable (customizable) and extensible.

The tools described in this section present UIs that allow exploring the literature in several ways. Specifically, the type of exploration that we pursue is the exploratory visual search that supports tasks such as analyzing, comparing and evaluating the content. The proposed UI design considers the exploratory visual search and the best usability practices of the tools described in this section.

3 The Pattern-Based User-Centered Design Approach

We apply a user-centered design (UCD) approach accompanied by the use of interaction design patterns for designing usable user interfaces for the biomedical literature search. Concretely, we cover the activities 2, 3, and 4 of the UCD process defined by ISO 9241-210:2010[6] as shown in Fig. 1:

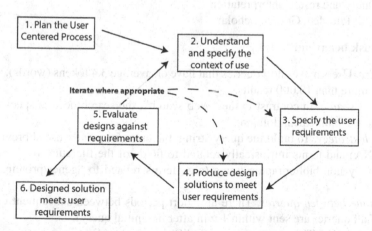

Fig. 1 User-Centered Design (UCD) approach based on ISO 9241-2010:2010

---

[4]https://en.wikipedia.org/wiki/Portal:Gene_Wiki.

[5]http://www.nextbio.com/b/nextbio.nb.

[6]https://www.iso.org/standard/52075.html.

2.—*Understand and Specify the Context of Use*. To know users, goals, tasks, and behaviours as well as the environment.

3.—*Specify the User and Organizational Requirements*. To specify the usability problems affecting user tasks.

4.—*Produce Design solutions*. To define and use interaction design patterns as design solutions to create a UI prototype.

4 Understanding and Specifying the Context of Use

Knowing the users and their goals are crucial to producing successfully designs. A tool commonly used by designers to know the users for whom the user interface is being designed is the *Personas*. Personas are useful for modelling users by describing the attitudes, goals, and behaviours of real people under study and represent them throughout the design process putting them in the center of the design process [14]. We defined a Personae by describing the *user's search behaviour* in this domain considering the information retrieved from the analysis of existing works in the literature [5, 15], interviews conducted with 2 genetic researchers working on genetic labs in Valencia, Spain, and 3 undergraduate students of bioinformatics from Polytechnic University of Valencia. For better organization of the Personae, we classified the user's research behaviour in two search tasks: *query* and *interpretation of results*.

Name: Clara Gonzales
Job: Genetic Biomedical research department
Tasks: Query and results interpretation
Tools used: PubMed, Google Scholar.

Query task behaviour

Query size. Users make short queries that have on average 3.4 tokens (words), which produce more than 10,000 results.

Type of search. In contrast to the "Web search", the search need is specific and related to the biomedical domain.

Search strategy. To build the query string, the users frequently use abbreviations (e.g., DNA) and terms intrinsically related to fields of the literature (e.g., author) followed by non-bibliographic terms (e.g., terms related to "genes/proteins" and "diseases").

The time between queries. There are short periods between subsequent queries (72% of all queries are sent within 1 min after the initial query).

Reformulation. The query string is modified continuously.

Persistence. Regardless of whether the results are many or none, the search is persistent; new queries are sent to obtain significant results.

Results interpretation task behaviour

Interpretation scope. The interpretation depends strongly on the repository used. For example, the results retrieved by PubMed are limited to the fields that it indexes (e.g., titles and abstracts) since it does not index full-text articles. On the contrary, Google Scholar indexes millions of articles from various domains including the biomedical domain. However, Google Scholar is not focused on human diseases searches, therefore, the results obtained overload valuable information.

Review trend. Users tend to select search results located in the top positions. The number of clicks in the documents located in the last pages decreases exponentially. In addition, the user accesses frequently the abstracts instead of the full-text article.

Selection probability. There is a low probability of selection of results when the result set increases in size. The greater the set of results, the user tends not to review the results.

Clara Gonzales is a fictitious name to identify our personae. Remember that a Personae is not a real person, but rather it represents to real people in our study. It comprises the behaviour characteristics becoming a distinctive model of the search behaviour of the user population in this domain and serves as a support instrument for the designer. In fact, Clara's search behaviour will serve to select the best design solutions that will make up the user interface.

5   User Requirements

We have considered the usability problems affecting the biomedical literature search UIs as requirements to be solved. We identified and collected seven (7) usability problems documented in the literature [5, 16]. The usability problems were categorized into two general lines: query and result interpretation. Within each category, each usability problem is identified with the prefix UP (usability problem), the assigned number and its distinctive name, as detailed in the following subsections.

5.1   Query Usability Problems

UP1-Correct query terms. Users experience problems when building the query string. These problems are caused mainly by the lack of information and the support mechanisms to structure and build the query string. From a practical view, these problems can be outlined in two specific usability sub-problems: "finding the correct term" (the search mechanisms provided by the repositories do not support searches by synonyms, but exact and well-written terms which usually produces 0 results) and "search by object ID" (object ID is a univocal and exclusive identifier number assigned to each article indexed in the literature database which is used to yield accurate results, however, in most cases, it is not used because the users do not know where or how to include it in the query).

UP2-Complex generation of the query string. The mechanisms used for building query strings are extremely simple or difficult to use. While the "standard search" mechanism becomes a solution relatively simple that often produces a lot of noise in the results, the "advanced search" becomes a difficult-to-use mechanism and requires special skills on the part of the user. For building complex queries, for example, the user must have an in-depth knowledge of the possible data fields to filter and deal with the logical operators. Especially, the syntax and semantics of the operators cause many problems among the users; users must deal with the order and combination of operators as well as their meaning (for example, some use "AND" another "+"), without obtaining any results. In that sense, the existing query mechanisms do not allow to correctly express the semantics of the query string.

5.2   Result Interpretation Usability Problems

UP3-Lack of the vision of the "big picture". Given the numerous query results, perceiving the trends in the result set is difficult. The user requires an entire visualization of the results that allow understanding the result set in a glance.

UP4-Manual Annotations. Users frequently use Microsoft Excel to manually document the findings found in the literature. This is a time-consuming task since, for each comment, the user must fill a row with several columns including the bibliographic reference to locate the source of the comment in the future.

UP5-Handling long lists of results. With more than 100 records, users behave in two ways: (a) Do not explore the results and reformulate the query string or (b) Focus on the first three results expecting them to be the most relevant (something that is not fulfilled in most cases).

UP6-Non-understandable ranking criteria. Several sorting criteria are used in lists of options or in data charts, however, many of them are not well explained leaving to the user's imagination the meaning of them.

UP7-Extract of the document does not allow understanding its content. The title and the abstract are not helpful to understand the document.

From these detected UPs, in the next section, we propose UI design solutions for facilitating the search and the interpretation of results.

6   Producing Design Solutions

In this section, we search for design solutions for the identified UPs and apply them to design a usable UI for analyzing biomedical literature. The UPs are resultants of inadequate design of the interaction between the user and the UI, therefore, we search for proved design solutions that enhance the manner in which the user interacts with the UI. These proved design solutions are known in the literature as *Interaction Design Patterns* (IDPs). The Interaction Design Foundation [17] defines an IDP as "a general repeatable solution to a commonly-occurring usability problem in interface design or interaction design". There are a plethora of IDPs collections documented and available in the literature [18, 19] and websites [20]. Our aim is to define a tailored catalog of IDPs that faces the identified UPs. To do that, we have followed a systematic process that consists of selecting the existing IDPs that covers the UPs and for those UPs that are not covered by the existing IDPs collections, we define new ones by analyzing existing UIs of similar applications and identifying the repeatable design solutions. The steps of the process are:

1. Select applications that implement UIs that addresses one or several UPs.
2. Analyze the UIs of the applications.
3. Select the design solutions with the highest frequency of use, those that have been used repeatedly for the designers to solve the UP's.
4. Compare the selected design solutions with existing solutions documented in the available IDP libraries. To do that, we use the UI-patterns [20] library because it is available online and very popular between UI designers.
5. If the design solution is documented in the UI-patterns library, we add it to the IDPs catalog.
6. If the design solution is not documented in the UI-patterns library, we documented it under a simple template consisting of three parts: *name* (i.e., short name to identify the IDP), *problem* (i.e., description about the problem that solve the IDP), and *solution* (i.e., explanation about how to solve the problem). The documented design solution is added to the IDPs catalog.

As a result of this process, our IDPs catalog contains the following IDPs:

IDP1: *Document network*
Problem: User needs to have contextual information related to a certain document.
Solution: Visualize the documents ordered by an spatiotemporal attribute common and provide context by highlighting the relationships between them.
Source: The authors

IDP2: *Annotation*
Problem: User needs to make notes about her findings.
Solution: Allow the user to make and save comments about the content without interrupting the development of the user's tasks.
Source: The authors.

IDP3: *Autocomplete*
Problem: The user needs aided search when performing search tasks that are difficult to remember or easily mistyped.
Solution: Provide an autocomplete search field that presents items which match with the user's input as they type. As the user types in more text into the search field, the list of matching items is narrowed down.
Source: http://ui-patterns.com/patterns/Autocomplete.

IDP4: *Live Filter*

Problem: The user needs to conduct a search using contextual filters that narrow the search results.

Solution: Refine search results in real time using one or more filters.

Source: http://ui-patterns.com/patterns/LiveFilter.

IDP5: *Continuous Scrolling*

Problem: User wants to stay on one page while she scrolls across a long list of items. The list of elements can grow as the results are delivered. The pagination of the list is not an adequate mechanism in this case.

Solution: Load automatically the items of a list as the user scrolls down.

Source: http://ui-patterns.com/patterns/ContinuousScrolling.

IDP6: *Highlight content*

Problem: The user needs guides that allow him to understand the meaning of the document content. The title and the abstract are not enough to understand the document.

Solution: Highlight the search terms and contextual information in the content of the document.

Source: The authors.

IDP7: *Advanced Search*

Problem: The user needs to build complex queries by using data fields and combining them with logical operators (i.e., AND, OR, NOT).

Solution: Provide a mechanism to build complex query strings where the user can easily sort the logical operators to express the suitable semantic.

Source: The authors.

Table 1 shows the UPs covered by each IDP that makes up the IDP catalog. The following section uses the IDPs catalog to design UI prototypes to solve the UPs.

6.1 UI Prototypes

Considering the Personae, the UP's and the IDPs catalog, we designed a UI prototype consisting of two UI's according to the two general lines: one for "query task" and

Table 1 Usability problems (UP) covered by interaction design patterns (IDP)

	UP1	UP2	UP3	UP4	UP5	UP6	UP7
IDP1			X		X	X	
IDP2				X			
IDP3	X						
IDP4					X		
IDP5					X		
IDP6							X
IDP7		X					

another for the "result interpretation task". In this section, we describe the design of each UI and its functionality, emphasizing how the usability problems described in the previous section have been addressed with the IDPs.

6.2 Result Interpretation UI

This UI has been designed to provide a global and detailed view of the results and allows the user to freely explore the literature through different connected content views. Figure 2 shows the design of this UI stating the IDPs incorporated.

The operation of the UI starts when the user enters a term in the search text box. This search text box implements the IDP3 to mitigate the UP1. The search text box helps the user to find the appropriate terms for searching and querying the heterogeneous biomedical data. Each term entered by the user is compared internally with terms of an underlying ontology [21] that contains the concepts of the domain and the relationships between them. Thus, even when the user commits a writing error, the system suggests the user correctly written terms related to the entered term. This achieves a query string with a high probability of obtaining accurate results.

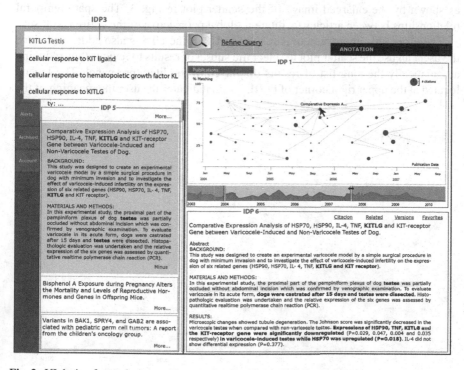

Fig. 2 UI design for exploring and interpreting the biomedical literature

The obtained results (the set of literature records) are listed implementing the IDP5 and mapped in the scatter plot that implements the IDP1.

The content of the UI changes according to the user's behaviour. For instance, when the user selects a circle that represents one of the articles published between 2004 and the last months of 2007 (as shown by the timeline bar), several things happen at the same time: (a) in the scatter plot, the lines that connect the selected article with referenced articles are highlighted, (b) in the document list that implement the IDP5, the corresponding publication (second publication of the list) is highlighted, (c) the IDP6 displays the full-text article with relevant information highlighted. In this way, the user can see highlighted not only the exact words that match with the search terms, but also the synonymous and the complete sentences that make the context of the document more understandable. This design solution, inspired by [11] and [1], addresses the UP7.

The scatter plot that implements the IDP1 is inspired by the Mastermind's scatter plot where the scientific-clinic articles are represented by circles of a variable area. The scatter plot shows the articles in three dimensions: number of citations (area of the circle), publication date (X-axis), and % match of the search terms within the article content (Y-axis). However, we have adapted the original Mastermind's scatter plot to show an additional dimension: the citation relationships between articles (lines that join the circles) to show the articles that have been referenced by a selected article, as shown by the enlarged image of the scatter plot in Fig. 3. The spatiotemporal relationships between articles facilitate a global perspective of the entire result set.

Therefore, this improvement is related to UP3. The UP5 is also addressed since the user can use the scatter plot to select the subset of results to review, thus reducing automatically the long list of results displayed in the literature panel. The legend located at the upper right corner of the diagram indicates the user the meaning of the

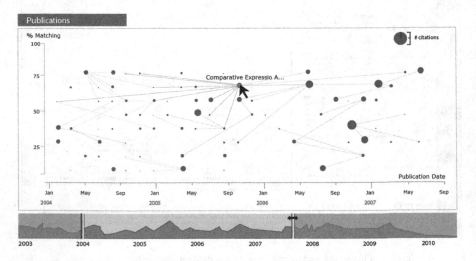

Fig. 3 Scatter plot chart showing four dimensions for publications

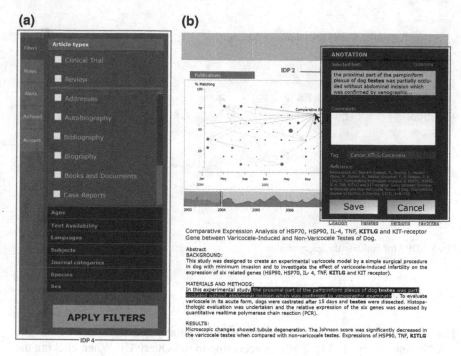

Fig. 4 a Filters. **b** Annotation form

circle area: the number of citations of the article, an important detail mentioned in the UP6. Therefore, each circle varies its area depending on the number of citations of the article.

The filters tab (Fig. 4a) implements the IDP4. It shows the filter conditions that help segregate the set of articles by some themes and categories related to the article attributes. The filters address the UP5 since through the filters the information overload is avoided by segregating the result set to one or another filter condition.

If the user is interested in an extract of the content of an article, the user can comment it by displaying the annotation form that implements the IDP5 (Fig. 4b) covering the UP4. When the form is displayed, it loads automatically the selected content by the user, the article citation, and provides a text box to add the respective comment. By accessing the "Notes" menu (Fig. 4a), the user can see all the notes made. This built-in functionality allows automating the manual annotation process improving the productivity of the user.

Fig. 5 IDP7 for building the query strings

6.3 Query UI

The Query UI deals with the tasks related to how to query and discover the data. The link "Refine Query" in Fig. 2 allows accessing to the Query UI. When clicking the link, the Query UI is displayed by showing a mechanism for building query strings (Fig. 5) that implements the IDP7 and covers the UP2 (i.e., complex generation of the query string). A query string is a set of terms related by logical operators (i.e., AND, OR, NOT). Building complex query strings can become a difficult task since it supposes to deal with nested logical operators and the order in which they must be executed. In this sense, the IDP7 facilitates the use of syntax and improves the semantic of logical operators. The mechanism consists of the "Query String" (Fig. 5a) and the "Query Builder" (Fig. 5b). The Query String is a read-only field that displays the query string formed automatically for each change made in the Query Builder. The Query Builder contains the "Search for" field, the first term of the query string, and the "matrix of terms" that contains the terms added to the first term by means of the syntax of logical operators AND, OR and NOT represented by the INCLUDE, OPTIONAL, EXCLUDE columns of the table, respectively.

To explain how to operate the mechanism, we will assume that the researcher wants to search for "*the relationship between the KITLG gene and testicular cancer in humans or in dogs*". To build this query string, the researcher enters the first search term "KITLG" in the "Search for" field as shown in Fig. 5b. Next, the researcher enters the "testis" and "human" terms in the INCLUDE column (using the corresponding text box at the top of the column) and the term "dog" in the OPTIONAL column since the researcher requirement states "*... in humans OR in dogs*". Note that, for each term entered, regardless of whether the term was entered in the INCLUDE, OPTIONAL or EXCLUDE column, the table creates a complete row to keep the term entry order, therefore, it is not possible to have two terms in the same row. For

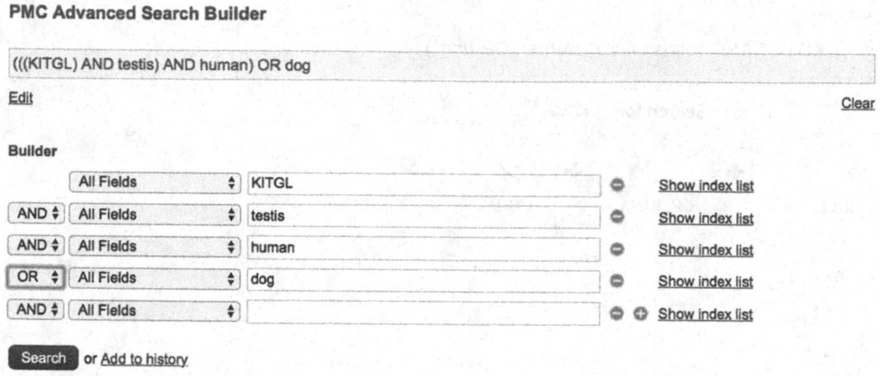

PMC Advanced Search Builder

(((KITGL) AND testis) AND human) OR dog

Edit   Clear

Builder

All Fields ⬍	KITGL	⊖	Show index list
AND ⬍	All Fields ⬍	testis	⊖	Show index list
AND ⬍	All Fields ⬍	human	⊖	Show index list
OR ⬍	All Fields ⬍	dog	⊖	Show index list
AND ⬍	All Fields ⬍		⊖ ⊕	Show index list

Search or Add to history

Fig. 6 NCBI's advanced search UI

each term in the table, the researcher can use the drop-down lists from the FIELD column to specify the field within the article (e.g., title, affiliation, publication year, author) to perform the query. The "Up" and "Down" actions allow altering the order of the terms in the query. The checkboxes of the GROUP column serve to express groupings between the terms, which we will see later. The result of this operation is the query string "(((KITLG) AND testis) AND human) OR dog" that yields 341,898 literature results.

So far, the query string formulation mechanism does not differ from those presented by the existing search repositories. In fact, the same query string can be built with the advanced NCBI search (Fig. 6) that yields the same number of results. However, the query string built by using the mechanism based on the IDP7 or the advanced NCBI search is incorrect since it does not express the correct semantics of the query. In fact, the end of the query string should be "*AND (human OR dog))*" instead of "*AND human) OR dog*". It is the reason for a large number of results.

What makes our mechanism different from existing mechanisms is the ability to allow expressing the correct semantics of the query string. For example, in the advanced NCBI search (Fig. 6), there would be no way of grouping the "*human*" and "*dog*" terms and connect them by using the "*OR*" operator, as the correct query should be. In addition, modifying the query string by adding a new term between the terms "*testis*" and "*human*" is impossible unless the query string is recreated from scratch. Instead, our mechanism allows freely grouping the terms and order them. For instance, to group the "*human*" and "*dog*" terms, in Fig. 5 the user checks the checkboxes corresponding to the "*human*" and "*dog*" terms and then clicks on the "*Group*" action link in the column header. Figure 7 shows the result of these actions. The broken lines state how the end of the query string has changed from "*AND human) OR dog*" to "*AND (human OR dog))*" by the grouping of the second-last and last rows. Note that the number of results has reduced from 341,989 to 9. These 9 results are appropriate since they come from a semantically correct query string that expresses the researcher's need for knowledge.

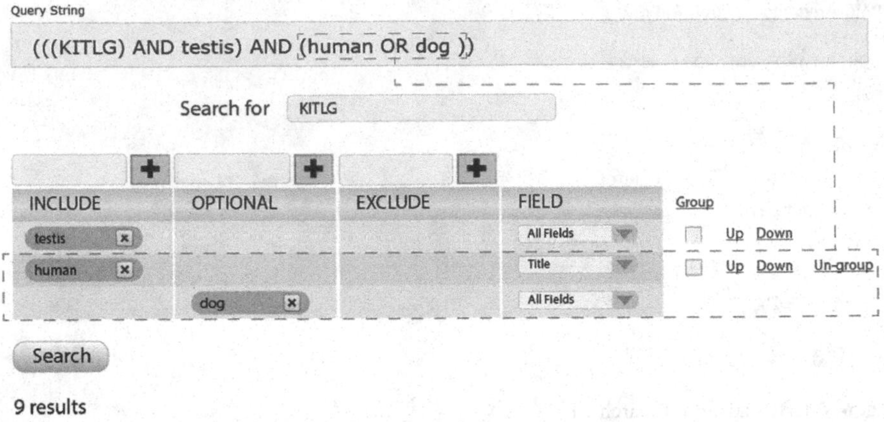

Query String

(((KITLG) AND testis) AND (human OR dog))

Search for   KITLG

INCLUDE	OPTIONAL	EXCLUDE	FIELD	Group
testis ✕			All Fields ▼	☐ Up Down
human ✕			Title ▼	☐ Up Down Un-group
	dog ✕		All Fields ▼	

Search

9 results

Fig. 7 IDP7 configured to show 9 results

7 Future Works

To complete the first iteration of the UCD process, we plan to carry out the usability tests with users using the proposed UI. The user feedback will be useful to refine the design before to implement it. Since the design pattern approach has been widely adopted in Software Engineering, capturing mainly the attention of designers and user interface developers, we strongly believe that a pattern approach can contribute to creating more user-centered bioinformatics applications. Therefore, our next aim is to evaluate the proposed pattern catalog and formalize it as a pattern catalog for designing UIs for exploiting genomic data. The UI implementation is totally feasible thanks to the web platform technologies (i.e., HTML, CSS, JavaScript) and especially to the FIWARE [22] platform that allows not only to implement the UI but also to implement the data layer that will provide the data to the UI. FIWARE is an open source software platform that facilitates the development of intelligent applications through the combination of components called Generic Enablers. Our plan is to use a Generic Enabler that allows us to integrate the diverse and heterogeneous biomedical databases and implement the proposed UI for searching and exploring the biomedical data.

8 Conclusions

In this paper, we apply a User-Centered Design approach for designing visual and interactive user interfaces for the efficient search of the biomedical literature. Our intention is to improve the productivity of practitioners in the biomedical domain by providing user interfaces designed to facilitate the visualization, analysis, and interpretation of relevant results. The approach we have used to design the UI includes the identification and understanding of the problems in the context, the identification of design solutions to solve such problems. In fact, the solutions incorporated in the proposed UI designs solve seven (7) current and concrete usability problems of the biomedical literature analysis, which have been detected and collected from the study and analysis of the available literature and interviews with domain practitioners. The usability problems that are addressed include the lack of a global vision of the result set, the handling of long lists of results, problems in the generation of query strings, among others.

For a better understanding of the usability problems, the problems were grouped considering the typical tasks of information search. Some problems are related to the query task and other problems are related to the result interpretation task. Indeed, the two user interface designs presented correspond to each of the two mentioned tasks.

The proposed UI design has implications for both the UI developers and the end users who consume the information. On the one hand, the improvement of UI usability positively impacts the productivity of end users (e.g., physicians, biologists, bioinformatics) allowing them to find more and better results either to generate biomedical diagnoses in their area or simply to keep updated with the advances in their research lines. On the other hand, the proposed improvements become heuristics of usability that can be applied by interface designers in the development of biomedical literature analysis and exploration software systems.

Although the usability problems analyzed in this paper are specific to the domain of the search of biomedical literature, the alternatives proposed to solve such problems can be extended to adapt to the usability problems in the UI of general literature search.

Acknowledgements The authors thank the members of the PROS Center's Genome group for fruitful discussions. In addition, it is also important to highlight that Secretaría Nacional de Educación, Ciencia y Tecnología (SENESCYT) and Escuela Politécnica Nacional from Ecuador have supported this work. This project also has the support of Generalitat Valenciana through project IDEO (PROMETEOII/2014/039) and Spanish Ministry of Science and Innovation through project DataME (ref: TIN2016-80811-P).

References

1. NCBI: PubMed homepage [Online]. Available: https://www.ncbi.nlm.nih.gov/pubmed/. Accessed 11 Mar 2018
2. Muin, M., Fontelo, P.: Technical development of PubMed interact: an improved interface for MEDLINE/PubMed searches. BMC Med. Inform. Decis. Mak. **6**, 36 (2006)
3. Alexander, G., Hauser, S., Steely, K., Ford, G., Demner-Fushman, D.: A usability study of the PubMed on Tap user interface for PDAs. Stud. Health Technol. Inform. **107**(Pt 2), 1411–1415 (2004)
4. Marill, J.L., Miller, N., Kitendaugh, P.: The MedlinePlus public user interface: studies of design challenges and opportunities. J. Med. Libr. Assoc. **94**(1), 30–40 (2006)
5. Islamaj Dogan, R., Murray, G.C., Névéol, A., Lu, Z.: Understanding PubMed® user search behavior through log analysis. Database, **2009**(0), bap018–bap018 (2009)

6. Tran, D., Dubay, C., Gorman, P.N., Hersh, W.R.: Applying task analysis to describe and facilitate bioinformatics tasks. In: Medinfo, 2004, pp. 818–822
7. Lu, Z.: PubMed and beyond: a survey of web tools for searching biomedical literature. Database **2011**, baq036
8. GoPubMed [Online]. Available: http://www.gopubmed.org/web/gopubmed/
9. VOSviewer: Visualizing scientific landscapes. Centre for Science and Technology Studies, Leiden University, 2015 [Online]. Available: http://www.vosviewer.com/
10. Douglas, S.M., Montelione, G.T., Gerstein, M.: PubNet: a flexible system for visualizing literature derived networks. Genome Biol. **6**(9), R80 (2005)
11. Genomenon: Mastermind—Comprehensive Genomic Search Engine [Online]. Available: https://mastermind.genomenon.com/. Accessed: 22 Apr 2018
12. DigitalScience: Dimensions [Online]. Available: https://app.dimensions.ai/discover/publication
13. Wu, C., Jin, X., Tsueng, G., Afrasiabi, C., Su, A.I.: BioGPS: building your own mash-up of gene annotations and expression profiles. Nucleic Acids Res. **44**(D1), D313–D316 (2016)
14. Cooper, A., et al.: The inmates are running the asylum: [Why high-tech products drive us crazy and how to restore the sanity]. Sams Indianapolis (2004)
15. Herskovic, J.R., Tanaka, L.Y., Hersh, W., Bernstam, E.V.: A day in the life of PubMed: analysis of a typical day's query log. J. Am. Med. Inform. Assoc. **14**(2), 212–220 (2007)
16. Bolchini, D., Finkelstein, A., Perrone, V., Nagl, S.: Better bioinformatics through usability analysis. Bioinformatics **25**(3), 406–412 (2009)
17. Interaction-design.org: Interaction Design Patterns [Online]. Available: https://www.interaction-design.org/literature/book/the-glossary-of-human-computer-interaction/interaction-design-patterns
18. Tidwell, J.: Designing interfaces: patterns for effective interaction design. O'Reilly Media, Inc. (2010)
19. Graham, I.: A pattern language for Web usability. Addison-Wesley (2003)
20. Toxboe, A.: Design patterns, 2007 [Online]. Available: http://ui-patterns.com/. Accessed: 05 Feb 2018
21. Rubin, D.L., Shah, N.H., Noy, N.F.: Biomedical ontologies: a functional perspective. Brief. Bioinform. **9**(1), 75–90 (2008)
22. Fiware.org: FIWARE, 2015 [Online]. Available: https://www.fiware.org/

Printed in the United States
By Bookmasters